PHONICS:
Why and How

PHONICS:

Patrick Groff
San Diego State University

Why and How

GENERAL LEARNING PRESS
250 James Street
Morristown, New Jersey 07960

PREFACE

Phonics: Why and How is a comprehensive, up-to-date treatment of one of the basic methods used to teach children how to read. It explores the rationale for using the phonics method to teach reading and explains the specific methodology utilized in such instruction. The Introduction discusses first the many controversies that have beleaguered the teaching of phonics. Second, the text describes the speech sounds of English and their spellings, pointing out what teachers should know about how words are syllabicated. Third, it depicts the principles of teaching that pertain to phonics. And fourth, it deals with organizing phonics into evolving stages of instruction.

Many examples and tables are provided, and references are given at the end of each chapter. A glossary defines the many terms needed to understand the phonics method. And an appendix contains suggestions for reading and spelling games that should be valuable to the teacher in the classroom.

The author hopes that *Phonics: Why and How* will aid teachers in their creative teaching of children to read. Both pre-service and in-service teachers should find the book an important tool in their classroom experience.

Patrick Groff

CONTENTS

III
The "How" of Phonics: Teaching Polysyllabic Words
199

INTRODUCTION

Phonics: Why and How has been written for two reasons. First, it is intended to provide teachers with the reasons why phonics should be taught to children learning to read. Second, the book deals with the specific methodology that is needed to be successful in this effort.

We need to discuss *why* phonics should be taught because this has been and is a controversial educational issue [Groff 1976]. The emphasis put on phonics over the years has waxed and waned. In the 1930s and 1940s, for instance, experts in reading instruction were advising teachers to use an "incidental" approach to phonics to make use of the knowledge of the relationships between the speech sounds of our language and the manner in which these sounds are written. It was said, if nothing else seems to help a child to learn to read, then the teacher should turn to phonics. During this period phonics was far down on the typical list of ways recommended by experts for teaching children to recognize words. Reading experts during this period published many erroneous notions about English sounds and their spellings with no fear of rebuke from linguists, who were, by and large, uninterested in the entire question of phonics instruction.

By the middle 1950s this "incidental" phonics methodology was coming under increasingly heavy attack. In his best-selling book of the decade, *Why Johnny Can't Read* [1955], Rudolf Flesch claimed that virtually no phonics was being taught in the elementary school. While this happened to be an exaggeration of actual conditions, it was true enough to receive widespread acclaim from disgruntled parents and other school critics (not from the reading experts of the time, of course). Beyond the fact that Flesch wrongly wanted teachers to revert to nineteenth century (prelinguistics) phonics, he was unwise in his attempt to reduce reading to phonics. That is, simply teach the child what each letter stands for and he can read. It is easy to demonstrate that reading is far more than just reading words aloud since it involves the very tricky matter of comprehending the meanings an author intended to convey.

It was not until the late 1960s that a more thorough and scientific study of phonics than Flesch's appeared. In *Learning to Read: The Great Debate* [1967], Jeanne Chall examined the pertinent research on the effectiveness of "code-emphasis" (phonics) methods as opposed to "meaning-emphasis" methods in teaching children to read. Chall found that phonics methods bring superior results not only in word recognition but in reading comprehension as well. Unlike Flesch's book, which could be dismissed as poorly documented, Chall's scholarly work has had a much greater influence.

Currently, despite Chall's conclusions, there remain objections to teaching phonics of any variety or degree. For example, Frank Smith declares in *Psycholinguistics and Reading* that "there is absolutely no evidence that he [a child] could ever actually use it [phonics] in the process of reading" [1973, p. 186]. He maintains that phonics "is far too complex and unreliable to be used as a tool for identifying unrecognized words, especially by beginning readers" [p. 84].

This very short history of phonics and antiphonics indicates the extent of the conflicting points of view that continue over phonics. Consequently, the *first* purpose of *Phonics: Why and How* is to bring these dissenting views of this subject into perspective in order to describe the degree to which phonics is a legitimate aid to children as they learn to read.

To teach phonics it is obvious a teacher needs to understand clearly what should be taught. Teachers of phonics need to be well versed, then, in the relationships between the speech sounds of English and how these sounds are spelled. Accordingly, *Phonics: Why and How* sets as its *second* goal a description of the speech sounds of English and their spellings. This section of the text also includes what teachers of phonics should know about the ways words are syllabicated, so that the most efficient approach to teaching children how to break up polysyllabic words can be undertaken.

But there is still more that the phonics teacher needs to know than reasons for teaching phonics and the linguistic information necessary to teach it. The *third* objective of *Phonics: Why and How* is to depict the principles of teaching that especially pertain to phonics. A discussion of the critical problems of classroom practice, the everyday procedures involved in helping children to learn phonics, naturally follows.

The *fourth* aim of *Phonics: Why and How* is to deal specifically with the matter of organizing the field of phonics into evolving stages or ongoing levels of instruction so that the child learning this information is taught with materials at slowly increasing levels of difficulty. The final chapters of this book indicate how phonics can be divided into ten increasingly difficult levels of instruction. For each of these ten progressively complex levels, many practical classroom activities with which they can be taught are given.

Phonics: Why and How limits itself to a description of the role that phonics plays in word recognition. While it recognizes the critical importance of reading comprehension, it does not venture to any significant extent into this area. Since reading comprehension is a field that is much less understood and agreed upon even than phonics, it is apparent that a reasonable treatment of comprehension is beyond the scope of this book.

This text does deal in detail with one concern outside phonics. *Context cues* (how the other words in a sentence, paragraph, or the discourse as a whole help the reader identify an unknown one) are used by all children along with phonics to recognize words. Chapter 19 discusses how context cues serve this collaborative function and makes it clear that phonics operates best as an aid to word recognition when context cues also come into play. John Bormuth [1975, p. 74] reminds us while phonics "do represent one of the most useful sets of skills one can employ to pronounce words" that "it is now clear, however, that the phonics skills cannot be employed to pronounce many words unless those skills are coupled with certain of the literal comprehension skills." The outline of the value of context cues in Chapter 19, therefore, allows us to stress the importance of the teacher's understanding the interdependency of these two cue systems.

Phonics: Why and How is based on research from linguistics and reading instruction and from studies of the nature of the child as a learner of phonics. Unfortunately, not all that the teacher needs to know about teaching phonics can be abstracted from these three areas of research. Some of the questions about phonics to which teachers need answers have not been researched thoroughly. In addition, some research on phonics contradicts other research. For these reasons, *Phonics: Why and How* is not offered as the final word on the teaching of phonics. Doubtless, there will be future research that will require changes in this book. For the present, the content of *Phonics: Why and How* represents the best of current research and judgments about its subject.

Phonics for Reading

It is helpful though to realize that despite some controversies still occurring about the place of phonics in the teaching of reading and spelling, certain conclusions are accepted generally.

Phonics teaching does, in fact, offer the child significant help in learning to read and spell. The research on the teaching of reading makes this clear. As Eleanor Gibson [1975, p. 298] puts it, "The heart of learning to read would seem to be the process of mapping written words and letters to the spoken language; a process of translating or matching one symbol system to another." After reviewing some of this evidence, Arthur Heilman was led to say, "The data from this study and from studies of the phonetic approach suggest that most basal reader programs might possibly be strengthened by more emphasis on phonic analysis in beginning reading" [1961, p. 242]. Louise Gurren and Ann Hughes' examination of twenty-two comparisons of various uses of phonics in teaching reading resulted in a more positive statement that early and intensive phonics instruction tends to produce superior reading achievement [1965].

A more comprehensive review of the findings of fifty-six studies that compared varied uses of phonics in teaching reading makes an even stronger case for phonics (code-emphasis reading programs). The director of this study, Jeanne Chall, concludes:

> . . . the research from 1912 to 1965 indicates that a code-emphasis method—i.e., one that views beginning reading as essentially different from mature reading and emphasizes learning of the printed code for the spoken language—produces better results, at least up to the point where sufficient evidence seems to be available, the end of the third grade.
>
> The results are better, not only in terms of the mechanical aspects of literacy alone, as was once supposed, but also in terms of the ultimate goals of reading instruction—comprehension and possibly even speed of reading [1967, p. 307].

As Helen Popp [1975, p. 104] rightly notes, "Several publishers of the conventional basal reader series seemingly have adjusted their programs in light of Chall's recommendations." These were that "school systems can improve reading standards by using one of the 'complete' code-emphasis [phonics] programs or one of the separate supplemental phonics programs as a replacement for the word-perception program in the conventional basal-reader series" [1967, p. 310].

Recent support for Chall's conclusions also has come from the twenty-seven *First Grade Reading Studies* [Stauffer 1967]. These studies were funded by the U.S. Office of Education and were designed to test the relative effectiveness of different approaches to first-grade reading instruction. The most significant finding of these studies, in our estimation, was the superior results found for *code-emphasis approaches* (using Chall's terminology). In the great majority of cases when a code-emphasis approach was compared to the traditional basal-reader approach, the former produced significantly better results. Looked at another way, the reading gains made

in the *meaning-emphasis approach* (again Chall's term) were very seldom
superior to those attained in code-emphasis approaches.

This advantage continued through the second grade. In his review of
the results of the second grade phase of this government-sponsored research,
Robert Dykstra concluded: "Early and relatively intensive teaching of
sound-symbol [sound-letter] correspondences appears to be highly related to
word recognition achievement at the end of second grade" [1968]. Not only
did these studies show the superiority of the phonics emphasis approaches
over the traditional basal reader in reading achievement in another way, "all
three [phonics emphasis] programs produced significantly superior spellers
after two years of instruction" [Dykstra 1968].

Phonics for Spelling

In reviews of the relationships of phonics and spelling, Ernest Horn has
commented on the potential value of phonics for the child in learning to
spell: "There is considerable evidence to suggest that a well-planned
instruction in sound-to-letter and letter-to-sound associations in appropriate
relations to other learning procedures may be of benefit both in spelling and
in reading" [1957, p. 424]. There is ample other evidence, of the nature
found by Karlene Russell, Helen Murphy, and Donald Durrell [1957], that
confirms the usefulness of phonics for teaching spelling. This study conducted exercises with six hundred middle-grade children in which these
students listened to spoken words and then wrote the graphemes for
indicated parts of these words. For example: "Listen to *farm*. Write the
letter for the first sound." In three months with this program these children
gained from six to ten months in standardized spelling test scores. A control
group of the same size given "customary spelling instruction" from traditional textbooks made slightly less than three months growth.

As early as 1941 George Spache concluded from a review of studies up
to that time that "there is ample evidence to conclude phonetic knowledges
and skills play an important part in spelling ability" [p. 573]. We reviewed
the research evidence on this matter from 1941 to 1965, and came to
substantially the same conclusion [Groff 1968]. Ronald Cramer's review of
this evidence also led him to a similar conclusion that "the weight of
evidence tends to support the view that instruction in phonics of various
types does provide some help in spelling achievement" [1969, p. 502]. From
the findings it is not unwarranted to insist that phonics can play an essential
part in learning to spell.

There is yet another position regarding phonics and spelling, which
says that phonics is best taught to children *exclusively* in the spelling
program. It is only after children have learned phonics by practice in the

spelling of words, it says, that they then can apply phonics to reading. As Jeannette Veatch explains this position, "All skills needed to break a word apart, to analyze it, to separate such into pieces in order to find out what it is, are spelling or writing skills" [1966, p. 363].

This theory of the teaching of phonics, however, has a serious flaw that invalidates it. As we shall demonstrate throughout this book, there are many more opportunities to use phonics in reading than in spelling. There are more phonics skills usable for identifying words than for spelling them. Thus, if phonics were taught only as an aid to spelling, children would not receive instruction in many of the phonics skills that can help them recognize words.

The Limitations of Phonics

Much evidence can be given regarding the complex nature of children's difficulties in learning to read and to spell. It is overly simplistic, then, to say that lack of phonics, alone, causes reading and spelling problems.

First, as Arthur Gates rightly concluded, a number of factors can cause difficulty for children in word-recognition tasks. Among these factors "a low intellectual level, inferior verbal aptitude, limited experience in hearing and speaking the language, a meager experiential background, speech defects, defects of vision and hearing, poor health, absence from school at critical times, emotional instability, misleading motivation, emotional blockings produced by unfortunate social adjustments" are all possible causes [1947, p. 206]. Add to this a bad teaching of inappropriate phonics, the misapplied use by the children of what phonics knowledge they have, and the list grows longer.

Spelling is also negatively affected by influences other than a lack of phonics knowledge. The fact that there are good readers who are mediocre spellers indicates that some children may dislike making the kind of mental effort needed to learn to spell over learning to read. Reading is obviously a more interesting task than spelling. Then, poor handwriting habits, which result in illegible writing, can contribute to what are often judged to be misspelled words.

The variety of factors that contribute to reading and spelling ability should convince one to be careful not to ascribe too much of the blame for reading or spelling disability just to a lack of phonics. We insist on the importance of phonics in developing a child's ability to decode or recognize words. On the other hand, we agree with findings such as John Bormuth's, which indicate that "only a negligible fraction of this problem [of illiteracy in older children] could be traced to the children being unable to sound out or otherwise identify words [1970, p. ii]. The evidence reviewed by Robert

Dykstra affirms this: "The superiority in word recognition of pupils in various phonics emphasis programs is not, as a general rule, demonstrated in the area of reading comprehension [1968, p. 65] (although other reviewers of the research [Chall 1967] find phonics-trained pupils are superior in reading comprehension to children who are taught little phonics).

A second generally accepted conclusion about phonics is that it is only one of the cue systems that a child learns to use to recognize words. The context of the sentence and the semantics involved (the special meaning of a word in a given sentence) also are cues children use in word recognition. Children do not read words just by "sounding" them out. This is even more the case as they mature in their reading skills. A mature reader cannot read aloud the following sentence, for example, without experiencing discomfort:

> The none and the buoy tolled hymn they had scene and herd bear feat in the haul.

This sentence may exasperate skilled readers because they are accustomed to using sentence cues and semantic cues along with phonics cues when they read aloud. To be read aloud the sample sentence requires the use of too many phonics cues, which makes it painful to read.

We believe that a reasonable delimitation of the function and value of phonics teaching for reading and spelling should in no way undermine one's confidence in the primary value of phonics instruction. In fact, we think it is vitally necessary to put definite restrictions on the importance of phonics. Otherwise phonics might parade, as it unfortunately has been made to do on occasion, as the panacea for all reading and spelling ills.

It is just as unreasonable, however, to assume that children learning to read and spell will effectively discover by themselves the phonics necessary to do this, if they are left to their own devices. Especially, it is important to deflate the notion that arises periodically that children learn to read in just the same way as they learned to talk. It has been held that if one simply surrounds beginners in school with written words, in much the same manner that they were surrounded with oral language as infants, they will instinctively discover the relationships between oral and written language, and thus on their own will learn to read and spell [Smith 1973]. We have illustrated how the great weight of experimental evidence questions this assumption. This research shows that what is needed in beginning reading for children to learn with ease and effectiveness is a careful examination of the ways the written language corresponds with the oral language, coupled with a systematic analysis of how children learn.

In short, this evidence indicates we cannot merely say that children *should* learn phonics. To the contrary, all the indications are they *must* learn it if they are to recognize and spell words. A study of phonics from kindergarten through high school makes this clear. The findings of this study indicated that the "simple phonological skills are significantly and substantially related to reading and spelling performance through high school. Poor readers have failed to master these skills at the syllable level at all grades" [Calfee, Lindamood, & Lindamood 1973, p. 298]. There seems little doubt, then, that the degree to which children are successful in word recognition and spelling depends to a large part on their success in learning phonics. Accordingly, the teacher of reading cannot settle for less than a good background of phonics information and an access to many details of how to conduct phonics lessons.

It is also highly likely that the demands on teachers of the future to know phonics will increase, not decrease. Robert Aukerman [1975] is studying the widely used basal readers in preparation for a book to be called *The Basal Reader Approach to Reading.* He reports that "in the 1980s, most basals will introduce a separate synthetic-analytic phonics program." That is, "within 5 to 10 years, the publishers of basals will have introduced separate, visible, structured phonics programs" [p. 11]. It seems clear that the basal readers of the future will teach more phonics than do those of the present.

This book follows a middle path between those, as Smith [1973], who contend they alone represent the "psycholinguistic" approach to reading instruction, and others, such as Fries [1964], who would deemphasize the use of context cues in beginning reading. Smith, who calls phonics "the great fallacy" of reading instruction [1973, p. 70], believes we should allow children to learn to read largely on their own. Unfortunately, Smith's attempts to prove this theory result in a revival of the use of the look-say or whole-word method of teaching reading, a method that has been thoroughly discredited by research. On the other hand, Fries would have us teach beginning reading with the use of clumsy appearing, artificial sounding sentences such as *The fat cat sat on a mat. Phonics: Why and How* opposes both these extreme points of view. We are convinced, instead, that learning to read proceeds most efficiently when phonics and context cues are taught together in a synchronized fashion.

To accomplish this purpose *Phonics: Why and How* offers the teacher the latest linguistic information and the principles of phonics teaching derived from educational research, as well as much practical guidance in the day-to-day problems in teaching phonics. Since this book is based upon research from linguistics and teaching methodology, it attempts, to the extent that this is possible, to document each important or crucial statement it makes about phonics.

But no book dealing with a subject about which so much debate rages can dare hope to please all its readers. *Phonics: Why and How* doubtless will challenge some of the beliefs of those who cling to the tenets of traditional phonics or antiphonics, both of which we believe to have been discredited to a substantial degree by recent experimental evidence from educational methodology and from linguistics research. The time is overdue to depart from old or radical beliefs about phonics and to attempt to arrive at a method of instruction that has a sounder justification. It is with this reform of phonics in mind that the suggestions in this text are offered to today's teachers.

REFERENCES

Aukerman, Robert C. "Look at Dick and Jane Now! (Plus a Peek at Their Future)." *Reading Informer,* 3(1975):9–11.

Bormuth, John R. *Literacy in the Suburbs.* Chicago: Department of Education, University of Chicago, 1970, mimeographed.

Bormuth, John R. "Reading Literacy: Its Definition and Assessment," *Toward a Literate Society,* eds. John B. Carroll and Jeanne S. Chall. New York: McGraw-Hill, 1975.

Calfee, Robert C., Lindamood, Patricia, and Lindamood, Charles. "Acoustic-Phonetic Skills in Reading: Kindergarten through Twelfth Grade." *Journal of Educational Psychology,* 64(1973):293–298.

Chall, Jeanne S. *Learning to Read: The Great Debate.* New York: McGraw-Hill, 1967.

Cramer, Ronald L. "The Influence of Phonic Instruction on Spelling Achievement." *Reading Teacher,* 22(1969):499–503.

Dykstra, Robert. "Summary of the Second Grade Phase of the Cooperative Research Program in Primary Reading Instruction." *Reading Research Quarterly,* 4(1968):49–70.

Flesch, Rudolf. *Why Johnny Can't Read.* New York: Harper, 1955.

Fries, C. C. *Linguistics and Reading.* New York: Holt, Rinehart and Winston, 1964.

Gates, Arthur I. *The Improvement of Reading.* New York: Macmillan, 1947.

Gibson, Eleanor J. "Theory-Based Research on Reading and Its Implications," *Toward a Literate Society,* eds. John B. Carroll and Jeanne S. Chall. New York: McGraw-Hill, 1975.

Groff, Patrick. "Research on Spelling and Phonetics." *Education,* 89(1968):132–135.

Groff, Patrick. "The Past, Present and Future of Anti-Phonics," *Fortieth Yearbook, Claremont Reading Conference*, ed. Malcolm P. Douglass. Claremont, Calif.: Claremont University, 1976.

Gurren, Louise, and Hughes, Ann. "Intensive Phonics vs. Gradual Phonics: A Review." *Journal of Educational Research*, 58(1965):339–347.

Heilman, Arthur W. *Teaching Reading*. Columbus, Ohio: Charles E. Merrill, 1961.

Horn, Ernest. "Phonetics and Spelling." *Elementary School Journal*, 57(1957):424–432.

Horn, Ernest. *What Research Says to the Teacher: Teaching Spelling*. Washington, D.C.: National Education Association, 1954.

Popp, Helen M. "Current Practices in the Teaching of Beginning Reading," *Toward a Literate Society*, eds. John B. Carroll and Jeanne S. Chall. New York: McGraw-Hill, 1975.

Russell, Karlene V., Murphy, Helen A., and Durrell, Donald D. *Developing Spelling Power*. New York: World, 1957.

Smith, Frank. *Psycholinguistics and Reading*. New York: Holt, Rinehart and Winston, 1973.

Spache, George. "Spelling Disability Correlates—Factors Probably Causal in Spelling Disability." *Journal of Educational Research*, 34(1941):561–586.

Stauffer, Russell G., ed. *The First Grade Reading Studies*. Newark, Del.: International Reading Association, 1967.

Veatch, Jeannette. *Reading in the Elementary School*. New York: The Ronald Press, 1966.

I

The "Why" of Phonics

1

A DEFINITION
OF PHONICS

What is meant by the term *phonics?* It is obvious from the stem of this word, *phon*, that it is related to the Greek word *phone*, which means *sound*. The words *telephone, megaphone, microphone, euphonious,* and *phonograph* also have something to do with *sound*. Phonics is no exception.

Phonics is related particularly to two other "sound" words, *phonetics* and *phonemics*. (See the Glossary for definitions of these and other technical terms used throughout this book.) As used in this book, the term *phonics* means two things: (1) it is an interpretation of *phonetics, phonemics,* and *graphemics* written for teachers of spelling and reading, and (2) it is a description of how the information given in phonetics, phonemics, and graphemics may be applied when one teaches children to recognize words (*decode* them) or to spell words (*encode* them).

We shall examine what it takes to teach children to understand the workings of the code or system, that is, the relationship between the way we speak words and the way we read and spell them. Children must learn this relationship if they are to learn to read and to spell. *Phonics: Why and How* describes how to conduct this teaching by illustrating how the teacher can make it possible for children to understand the relationship between the spoken language and the written language.

Phonetics

The first step in understanding phonics is to learn what is meant by the word *phonetics*. Phonetics is the study of the sounds made in a dissection of the living stream of speech. Just as a specialist in anatomy can divide the human body into its separate parts and can name each of these parts, so can a specialist in phonetics separate the flow of live speech into separate sounds, each of which is given a name.

But phonetics is much more than a guide to the pronunciation of written language. It is a broad field concerned with the symbolic nature of speech; the way in which speech sounds are produced; the physical mechanisms involved in this production; the psychological problems attendant to speech perception; the varieties of usage and style; and the variant pronunciations of speech sounds in different regions of a given part of the world in which a certain language is spoken. It sometimes deals with acoustics, the origin and history of speech sounds, the teaching of speech correction, and the teaching of English as a foreign language.

Most phoneticians purport to only hear speech sounds. Acoustic phoneticians can "see" sounds as these are recorded on machines that print out the wave lengths of sounds. Other phoneticians draw visual diagrams of sounds [Barrutia 1970]. For phoneticians to prove that they can hear separate, distinctly different speech sounds—*phonemes*—they usually use a written symbol for each. These symbols can also be used by others to write down spoken language. But as Burt Liebert rightly puts it:

> To try to write the sounds of a language is a little like trying to describe what it is like to be kissed. Words and symbols are only substitutes. Nevertheless, poets and philosophers have been talking about kissing since the dawn of literature, and linguists have developed a system, known as the *phonetic alphabet*, to make it possible for you and me to discuss speech sounds without hearing each other's voices [1971, p. 71].

Having a separate written character for each sound in English is an absolute necessity in phonetics, as well as in the application of this knowledge, which we call phonics. A "frequency phonetic alphabet," based on the most common spellings given to sounds, is shown in Table 1. In each case the indicated letter or letters used most frequently to represent the sound is underlined in the word [Hanna et al. 1966].

An inspection of this frequency phonetic alphabet shows that it is easier to criticize such an alphabet than to create one. One cannot contrive a phonetic alphabet that is based entirely on the letters that are most frequently used to spell speech sounds. We can see from this frequency phonetic alphabet that the vowel letters, *a-e-i-o-u,* are called upon for double, triple, and quadruple duty: *u* for *put* and *union; o* for *both, odd,* and *carton; a* for *at, vary, angel,* and *arm.* Even the consonant letters do not match up one to one with sounds. For example, *g* is used most often to represent both [g] and [j] sounds; *s* represents three sounds more often than does any other letter; *y* and *z* are not the letters most often used to represent [y] and [z]; *c* is used most frequently to represent the beginning sounds in both *cat* and *keep.*

TABLE 1. A FREQUENCY PHONETIC ALPHABET

Vowels

i—*it*	a—*a*ngel	a—*a*rm
a—*a*t	i—f*i*nd	ou—*ou*t
u—p*u*t	oo—b*oo*t	oi—b*oi*l
e—b*e*d	o—b*o*th	u—*u*nion
a—v*a*ry	o—*o*dd	er—h*er*
e—b*e*		o—cart*o*n

Consonants

b—*b*at	h—*h*ot	n—*n*ot	v—*v*at	ch—*ch*ap
c—*c*at	g—*g*em	p—*p*at	w—*w*et	th—*th*in
d—*d*og	c—*k*eep	qu—*qu*ick	x—fo*x*	t—ac*t*ion
f—*f*at	l—*l*ap	r—*r*un	i—sen*i*or	th—*th*e
g—*g*ot	le—ab*le*	s—*s*at	s—*z*ip	s or si—fu*si*on
	m—*m*an	t—*t*op		ng—si*ng*

Adapted from Hanna et al. [1966].

Notice the brackets, [ ], used here to indicate phonetic spellings of a word. For example, *Jim* and *gym* if spelled phonetically could be written [jim] and [jim].

It is a reminder that there are not enough letters in our alphabet to match all the sounds of language. How can one describe all the sounds of the language in *written* symbols? In *Phonics: Why and How* we shall use diacritical marks, when needed, for this purpose. For example, the "a" sound in *a*ngel is written as /ā/. Chapter 3 describes this system in detail.

An examination of phonetics makes it clear that much of the science of speech sounds and the application of this science to the understanding and speaking of languages is useful in phonics. It is equally apparent that large amounts of phonetics information is not useful in phonics. The phonics teacher must decide what is relevant and what to omit. To help make this decision it is important to talk about phonemics.

Phonemics

Phonemics is a somewhat narrower field of information about speech sounds than phonetics. According to one linguist, "The study of the actual sounds of language is called *phonetics* and the way in which these sounds are used, put together and organized in any one language is called *phonology* (or more usually *phonemics* in America)" [Wallwork 1969, p. 23]. *Phonemics* is that area of linguistic study concerned with the identification of the significant sounds of a given language. These significant speech sounds or *phonemes* are sounds in English that make a distinction, or that distinguish, between words *regarding their meanings.* A single phoneme distinguishes the meanings of *till* and *dill* and *fill* and *pill* and *bill.* This is rather obvious. But most of us would probably be surprised to learn that one phonetician has discovered that the first sound in *till* is only one of ten different ways to pronounce /t/, none of which distinguish between words in regard to their meanings [Wise 1957, pp. 75–76]. (Notice that in phonemics slant lines, / /, are used to transcribe speech sounds.) The "t-sound" is really a family of sounds. *Allophones* is the name given the different sounds of a phoneme.

Graphemics

The teacher of phonics also must rely on the field of *graphemics* for information as to what to teach in phonics. *Graphemics* is the study of writing or spelling systems and of their relationships to phonetics and phonemics. Graphemics deals with how we usually transcribe spoken language. In ordinary terms we call this *spelling* or *orthography.*

✳ Reading and Phonics

The place phonics has in the teaching of reading depends as well on what one means by *reading.* By the term *reading* we mean:

1. A person's ability to recognize single words in sentences. By *recognize* we mean the act of converting a printed word into spoken language, either spoken aloud or subvocalized. This act is also called *decoding.* The terms *decoding* and *word recognition* cannot be used interchangeably, however, since context cues are also involved in word recognition.

2. Reading also refers to the reader's understanding of what the author of a piece of printed material apparently intended to convey. We do not always know precisely what this meaning is, of course, since we cannot read an author's mind. In poetry, for example, where an author is deliberately ambiguous, we have additional misgivings. As Roger Brown notes, "No one has offered an explicit formulation of the total process of sentence comprehension for either the reading or the hearing case. What we have is a rough general conception and a collection of isolated clues and conceivable heuristics" [1970, p. 186]. Being able to understand what a written passage means after it has been read has been called *recoding.*

To recognize a word in a sentence, children always use all three sources of information: (1) knowledge of phonics, or letter (grapheme)-sound (phoneme) correspondences, (2) understanding of where in the structure of the sentence a given word rests, and (3) awareness of at least one meaning of the word. *Phonics: Why and How* is concerned primarily with the first of these means of word recognition: phoneme-grapheme correspondences. Sentence structure cues to word recognition, however, are not neglected (see Chapter 19).

A good test of whether children are reading, in the first meaning of the word, therefore, is to listen to them read aloud. As Frederick Brengelman notes, a child's progress in learning to read "will be indicated by his supplying suitable patterns of intonation" [1970, p. 108] (and by paraphrasing or transforming what he has read). If children read sentences with what the listener deems to be proper pitch, stress, and juncture, one can say they are reading well in one sense of the term. However, if children, after reading sentences in this fashion, cannot answer questions regarding the intended meaning of their author in a satisfactory manner, then it can be said they are not reading well in the full, complete, higher or second sense of the term.

A problem appears here immediately, however. It is easy to tell when children are reading aloud in an unnatural, singsong, "shopping-list" fashion, or in a way that impresses one as using natural intonation. Thus, a reading test of whether children can recognize a word in a sentence is relatively simple and reliable (that is, it can be administered by several testers with the same results). But this is not true of the second kind of reading. For example, how many of the 172 meanings of *run* given in a large, modern dictionary would children have to indicate they know before a tester says they can "read" *run*? Or should we say that children cannot read *run* until they can show comprehension of *all* 172 meanings? Should we expect children to learn to read *x* number of meanings of *run* per school year? Obviously these questions about the meaning of reading in its second sense perhaps never will be answered.

Some scientific attempts have been made to determine what unique comprehension skills (the second meaning of reading) exist in reading. The ones Frederick Davis found to be operative with secondary school students' reading could also be those used by pupils in lower grades. To this extent we agree that the elementary grade teacher should do the following:

1. Make pupils familiar with the meaning of as many words as possible. . . .

2. Encourage pupils to draw inferences from what they read and to do this accurately. . . .

3. Provide supervised practice for pupils in
   a. following the structure of a passage;

    b. finding answers to questions answered explicitly or in paraphrase in the material read;

    c. recognizing an author's attitude, tone, mood, and purpose [Davis 1968].

Further analyses by Donald Spearritt support this conclusion, with the exception that his "analyses do not support the hypothesis that . . . finding answers to questions answered explicitly, or in paraphrase, is an additional, separately distinguishable skill" [1972]. Spearritt also discovered that the "present types of reading comprehension tests, as distinct from word knowledge tests, largely measure one basic ability, which may well correspond to the label of 'reasoning in reading'" [1972]. This kind of well-done analysis explodes the notion, given by basal-reader manuals particularly, that there are dozens of comprehension skills one should teach children. For example, the Macmillan Reading Program [1966] contends that it teaches forty comprehension skills in its readers for grades five and six. The Harper & Row Basic Reading Program [1966] purports to teach seventy such skills at these grade levels.

In making this distinction between phonics and certain kinds of comprehension, we do not mean to downplay the importance of comprehension in reading. We agree entirely that the phonics teacher should proceed on the assumption that reading is always a meaning-getting exercise. Keeping this in mind the phonics teacher—as nearly as possible—uses words inside sentences. It is appropriate to stress that the teacher of phonics, in addition to teaching children the relationships between the ways words are spoken and spelled, helps pupils to understand that reading is a way to get meanings. This is best done by teaching them from the beginning to combine knowledge of sound-spelling relationships with intelligent guesses as to the identity of a written word from context cues—the slot in the sentence in which it fits.

Spelling and Phonics

Good spellers are seldom poor readers, and poor readers are seldom good spellers [Plessas & Ladley 1965]. But it is apparent to most literate people that spelling is more difficult to master than is reading. In learning to spell one must first say, subvocalize, or think of the word one wants to write. Second, one must remember the precise sequence or serial order of letters or graphemes that are used to correctly represent the sounds to spell them in a socially acceptable fashion. A child, for example, may want to spell /bred/ as in *bread and butter*. The vowel sound in /bred/ can be spelled either as *e* or *ea* (bred-bread). In reading the child does not face this difficulty. The sentences *The bread is good* and *The man bred horses* provide many cues that help the reader recognize the difference between the two words.

Thus, for the teacher of phonics, one fundamental difference between reading and spelling has to do with the kind and degree of memorization, or visual recall, required of pupils in each activity. In spelling, pupils must visually remember the serial order of graphemes. In reading, these are given to them as cues as to how the word is sounded. If children use phonics in spelling, they will learn that there are certain predictable ways that sounds are spelled. When the word is spelled, it also must "look right." The effect of the "right look" of words on fifth-grade children was demonstrated by Michael Wallach [1963]. Using a tachistoscope, he flashed pseudowords for these children, which were made up of a random sample of letters, for example, *cvgjcd.* Then a second group of pseudowords that take into account strings of four letters that actually occur in English were so given, e.g., *mossia, onetic.* After twelve presentations of the latter type of "words," the children improved in their ability to recall letters in these latter "words" by 197 percent. After twice as many presentations of the first kind of "words," the children improved in their recall of letters in them by only 12 percent.

It is clear that attention must be given to the visual imagery of words in spelling instruction. After children have utilized phonic cues to the spelling of a word, they must then decide if the word "looks right." "No doubt the sense of sound plays a bigger part in writing, but here, too, the eye is at least as important as the ear. When, for example, we are doubtful of a spelling, we often write down two possible forms of the word concerned and choose the one which 'looks right.' Our umpire is the eye; if sound comes into it at all, it is as the umpire at the other end, as it were, who is appealed to only when his colleague cannot decide for himself" [Vallins 1965, p. 15]. How this matter is to be resolved, how children are best taught to develop visual memory for spelling, is far from clear, however.

It appears, then, that spelling is inherently more difficult than reading not only because it is an essentially more complex linguistic task, but because it requires more visual memorization. Research to this effect [Aaron 1954; Comerford 1954] is supported by the common assertion of phonics teachers that children make fewer mistakes in reading a word than they do in spelling this same word. Teachers also generally insist that children can respond to, are ready for, reading instruction before they can go on to spelling.

We cannot say, therefore, that spelling and reading are merely reverse aspects of the same linguistic act, although spelling relates to reading in a statistical sense as closely as anything one can find. In a review of the research on this matter Eve Malmquist [1960] reports moderate to high correlations (0.65 to 0.81) between these two linguistic acts.

Unfortunately, the attempts that have been made to theorize about spelling are of little help. For example, Carl Personke and Albert Yee [1971] have constructed an intricate-appearing (yet inadequate) model for the analysis of spelling behavior. According to their model spelling has seven "phases": (1) feeling a need to spell, (2) making use of one's knowledge or information and attitude about spelling, (3) deciding how much of this information is necessary, (4) making an "initial spelling response," (5) using a helpful external resource, such as a dictionary, (6) actually writing a word, and (7) "self-evaluation and scanning other people's responses" [p. 16].

This model proclaims that to spell a word children must either rely on memory or depend on other external supports (books, the teacher, etc.). The fact that children can confirm the spelling correctness of a needed word either *before* or *after* they attempt to write it is also common knowledge or opinion, as is the fact that their attitudes toward correct spelling, either positive or negative, play a role. This model gives us little about spelling that common sense would not dictate.

Personke and Yee's model for spelling gives no inkling as to which kinds of words hypothetically should be taught as "memory words," or which should be taught as needful of external input or phonics generalizations, or why redundancy cues used in reading do not always transfer to spelling. No theory of spelling behavior can be useful without giving attention to these various elements. These writers avoid doing so, merely noting that "the Internal Input [phase 2] must be stocked, for example, with a large number of learned responses, or words for which the spelling is known," while "the attainment of these learned responses must be a primary goal of the spelling program" [p. 33].

We can agree, however, that

> it is true, of course, that one can learn to spell without being able to hear or speak—perhaps by gaining a visual memory of the word as a whole and its separate graphemes, and transcribing this visual image into writing. But if a person relies solely on visual processes, he fails to capitalize on the premise on which American-English spelling is based: that *in an alphabetic orthography, the act of spelling is basically one of encoding the phonemes of speech into the graphemes of the writing system* [Hanna, Hodges, & Hanna 1971, p. 103].

Yet the question remains: which comes first in spelling, visual memory or one's application of phoneme-grapheme correspondences? Some writers insist that visual memory comes first. The child will "check the success of his encoding effort by comparing it with a visual recollection of the word," a recollection that is easy to make since he will have "abundant visual memories" of words from his past reading of them [McKee 1966, p. 103].

This would force us to *disagree,* however, with McKee's conclusion that "it is almost impossible to teach about vowels what might be profitable for purposes of spelling without doing serious damage to the teaching of reading itself" [p. 109]. Or that, a "questionable matter" is "the notion that what the pupil could be taught profitably about letter-sound associations for vowels as a part of instruction in spelling is also what he needs to know about those associations in order to do well in beginning reading" [pp. 133–134]. On the contrary, we know of no evidence that suggests that ability in spelling, which involves the awareness of vowel phoneme-grapheme correspondences and redundancy cues, interferes with reading ability.

By sequential redundancy cues we mean that if certain letters are seen in certain places in a word, then it is predictable that only certain other letters will follow. You are readily aware that *u* almost always follows *q* in words (*quick*). This kind of predictability for other letters is less obvious to most of us. For example, if the letter *t* is seen as the first letter in a word, this means that only *h, r,* or *a, e, i, o, u,* or *y* may follow. As children learn to use the sequential redundancy of letters of a word as a cue to its recognition, this doubtless transfers over and helps in spelling the word.

One's spelling is handicapped, moreover, by the requirement that we have to spell words in socially correct, yet unpredictable ways. Reading, for mature readers at least, is not so greatly handicapped by these demands on the spelling system [Chomsky & Halle 1968]. In fact, the variant spelling system in English presents many cues that aid one in learning to read. For example, seeing the morpheme *bomb* in *bombard* (although it is not pronounced as *bomb* here) indicates to the reader the latter word has something to do with a bomb. The different spelling of *sitting* and *siting* tell us these have different meanings. The marker *e* on *site* shows this word will have a different sound and meaning from *sit*.

Phonics: Why and How agrees that our spelling system is far from the chaotically confused state some see it in. While obviously not a simple system, it is *systematic* to a great extent. Other recent comment on the relationships of sounds and their spellings questions whether the spelling of words is, however, "merely a letter-to-sound system riddled with imperfections." It is viewed instead as "a more complex and more regular relationship wherein phoneme and morpheme share leading roles." The idea "that deviations from a perfect letter-sound relationship are irregularities" also is a "purblind attitude," according to Richard Venezky [1967, p. 77]. G. H. Vallins agrees that the eccentricities of spelling have been exaggerated. "Looked at in historical perspective, [they] are nothing more than pleasant variations from a reasonably intelligent pattern" [1965, p. 26]. Viewed historically, Albert Marckwardt believes that "the language and its writing system are not something indescribable, inscrutable, unexplainable, and uncontrollable, but that in their own highly peculiar way, they do make sense" [1966, p. 90].

REFERENCES

Aaron, Ira A. *The Relationship of Auditory-Visual Discrimination to Spelling Ability.* Ph.D. dissertation, University of Minnesota, 1954.

Barrutia, Richard. "Visual Phonetics." *Modern Language Journal,* 54(1970):482–486.

Brengelman, Frederick. *The English Language.* Englewood Cliffs, N.J.: Prentice-Hall, 1970.

Brown, Roger. "Psychology and Reading: Commentary on Chapters 5 to 10," *Basic Studies on Reading,* eds. Harry Levin and Joanna P. Williams. New York: Basic Books, 1970.

Chomsky, Noam, and Halle, Morris. *The Sound Pattern of English.* New York: Harper & Row, 1968.

Comerford, Joseph F. *Perceptual Abilities in Spelling.* Ph.D. dissertation, Boston University, 1954.

Davis, Frederick B. "Research in Comprehension in Reading." *Reading Research Quarterly,* 3(1968):499–545.

Hanna, Paul, et al. *Phoneme-Grapheme Correspondences as Cues to Spelling Improvement.* Washington, D.C.: U.S. Office of Education, 1966.

Hanna, Paul R., Hodges, Richard E., and Hanna, Jean S. *Spelling: Structure and Strategies.* Boston: Houghton Mifflin, 1971.

Liebert, Burt. *Linguistics and the New English Teacher.* New York: Macmillan, 1971.

Malmquist, Eve. *Factors Related to Reading Disabilities in the First Grade of the Elementary School.* Stockholm: Almqvist and Wiksell, 1960.

Marckwardt, Albert A. *Linguistics and the Teaching of English.* Bloomington: Indiana University Press, 1966.

McKee, Paul. *Reading.* Boston: Houghton Mifflin, 1966.

Personke, Carl, and Yee, Albert H. *Comprehensive Spelling Instruction.* Scranton: Intext Educational Publishers, 1971.

Plessas, Gus P., and Ladley, Dorothea M. "Some Implications of Spelling and Reading Research." *Elementary English,* 42(1965):142–145.

Spearritt, Donald. "Identification of Subskills of Reading Comprehension by Maximum Likelihood Factor Analysis." *Reading Research Quarterly,* 8(1972):92–111.

Vallins, G. H. *Spelling.* London: Andre Deutsch, 1965.

Venezky, Richard L. "English Orthography: Its Graphical Structure and Its Relations to Sounds." *Reading Research Quarterly,* 2(1967):75–105.

Wallach, Michael A. "Perceptual Recognition of Approximations to English in Relation to Spelling Achievement. *Journal of Educational Psychology,* 54(1963):57–62.

Wallwork, J. F. *Language and Linguistics.* London: Heinemann, 1969.

Wise, Claude M. *Applied Phonetics.* Englewood Cliffs, N.J.: Prentice-Hall, 1957.

2

THE PHONEMES
IN AMERICAN ENGLISH

Phonemes—the speech sounds of our language—are linguistic units that help us determine meaning in language. By linguistic units we mean any part of the spoken language that can be heard as significantly different from any other part. For example, we hear *hat* and *rat* as different words partly because we recognize the differences between the sounds /r/ and /h/. There are different phonemes in *hat* and *rat*. *Flower* and *flour*, on the other hand, have the same phonemes. When we hear *flower* or *flour*, spoken without support as to their meaning from the sentence they are in (e.g., "Which flour/flower is best?"), no differences of sound or meaning are noted. Thus, one difference between *hat* and *rat* is a *phonemic* difference. No such phonemic difference exists between the words *flower* and *flour* in the above sentence, although they obviously do not have the same meaning.

By *meaning*, we refer to the communication of ideas between one person and another via oral language. "Watch out! There goes a rat!" doubtless evokes a different response than would, "Watch out! There goes 'r hat!" When we hear *phonemic* differences in words, we immediately think of something different. This fact is generally well known to the adult reader, and the phonics program in this book assumes this to be the case. One special purpose of *Phonics: Why and How* is to separate and identify *all* these well-known speech sounds (phonemes) in our language so that this knowledge can be used, in turn, to help children learn to read and spell.

What Is a Phoneme?

To describe the nature and limits of the separate speech sounds, or phonemes, of English is to ask the question, "How many different sounds are
there in our language?" As we answer this question, we will note that a
certain number of phonemes are used in each dialect of English.

If we say that one phoneme is different from another, we must prove
that the use of a different phoneme in a word would affect the meaning of
what we want to say. A phoneme is a speech unit that is not identical with
any other speech sound. It must be so different that it will definitely affect
the meaning of what is said. Later, we shall describe how certain small
differences within a speech sound do not do this.

Phonemes, therefore, are partially the way we determine word
meanings (e.g., *hat-rat*). But phonemes also are units of sound that can be
used interchangeably within words without affecting the meanings of words.
For example, in the words *mat, fat,* and *cat,* we hear the same middle and
final speech sounds. The regularity of the way we say /at/ in any word
indicates why it is possible for us to speak a complicated, extensive language
and yet use only a limited number of speech sounds. For example, *ten* and
net have identical phonemes. The different *sequence* of phonemes allows us,
while saying the same sounds, to say two different words. This illustrates
how we can use the same sounds over and over in different words without
confusing our listeners.

In learning to speak as children, we learned to detect and reproduce at
will the minor differences in sounds we hear, for example, in *mat, fat,* and
cat. We also realized at a very young age that these phonemic differences
carried differences in meaning. By the time normal children come to school
they *comprehend* all of the sounds in their dialect. They also can say or
produce almost all of these sounds.

The differences in phonemes or speech sounds, however, are not quite
so limited as this suggests. We must mention one other distinctive aspect of
phonemes—*allophones.* Generally, we accept the sounds we hear represented by *t* in *teem* and *butter,* for example, (or *ten* or *net*), to be the same.
That is, we are aware of no difference in these sounds. We also say that the
beginning sounds of *law* and *lit* are the same. And, yet, if you say *teem* and
butter aloud, you will notice that your tongue is not in exactly the same
place for both these /t/ sounds. If one's tongue is not in the same place for
each of the /t/ sounds, the two sounds cannot be exactly the same. The same
test can be made with *law* and *lit.* A difference in the position of your
tongue in saying the two *l's* is again noticeable. We may say, then, that these
two pairs of sounds, /t-t/ and /l-l/, are acoustically different.

However, if the /t/ sound from *butter* were to be used in *teem,* and
vice versa, to a listener the meaning of the two spoken words would not be

changed. Thus, we have evidence that we can hear, and tolerate, slight differences in the sounds of /t/ and not let these differences affect meaning. And if the two differences in the sounds of /t/ do not affect meaning, we do not consider it important enough to classify them as separate phonemes. "In order to indicate all these facts, one says that the two *t* sounds are different allophones of the phoneme /t/" [Carrell & Tiffany 1960, p. 19]. In a technical or acoustic sense, adults can detect the allophones of /t/. For the practical purposes of teaching children to read and spell, however, this aspect of phonemes can best be ignored, as it is too difficult for children to understand. Accordingly, we will neither discuss allophones as a subject for instruction elsewhere in this book, nor include them in our list of sounds to be used in teaching phonics (see Tables 2 and 3).

To sum up, the following are important considerations that are made in order to answer the questions: "What are the different speech sounds?" and "How many of these are there?"

1.   Any phoneme to be a phoneme must be a speech sound different from any other phoneme. But to be called a phoneme this speech sound must also be so *different* from any other that a substitution of it for one other phoneme in a word would change the meaning of the word. Therefore, slight differences in speech sound, which do not change meaning (*allophones*), are not counted as separate phonemes. Since the exchange of allophones in words does not change the meaning of words, this aspect of phonemics need not be taught to children.

2.   Phonemes are interchangeable speech units. For example, each of the individual syllables in the hundreds of thousands of words in English contains only one of the vowel sounds. Since speech sounds largely are interchangeable, we need to use only a limited number of speech sounds to speak our complex language. We do this by using this limited number of sounds over and over again.

3.   Some words that have different meanings are made up of identical phonemes (e.g., *flour-flower*). A knowledge of the speech context in which such words are spoken is therefore necessary if one is to understand their meanings. This illustrates one basic principle of phonemes: no phonemic difference—no meaning difference, unless this is given in the ongoing speech context.

4.   Some American linguists say they hear more or fewer phonemes than do other linguists. Some include in their list of phonemes all the vowel sounds that are possible in all the dialects in English. Whether or not the diphthongs (blends of two vowel sounds that are initiated as one vowel sound, gradually gliding to the sound of the second vowel) are counted as phonemes makes a great difference.

Vowels and Consonants

The phonemes in English are of two general categories. One of these groups of sounds is called *vowels,* the other is called *consonants.* The distinctions that phoneticians have discovered between these two major kinds of sounds are important for the phonics teacher to understand.

If you open your mouth widely, say "ah," and allow the sound to escape freely, you will produce a *vowel.* If you continue to say "ah" and now move your tongue around so that it touches or very nearly touches the roof of your mouth, or touches your teeth, or if you close your mouth, you will produce a *consonant.* Try this. This is one way to distinguish between what linguists call vowels and consonants.

A *consonant* occurs, then, when one blocks or partially obstructs the breath and causes rubbing noises by forcing one's breath around obstacles or through a gap. To the contrary, when the air stream of speech escapes unrestricted, without rubbing noises, one makes a *vowel* sound.

Another way of distinguishing vowels from consonants is to say that vowels have more *prominence* in syllables than consonants do; that is, they are louder, of longer duration, of higher pitch, and have greater sonority or resonance than do consonants. Vowels, in short, are released with greater energy and pressure than are consonants. When this difference, called prominence, is great, it is relatively easy to hear.

There have been impressionistic notions as to the differences between vowels and consonants. Robert and Marlene McCracken assert, for example, that "each consonant acts as an interruption, but each succeeding vowel continues the flow of sound" [1972, p. 89]. To the poet Robert Duncan [1968, p. 132],

> The vowels are physical
> corridors of the imagination
> emitting passionately
> breaths of flame. . . .

> The consonants are the church of
> hands interlocking, stops
> and measures of fingerings,
> that confine the spirit to
> articulations of space and time. . . .

While these are all interesting suppositions, they do not accurately describe the linguistic role of vowels and consonants.

A more precise way to separate vowels and consonants is to test the initial letter of a word to see whether it begins with a vowel or consonant. Take *bear,* for example, and place before it this pair of words: *a-an.* If the first word of this pair (*a*-an) accommodates itself to the succeeding sound in a fitting way, the succeeding sound is a consonant (*a bear*). If the second word so accommodates itself, the succeeding sound is a vowel. For example, say: *a* orange—*an* orange, or *a* dog—*an* dog. Our test shows /ô/ as a vowel and /d/ as a consonant.

Phoneticians say that all vowels but not all consonants are characterized by voicing. Voicing means that sounds "are normally produced with the vocal cords in vibration" [Kantner & West 1960, p. 68]. Voicing means vocal cord vibration. When a person speaks, the vocal cords can be in a wide open position, in a partially closed position, in a phonating position (rapid closing and partial opening), and in a closed position. Vowel sounds also are "made with the vocal cords closed to the point of vibration" [Kantner & West 1960, p. 140]. Vowels are always voiced and are continuant or continually flowing sounds.

Some *consonant* sounds are voiceless and are thus made while the vocal cords are more at rest. Voiced consonants sound as if "whispered," while voiceless ones are characterized by hisses and clicks. Pairs of voiced-unvoiced consonants can be noted. These are pairs that are allied or similar in nature and quality, that is, pairs that are produced with (1) a similar degree of closure of the sound channel through which the speech breath passes, (2) a similar position of tongue, teeth, and lips, and (3) a similar degree of pressure and release of speech breath. The conventional pairings of voiceless-voiced consonants are as follows:

Voiceless: /p t k f th (as in *thigh*) s sh ch wh h/

Voiced: /b d g v th (as in *thy*) z zh j w/

Additional voiced consonants are /l, m, n, ng, y, r/.

You can feel the vibration of the voiced consonant sounds by placing your hand against your throat with the crotch of your thumb/forefinger just below the Adam's apple. Say, s-s-s-s-. Then say, z-z-z-z-. Try this with the other pairs given above.

The vowel sounds can be called the voice or "color" of language. The speech one hears, whether it is clipped, drawled, or jerky depends on the way vowels are said. One can best speed up or retard one's rate of speech by shortening or lengthening vowel sounds.

On the other hand, communication of meaning through language is more dependent on consonant sounds than on vowel sounds. This may be partially due to the fact that although each vowel sound differs from every other vowel sound, it does not appear to us for some reason that these differences are as great as those among the consonant sounds. The relative importance of consonant letters over vowel letters in transmitting *written* messages also can be demonstrated by attempting to read sentences with the consonant letters removed rather than those with the vowel letters removed.

For example, one can read this sentence rather easily: Th_ m_n w_nt t_ t__n. (The men/man went to town.) Now try to read this one: __e _i__ _oo_ _e_ _o__.[1]

One other difference between consonants and vowels has to do with the places they occupy in words. Consonants can occur at the beginning, middle, and end of words, but this is not true for all vowels. Some vowels can begin a word, as in *add, aid, odd, ode, out, ice,* and so on. Some can end a word, as in *tea, two, say, so, saw, buy, boy, now.* But some vowels can never end a word or syllable, as those heard in the middle of *bit, bet, bat, hut, foot.*

There are several other complexities about consonant and vowel articulation that we will *not* discuss at any length in *Phonics: Why and How.* It is not that these additional aspects of phonation are not important. Rather, in our judgment we can avoid a discussion of them and yet describe enough of consonant articulation to make it possible for the teacher to develop an authentic use of phonics.

Regional and Socioeconomic Variations in Pronunciation

We have shown that the number of phonemes in American English depends on whether the speech sounds in our language make a difference in the meaning of words. The number of speech sounds in American English is also conditioned by the geographical region in which one learned to speak. For example, *tot* and *taught,* as spoken, are rhyming words on the West Coast. In New England these words often are given different vowel sounds and therefore are not rhyming words. Thus New Englanders would have an additional phoneme in their spoken language that would not be heard in the speech of native Californians. This brings us to what are "right" or "wrong" speech sounds.

In our description of phonemes thus far, we have discussed to some degree the production of speech sounds, that is, the speaker's ability to formulate the sounds in words with sufficient accuracy to make those words easily distinguishable, one from the other. At this point we can say that a word is mispronounced if in this sense it has wrong sounds, or if any of its sounds have been omitted, added, or shifted around.

To decide what is a "wrong" sound, we also must concern ourselves with regional variations in pronunciation. We know that the region of the United States in which one has learned the language as a child also influences one's judgment as to what is the proper pronunciation of words. To a

---

[1] The girl took her doll.

New Englander, the Californian's use of the same vowel sound in *tot* and *taught* seems inaccurate or faulty. To a Californian, on the other hand, the use of different vowel phonemes for these two words sounds odd and unnecessary.

Linguists who have studied such regional variations in pronunciation say there are three or four great geographical speech regions in the United States. These are (1) *Eastern American* (New England and New York City), (2) *Southern American* (the old Confederacy and Kentucky, with west and central Texas excluded), and (3) *General American* (the remaining states) [Carrell & Tiffany 1960]. Others call these regions (1) North, (2) South, (3) Midland ("Pennsylvania and adjoining areas to the east, west, and southwest"), and would add (4) Middle West and Far West [Kurath 1964, p. 5]. Yet another phonetician notes that the information needed to draw boundary lines that separate the major speech areas of the Middle West and beyond are not available.

We can, however, draw some conclusions from the evidence already in: (1) A clearly defined Midland Speech separates the regional dialects of the North and South in the eastern part of the United States. (2) The political boundaries of the North and the South have proved inaccurate for designating regional speech areas. (3) The older designations, "New England Speech," or "Eastern Speech," are misleading. Coastal New England, western New England, New York City, and the Hudson Valley are fairly distinct speech areas. . . [Bronstein 1960, p. 51].

"Western" Dialect

The phonemes in *Phonics: Why and How* are adopted from what we shall call "Western" dialect. We recognize that the term "Western" poorly applies to some geographical regions (see above) speaking this dialect, but it does give us a term distinct from "Eastern" and "Southern," although the boundaries of "Western" touch these areas. We accept Claude Wise's statement that the term *Northern speech* for this speech region is "an obvious misnomer" [1957, p. 171].

Accordingly, Tables 2 and 3 in Chapter 3 are based on the phonemes used in the *General American/Midland-Middle West/Far West* dialects. The teacher of children from other speech regions than these has the right to ask, "Why so?" Why should the dialect called "Western" be chosen for the list of phonemes in a book on phonics? There are several reasons why we have accepted the sounds in "Western" dialect for the standard list of phonemes found in this book. First, as most linguists agree, "GA [General American] comes closest to the common currency of speech in this country. It is accepted anywhere and is spoken far more widely in the United States than are either EA or SA" [Carrell & Tiffany 1960, p. 7]. Second, changes in pronunciation habits in the United States will probably continue to be in the direction of "Western" dialect because the population shifts in the country are generally in this direction. The westward tilt of the nation's population will result in ever more children hearing "Western" dialect in their schools and communities and from their teachers. Third, as Wise has said, "America is now suddenly an almost completely mobile country, with nearly everybody traveling nearly everywhere and finding employment in every part; in such a situation, numbers count heavily. What has been called the General American dialect will presumably have the advantage" [Wise 1957, p. 180]. Fourth, among the most important influences on uniform American speech are television, radio, and movies. These mass media tend to use "Western" dialect. For example, our "Western" dialect is almost identical to the dialect of national TV [Crowell 1964]. Fifth, with few exceptions, dictionaries use "Western" dialect in their phonemic spelling of words. For all these reasons it seems appropriate for us to use this "Western" dialect as our guide for the phonemes needed to explain how phonics can be used in teaching reading and spelling.

Regional differences do not mean, however, that a New Englander and a Californian could not understand each other. It is true that "good-quality speech from one linguistic area is rarely unduly conspicuous in another dialect region" [Carrell & Tiffany 1960, p. 6]. "Actually, the really conspicuous regional differences among educated speakers from each of these three areas [EA, SA, GA] are relatively few; most of the more obvious distinguishing features center around the way the r sound is handled and upon the pronunciation of the a vowels. Careful analysis, of course, will reveal a number of fine points of difference, but these are not apparent to the average listener" [p. 5].

Nonetheless, for the teacher of phonics, these points of difference can be important. To use a given list of phonemes (as shown in Tables 2 and 3 of Chapter 3), the teacher of children who speak dialects that differ from this given list will have to make adjustments for these differences. We do not assume that teachers of phonics should teach phonics in any other dialect than that considered standard for their speech region. To do otherwise would be impractical, if not impossible. In the United States we do not have a standard form of pronunciation that is used by educated people in all geographical regions. As one phonetician says, "The speech of educated Bostonians is no more 'standard' than the educated speech of Tulsa, except in Boston. And the educated patterns of speech of Chicago or Charleston are not more accepted than are those of New York. The speech you use in this country, then, is considered standard *if it reflects the speech patterns of the educated persons in your community*" [Bronstein 1960, p. 6]. The "Western" dialect presented in *Phonics: Why and How*, therefore, is neither better nor worse than any other regional dialect.

REFERENCES

Bronstein, Arthur J. *The Pronunciation of American English.* New York: Appleton-Century-Crofts, 1960.

Carrell, James and Tiffany, William R. *Phonetics.* New York: McGraw-Hill, 1960.

Crowell, Thomas L. *NBC Handbook of Pronunciation.* Thomas Y. Crowell, 1964.

Duncan, Robert. *Derivations.* London: Fulcrum Press, 1968.

Kantner, Claude E. and West, Robert. *Phonetics.* New York: Harper & Row, 1960.

Kurath, Hans. *A Phonology and Prosody of Modern English.* Ann Arbor: University of Michigan Press, 1964.

McCracken, Robert A. and McCracken, Marlene J. *Reading Is Only the Tiger's Tale.* San Rafael, Calif.: Leswing Press, 1972.

Wise, Claude M. *Applied Phonetics.* Englewood Cliffs, N.J.: Prentice-Hall, 1957.

3

HOW PHONEMES
ARE WRITTEN

Chapter 1 indicated that there are more speech sounds in English than there are letters to represent these sounds. Thus, a given letter or combination of letters sometimes must be used to represent more than one speech sound or phoneme. To avoid any ambiguity in reading about speech sounds it is necessary, therefore, to decide upon one, and only one, way to transcribe each speech sound. To do this we must first decide how many phonemes there are in English.

How Many Phonemes Are There?

It can be seen from Tables 2 and 3 in this chapter that we have identified forty-one phonemes. (We shall discuss later why the twenty-six letters of English are not enough for a one-to-one match with the sounds in American English.) As we have shown in the previous chapter the number of phonemes one hears depends on the geographical speech region one uses as a base for this determination. Some speech regions have more or fewer phonemes than others.

The reduction of our "Western" dialect to written language also requires that either certain accepted written symbols for speech *or* diacritical markings be used to transcribe its phonemes into writing. The latter type of transcriptions, *diacritical markings,* are marks added to conventional letters. For example, the vowel sound in *be* would be transcribed as /ē/. The speech symbols do not usually add an additional mark to conventional letters to indicate their phonemic character. For example, the vowel sound in *at* in this system would be transcribed as /æ/. Both systems of transcribing speech sounds are given in Tables 2 and 3.

Tables 2 and 3

Table 2 presents twenty-four consonant sounds and the consonant cluster /hw/ as heard in *what.* (Letters or symbols within slant lines, / /, indicate the phonemic transcriptions of sounds.) Table 3 presents seventeen vowel sounds. This is the sum of forty-one phonemes of "Western" dialect American English.

Column one of Tables 2 and 3 gives some typical spellings of the indicated sounds. Thus, for the phoneme /p/ we find the word *pat.* The phoneme /p/ is spelled as *p* in the word *pat.*

Column two of these tables is headed "percent of occurrence." The numbers found in this second column indicate the percent of times, in the 17,000 most frequently used words having the given phonemes, that phonemes are spelled with the indicated letters. For example, the phoneme /p/, when heard in these 17,000 words, is spelled with the letter *p* 96 percent of the time [Hanna et al. 1966].

Column three of Tables 2 and 3 indicates different numbers of ways the indicated phoneme can be spelled. The phoneme /p/ can be spelled two ways: *p* and *pp.*

All the percents and numbers in columns two and three of Tables 2 and 3 are based on data from the Paul Hanna, et al. study of phoneme-grapheme correspondences in the 17,000 most frequently used words [1966]. In certain instances the data from Hanna have been combined and recalculated for these tables. This is done when phonemes that were used by Hanna do not correspond with the set of "Western" phonemes used in *Phonics: Why and How.*

Columns four and five of Tables 2 and 3 indicate respectively the transcription symbols that are commonly used by linguists for writing sounds, and the dictionary diacritical marks used for this purpose. The phonemic transcription symbols in column four are taken from Hans Kurath [1964]. They are somewhat changed forms of the International Phonetic Alphabet.

A description of one other aspect of phonemes is given in Tables 2 and 3. These are the linguistic designations *plosives, fricatives, nasals, laterals,* and *semivowels* for consonants; and *checked, free,* and *free, less accented* for vowels.

The consonant designations describe the degree to which these sounds are blocked or held back in the throat, mouth, or nasal cavities when spoken. Plosives are produced by blocking the breath channel and then exploding the breath. Fricatives are formed by narrowing the breath channel and then forcing breath through it. Nasals, laterals, and semivowels escape more freely through the mouth and/or nasal cavities. The ease with which breath escapes when one speaks determines the loudness or sonority of consonants. Therefore, semivowels are the loudest, followed in this quality by laterals and nasals. Plosives and fricatives are the least loud of all consonants.

The vowel designations in Table 3—checked, free, and free, less accented—also have significance for the teacher of phonics. The importance of these distinctions will become especially clear as we discuss later how they should be taught. For now the reader can see that checked vowels are generally or typically seen in "closed" syllables.

"Free vowels, on the other hand, appear both finally and before consonants" [Kurath 1964, p. 17]. Closed syllables are those syllables with vowel-consonant(s) endings as in *cat*.

Free vowels are typically heard in both closed and open syllables, an open syllable being one that ends in a vowel phoneme, as in *go*. Free vowels can be heard, therefore, in beginning, middle, and end positions in syllables and one-vowel words (*oat, goat, go*). Checked vowels do not appear in ending positions.

The terms *long* and *short*, while usually used by phonics writers to classify vowel sounds, are not useful for this purpose. *Long* and *short* vowel sounds are said to be heard in these words:

Long	Short
hate	hat
Pete	pet
site	sit
hope	hop
cute	cut

This classification does not work out, however, since some *short* vowels in the above list are not always shorter in duration than the *long* vowels. This can be shown by arranging eight of the above words into the rank order of the length of the duration of their vowel sounds: *hat, hot, hope, Pete, hate, pet, cut, sit.* Notice that some "short" vowels are the longest of all and that "long" sounds here are actually median length vowels [Berg & Fletcher 1970, p. 66].

The free, less accented vowel sound, called a schwa /ə/, is found in less accented syllables, such as *arise, father*. This schwa sound, it can be noticed, resembles a lightly accented checked /u/ sound, as in *up*.

Using Tables 2 and 3

The phonemic data presented in Tables 2 and 3 are very important to the phonics teacher, who will be able to understand how to teach phonics well *only* if he or she understands the linguistic material given in them. Therefore, before proceeding further, study carefully the spellings, figures, symbols, and diacritical markings given in Tables 2 and 3.

Read as much as possible of the material from Tables 2 and 3 aloud to yourself. To hear the "exploding" nature of plosives, for example, say *pat, tap, chap, cat, bat, dot, jet,* and *got.* Pay especial attention to the formations of your tongue and lips and to breath pressure and its release.

For the sake of readability, we will use the dictionary diacritical markings as our phonemic transcriptions. These are given in column five of Tables 2 and 3. Note that some of these diacritical markings are not the same as the typical spellings one would expect for the phoneme in question. This can be noted for free vowel phonemes especially. For example, in *be* the free vowel is spelled *e.* The diacritical marking of this free vowel is /ē/.

The Phoneme /r/

The /r/ phoneme is distinct enough from other consonant phonemes to warrant a separate discussion. No voiced sound in our language is more variable than /r/: "*r* is a sound, that even more than *t, k,* and *l,* is influenced by neighboring sounds. We will not be far wrong if we think of *r* as being dragged all over the mouth cavity by the various sounds with which it happens to be associated" [Kantner & West 1960, p. 169]. Thus, /r/ is called a glide sound. "Like all other glide sounds, it is characterized by a rapid change of resonance[1] produced by a gliding movement of the organs of articulation involved in its production" [Carrell & Tiffany 1960, p. 213]. It is this gliding characteristic that complicates the sound of /r/.

It can be noted in Table 3 that certain vowel phonemes that precede /r/ are distinguished, for easier identification. We say in Table 3 that

1. /e/ is heard in v*ar*y, c*are,* h*air,* and th*ere*

2. /ô/ is heard in c*ore.*

3. /o/ is heard in *ar*m.

4. /ûr/ is heard in h*er,* b*ur*n, and f*ir.*

5. /i/ is heard in f*ear,* m*ere,* b*eer.*

6. /ər/ is heard in aft*er* (/ər/ is considered an allophone of /ûr/).

---

[1] For example, /m/ has much resonance; /t/ does not.

TABLE 2. TWENTY-FOUR CONSONANT PHONEMES:
THEIR SPELLINGS AND TRANSCRIPTION SYMBOLS

Type of Consonant	Typical Spelling	Percent of Occurrence	Number of Spellings	Linguistic Transcription Symbol	Diacritical Marking
Plosive	1. *p*at	96	2	/p/	/p/
	2. *t*ap	97	9	/t/	/t/
	3. *ch*ap	55	5	/č/	/ch/
	cul*t*ure	31			
	4. *c*at	73	13	/k/	/k/
	*k*eep	13			
	5. *b*at	97	3	/b/	/b/
	6. *d*ot	98	3	/d/	/d/
	7. *j*et	22	8	/ǧ/	/j/
	*g*em	66			
	8. *g*ot	88	7	/g/	/g/
Fricative	9. *f*at	78	6	/f/	/f/
	10. *th*in	100	1	/θ/	/th/
	11. *s*at	73	10	/s/	/s/
	*c*ent	17			
	12. *sh*ut	26	15	/š/	/sh/
	a*cti*on	53			
	13. *h*it	98	2	/h/	/h/
	14. *v*at	99.5	3	/v/	/v/
	15. *th*e	100	1	/ð/	/ᵭ/
	16. *z*ap	23	8	/z/	/z/
	a*s*	64			
	17. u*s*ual	33	5	/ž/	/zh/
	fu*si*on	49			
Nasals	18. *m*an	94	6	/m/	/m/
	19. *n*ot	97	6	/n/	/n/
	20. si*ng*	59	3	/ŋ/	/ng/
	ba*n*k	41			
Laterals	21. *l*ap	91	4	/l/	/l/
	ab*le*°	95	5		
	22. *r*un	97	4	/r/	/r/
Semivowels	23. *w*et	92	3	/w/	/w/
	24. *y*et	44	3	/j/	/y/
	sen*i*or	55			
	*wh*en°°	100	1	/hw/	/hw/

° Heard in less accented syllables.

°° Not truly a separate phoneme. Included here for other reasons. See text.

Note Well: Consonant sounds can indicate the beginning of, or termination of, syllables. Consonants are classified in Table 3 according to the degree of closure or blockage of the breath stream in the mouth or throat at the time these sounds are made.

The complex sound of /r/ should not, however, lead us to assume that it is especially difficult for children to hear and speak. James Carrell and William Tiffany are mistaken, therefore, when they state that the /r/ sounds "are typically the last to be acquired during the developmental period" [1960, p. 215]. Research has shown that children learn to pronounce correctly all the following sounds *after* they speak /r/: /s/, /sh/, /ch/, /t/, /th/, /v/, /l/, /ᵭh/, /zh/, and /j/ [Templin 1957].

While all the vowel letter-r spellings must be given special care in phonics, one of these is particularly confusing. It is the *o* before *r* spelling, as in *more*. Our survey of the opinions expressed in leading phonetics texts showed a rather general agreement that the vowel sound represented by *o* before *r* is /o/ or /ō/, depending on one's dialect. Then, we asked phoneticians in forty-three different state universities (which represent all the speech regions of the United States) for their views on the problem. A large majority of these professors of phonetics agreed that the vowel sound represented by *o* before *r* was /o/ or /ō/. They noted there were other vowel sounds heard here, however, since this depended on the dialect one uses [Groff n.d.].

We can say with confidence that the vowel sound in *more* and *rope* are different sounds. We use the symbol /ô/ to indicate the vowel sound heard in *more*, and /ō/ the vowel sound heard in *rope*. Doubtless almost all phonics teachers will hear the /ō/ sound in *rope*. (Phonetics texts and phonetics professors do agree on this.) Each phonics teacher must personally decide what vowel sound he or she hears in *more*, however, since this varies from dialect to dialect. Hence, we use the special diacritical marking /ô/ for *more*.

Table 2 Footnotes (continued)

When *plosives* or *stop plosives* (including *affricatives*) are produced, the closure is complete; the breath is almost entirely blocked. This blockage is made by the tongue or lips.

If this closure or blockage is incomplete, a *fricative* is produced. *Fricatives* are continuants, that is, they are made with a continuously flowing, but in this case partially constricted, breath stream. The fricative sounds are made when the continuous pressure of the breath is directed against the mouth, teeth, or lips. This friction makes for a hissing noise, which characterizes fricatives.

Nasals are so called because the especially resonant sound imparted to them comes as a result of the passage of breath into the nasal passages. This special resonance sounds pleasing to our ears when heard in /m/, /n/, and /ng/. This is not the case when nonnasal sounds are given a nasal quality.

Laterals denote the fact that the breath for these sounds is blocked and then allowed to escape laterally over the sides of the tongue. You can hear that these sounds are more closely related to nasals than the other consonant sounds. Some experts insist that /l/ is the only true lateral sound.

Semivowels as a term implies that these sounds can stand as either vowels or consonants. In some cases these sounds function as the syllabic (prominent sound) of a syllable. (For that matter, so can /l/, /m/, /n/, and /r/. But we believe that these sounds are better classified from their other phonetic characteristics since the vocal passage is not entirely open when they are produced.)

In some sources /w/, /r/, and /y/ are called *glides* since with these sounds the sound-producing articulators move rapidly from one position to another as these sounds are made. When these sounds are made in syllables, the position of the mouth, teeth, and lips are much influenced by the vowel sound with which /w/, /r/, and /y/ are associated.

TABLE 3. SEVENTEEN VOWEL PHONEMES

Type of Vowel	Typical Spelling	Percent of Occurrence	Number of Spellings	Linguistic Transcription Symbol	Diacritical Marking
Checked	1. *it*	66	22	/ɪ/	/ĭ/
	m*y*th	23			
	2. *at*	96	3	/æ/	/a/
	3. *foo*t	31	6	/u/	/o͝o/
	p*u*t	54			
	4. *up*	86	6	/ʌ/	/u/
	5. b*e*d	91°	13	/ɛ/	/e/
	v*a*ry	29°°	9		
	c*a*re	23			
	h*ai*r	21			
	th*ere*	15			
Free	6. b*e*	70	16	/i/	/ē/
	*ea*t	10			
	f*ee*l	10			
	7. *a*ngel	45	16	/e/	/ā/
	*a*te	35			
	8. f*i*nd	37	14	/aɪ/	/ī/
	*i*ce	37			
	b*y*	14			
	9. b*oo*t	38	16	/u/	/o͞o/
	tr*u*th	21			
	wh*o*	8			
	r*u*de	8			
	10. b*o*th	73	16	/o/	/ō/
	c*o*de	14			
	11. c*o*rd	not available	not available	/ɔr/	/ôr/
	12. *o*dd	79°	13	/ɔ/	/o/
	*a*rm	89°°	6		
	13. *ou*t	56	5	/aʊ/	/ou/
	h*ow*	29			
	14. b*oi*l	62	4	/ɔɪ/	/oi/
	b*oy*	32			
	15. *u*nion	69	11	/ju/	/yo͞o/
	c*u*te	22			
	16. h*er*	40	14	/ɜr/	/ûr/
	b*ur*n	26			
	f*ir*	13			
	aft*er*	70†	9	/ər/	/ûr/
Free, Less Accented	17. cart*o*n	27	22	/ə/	/ə/
	c*a*nal	24			
	pen*c*il	22			
	reb*e*l	13			

Tables 4 and 5

Tables 4 and 5 are lists of the spellings given to the twenty-four consonant and seventeen vowel sounds found in Tables 2 and 3. For each sound given in Tables 4 and 5 the dictionary diacritical marking is presented, and some examples of the ways the sound is spelled are given. For example, the phoneme /p/ is spelled in two ways, *p* and *pp*, as seen in *pat* and *happy*. Table 4 shows that these two ways are the only ways the phoneme /p/ is spelled.

Tables 4 and 5 do not list all the possible spellings that can be given a phoneme. (A more complete list of spellings of vowel and consonant phonemes is given in Chapter 4.) For example, the phoneme /t/ has nine possible spellings. Table 4 gives only two of these, *t* and *tt*, as seen in *pat* and *putt*. The other seven spellings of /t/ are not included because as a group they constitute less than 1 percent of the total possible spellings of /t/. In other words, over 99 percent of all the words with the phoneme /t/ are spelled with *t* or *tt*. The phoneme /t/ can be spelled as *ed* as in *paced*, but this spelling is uncommon. It constitutes only about 0.35 of 1 percent of the ways /t/ is spelled in the most frequently used 17,000 words in English [Hanna et al. 1966]. In Tables 4 and 5 no spelling is indicated if it constitutes less than 1 percent of the total of spellings in these 17,000 words.

The first spelling in the row of spellings given for each phoneme in Tables 4 and 5 is the most common spelling for that phoneme. From Table 4 one can see that for /p/, /t/, /ch/, and /k/ the most common spellings are *p* (*pat*), *t* (*tap*), *ch* (*chart*), and *c* (*cab*). That *c* is the most common spelling for /k/ may seem surprising, which suggests that in American English the diacritical marking *c* might well be a better one for this phoneme than *k*. Tradition dictates the use of *k*, however.

Table 3 Footnotes

° Percent refers to vowel phoneme pronounced before phonemes *other than* /r/.

°° Percent refers to vowel phoneme pronounced before /r/.

† Percent refers to spelling in *unaccented* syllables only. For our purposes /ər/ is considered an allophone of /ûr/.

Note Well: Diphthongs, the compound vowel sounds generally said to be heard in *ate* /ā/, *feet* /ē/, *fight* /ī/, *note* /ō/, *boot* /o͞o/, *house* /ou/ and *boil* /oi/ are not considered as such in this list of phonemes. We do not disagree with the fact that diphthongs are distinguishable, as such. We avoid the term *diphthong* throughout *Phonics: Why and How*, however, because we do not believe it necessary to teach children the distinction between simple vowel sounds and diphthongs. Diphthongs are examples of a complicated linguistic fact that is not required for children to know in order to learn to use phonics.

Also noticeable is that /yo͞o/ is two vowel sounds but is not taught as such. Note, too, that /ûr/ is a combination of sounds that is taught together in all instances. No distinction is made between *er* in h*er* and in aft*er*.

In Tables 2 and 3 we have given the percent of occurrence of the most common spellings of a phoneme. For /ch/, for example, we find the spellings *ch* about 55 percent of the time, and *t* about 31 percent. The importance to the phonics teacher in knowing the most common spellings of phonemes will become readily apparent later as we discuss how this affects the sequences for teaching phonics. In teaching children to make the best use of phonics in reading and spelling it is important to first teach the phoneme-spelling correspondences that are the most frequent and then move to those that are less frequent.

Using Tables 4 and 5

Tables 4 and 5 also provide practice material for the teacher of phonics. To learn thoroughly the correspondences between sound and spelling presented in these tables, go through the tables reading aloud the words in which the separate sounds appear. By doing this you will become accustomed to hearing the same phoneme over and over as it appears in various spellings. This is important since phonics teachers sometimes have trouble in making some of these associations. As adults they are not accustomed to hearing and seeing such sound-spelling correspondences in this manner because mature readers reduce such cues to word recognition to a semiconscious level of recognition. Since the child learning to read must first develop a fully conscious recognition of these correspondences, the phonics teacher, in turn, must go back to this prior level of recognition.

If a tape recorder is available, it is useful to read the words presented in Tables 4 and 5 into the recorder and then listen to them. In addition, an easily arranged personal listening test can be put together with the use of a taped reading. To do this the phonics teacher should read the words in Tables 4 and 5 that represent the separate sounds into the tape recorder in random order. That is, jump around and select words that represent different phonemes out of the order in which they are given in the tables. For example, go through the tables reading every third word: *pat, cab, gem, ether, hot, zoo, nap, rap, what, chart,* and so on. Then listen to the tape and see if you can identify the first consonant phoneme of each of these. For the vowel sounds in Table 5, you could, of course, do the same thing. It would also be worthwhile in this drill to identify the sounds with their dictionary diacritical markings as they are given in the tables.

Another way to use such a tape recording is to listen to the random list of words and to identify the *number* of different phonemes as well as the markings of these phonemes in each word. This is most effective if you leave a pause between the spoken word in the recording to give yourself time to name the phonemes as you identify them. For example, "School" (pause). The answer would be "four phonemes: /s/—/k/—/ōō/—/l/." "Dad" (pause). "Three phonemes: /d/—/a/—/d/."

TABLE 4. SPELLINGS OF TWENTY-FOUR CONSONANT PHONEMES

Plosives

---

1. /p/ *p*at, ha*pp*y
2. /t/ *t*ap, pu*tt*
3. /ch/ *ch*art, cul*t*ure, wa*tch*, ques*t*ion
4. /k/ *c*ab, *k*ing, ba*ck*, s*ch*ool, e*x*it, oc*c*upy
5. /b/ *b*ad, e*bb*
6. /d/ *d*ad, a*dd*
7. /j/ *g*em, *j*am, bu*dg*et, e*d*ucate, a*dj*ust, re*g*ion
8. /g/ *g*o, e*gg*, e*x*act, ro*gu*e

Fricatives

---

9. /f/ *f*arm, *ph*one, o*ff*
10. /th/ e*th*er
11. /s/ *s*it, *c*ent, pa*ss*, *sc*ent
12. /sh/ a*ct*ion, *sh*ip, *s*ocial, mi*ss*ion, pen*s*ion, o*c*ean, *ch*ef, nego*t*iate, *s*ugar
13. /h/ *h*ot, *wh*o
14. /v/ *v*at
15. /th̸/ ei*th*er
16. /z/ a*s*, *z*oo, bu*zz*, de*ss*ert, e*x*act
17. /zh/ fu*s*ion, mea*s*ure, re*g*ime

Nasals

---

18. /m/ *m*an, mu*mm*y
19. /n/ *n*ap, i*nn*
20. /ng/ si*ng*, ba*n*k

Laterals

---

21. /l/ *l*ad, a*ll*, ab*l*e, easе*l*
22. /r/ *r*ap, pu*rr*

Semivowels

---

23. /w/ *w*et, liq*u*id
24. /y/ sen*i*or, *y*es

Fricative/Semivowel

/hw/ *wh*at

TABLE 5. SPELLINGS OF SEVENTEEN VOWEL PHONEMES

Checked

1. /i/ in, give, senate; and before /r/: hero, hear, deer, here, pier, souvenir, fierce, weird
2. /a/ bad, bade
3. /o͝o/ put, foot, could, woman, sure
4. /u/ up, oven, touch, come, budge
5. /e/ end, head, many, edge; and before /r/: vary, care, hair, there, bear, heir, bolero, millionaire

Free

6. /ē/ senior, feel, eat, eve, elite, ski, chief, ease, baby
7. /ā/ angel, ate, aid, way
8. /ī/ ice, find, by, night, pie, dye
9. /o͞o/ boot, truth, who, rude, you, threw, true, choose, lose, fruit
10. /ō/ both, code, oak, own
11. /ôr/ four, cord, oar, hoarse, horse
12. /o/† odd, all, faucet, dawn, ought, caught, broad, dodge; and before /r/: arm, are, heart
13. /ou/ out, owl, ounce
14. /oi/ oil, boy, voice
15. /yo͞o/ union, use, feud, cue
16. /ûr/ and /ər/° her, burn, fir, word, verse, earn, journey, urge; and in the unstressed syllables of after, honor, altar

Free, Less Accented

17. /ə/ carton, canal, pencil, rebel, pious, medium, science

† Dictionaries also give these diacritical marks for this phoneme: ä, ô. In "Western" dialect /ä/ (calm) and /o/ cough are the same vowel phoneme.

° These two phonemes are considered the same for the purposes of teaching phonics. The phoneme /ər/ is considered an allophone of /ûr/.

Practical Advice

With such practice on the identification of speech sounds, the phonics teacher is strongly advised to keep the following in mind:

1. It is necessary to isolate, identify, and discriminate speech sounds although individual, isolated phonemes cannot be pronounced in isolation without a resultant distortion. We have seen that this is especially true for consonant phonemes.

2. It is necessary to listen to *how* something is said not to *what* is being said. It is our habit as mature listeners to gloss over sounds and/or to be unaware of deviations in pronunciation, to tolerate them, and yet to get meaning from what we hear. When meaning is not listened for, however, the speech sounds we hear take on added significance. We listen then with a different, more demanding ear.

3.   It may be that many pronunciations of a word will be necessary before the phonics teacher will hear an indicated phoneme in Tables 4 and 5.

4.   If you do not readily identify a particular phoneme in a word as given there, keep on saying the word. The sound will eventually emerge out of the word and into your consciousness. It is a truism, but a useful one, to say that the sounds of phonemes can best be studied by listening to them, *and not simply by reading about them.*

5.   The phonics teacher in developing the ability to hear all the speech sounds as isolated units should not always think of speech in terms of conventional spelling. Instead of thinking of the spellings of words when you hear them, concentrate on an auditory translation of these words into discrete sounds. Then, transcribe these sounds with the diacritical marking system given in Tables 2 and 3. For example, when you hear the word *palm*, momentarily repress your visual memory of the customary spelling of the word and think /pom/.

6.   As the phonics teacher practices with Tables 4 and 5, he or she should note which phonemes appear relatively difficult to discriminate. This personal difficulty should be a signal that the sounds that have been troublesome are likely also to be hard for the pupils. Such bothersome differences between phonemes for the teacher's mature hearing abilities should probably be taught to children *after* those the teacher recognizes with untroubled ease. There also have been notable instances when teachers have tried to have pupils hear differences between sounds when these differences were not even clear to the teacher. This usually happens, of course, when teachers are uninstructed in phonics.

7.   Tables 2 and 3 represent the sounds of our language and their spellings that the teacher of phonics needs to know in teaching children to use phonics in learning to read and spell. The consonant phonemes found in Tables 2 and 3 are not difficult to hear and thus perceive as individual, unique, and important sound units. Therefore, we can say without hesitation that the consonant sounds found in Table 2 are the ones *all* teachers of phonics should use.

8.   The list of the vowel phonemes found in Table 3 demand explanation and justification. It is less easy to justify the teaching of this specific list of vowel phonemes than the consonant phonemes found in Table 2. We have noted that one reason for this is the fact that there are different dialects of American English. Certain vowel sounds are used, or not used, in different parts of our country. An obvious example of this in Table 3 is the phoneme /o/. We have described the words *box,*

calm, and *fall* as all having the same vowel sound, even though we know that in certain parts of the country additional vowel sounds will be heard for the words *calm* and *fall.* At this point we can only suggest that if you have pupils who speak a dialect that distinguishes between the vowel sounds in *box, calm,* and *fall* add the other vowel sounds to their instructional program in phonics. Do not hesitate to make other such substitutions in vowel phonemes given in *Phonics: Why and How* when these phonemes are not those of your pupils.

Our previous discussion gave as one reason for the adoption of a "Western" dialect for our guide to the list of phonemes that the mass media, especially radio and television, use this system of pronunciation. In Tables 2 and 3 we make only two deviations from the *NBC Handbook* [Crowell 1964] list of vowel phonemes and no deviations from their list of consonant phonemes. One of these vowel deviations is with the phoneme /o/, as in *hot.* NBC would say that *bah* and *raw* are not rhyming words but that they have different vowel sounds. We say that they have the same vowel sound in "Western" dialect and therefore are rhyming words.

NBC also notes the difference between the vowel sounds in *hurt* and in the second syllable of *father.* While we recognize that these vowel sounds are different (*hurt* is an accented syllable, *er* in *father* is a less accented syllable), we make no distinction in their sounds in Table 3. We see /ər/-fath*er* as an allophone of /ûr/-h*er.* We do this to simplify the teaching of phonics and so to ease the probable difficulties in learning phonics. We suggest the teaching of *all* vowel phonemes as if they occurred in stressed or accented syllables of words.

9.   Teachers using phonics with children who say /aftə/, instead of /aftər/, will also have to make some adjustments. This is not the same problem as teaching additional vowel sounds, however. The child who says /aftə/ must be taught that the final phoneme in that word is spelled *er,* just as must the child who says /aftər/.

10.   Vowels that occur before the letter *r* in words have different sounds in different speech regions. We refer here to *vary, care, hair, there, cord,* and *arm.* Such words in our list all "sound" the *r.* That is, our "Western" dialect speaker says /her/ for hair. We have noted that vowels before *r* in words like *fir* and *after* are considered the same sound in this book because of the special problems of teaching them to children.

11.   Linguists consider the sound /ûr/ in *her* and /ər/ in *after* to be vowels, not consonants. They are said to be vowels with "r-quality" or "r-colored" vowels. They appear as such "in almost all texts on the

phonetics of American English" [Bronstein 1960, p. 176]. Accordingly, these vowels are sometimes given special transcription symbols: /ɝ/ and /ɚ/. For the sake of simplicity, however, we will refer to them throughout this book as /ûr/ and /ər/. Since this, too, is a difficult distinction, only /ûr/ is taught to children in *Phonics: Why and How*.

12. It can also be seen from Tables 3 and 5 that checked vowel sounds are not heard in the final position in syllables. The teacher should also be careful not to see the final *e*, in words such as *there, idle, come*, as representing a sound.

13. It is equally noticeable from Tables 3 and 5 that free vowel sounds can occur any place in a word, either in the initial, medial, or final positions. Thus we hear the same vowel sound in *odd, hot*, and *law* but in three different places, including the final position.

14. The relatively higher number of spellings (column three of Tables 2 and 3) for vowel versus consonant phonemes can be seen. The average number of spellings for consonants is 5.4. The average number of spellings for vowel sounds is 13.8, over 2.5 times that for consonants [Hanna et al. 1966]. This matter is of great importance, as we shall see in later chapters.

More Practice with Sounds

The following exercises have been designed to allow the phonics teacher to get a more conscious "feel" of the separate sounds that are made when we speak. As with all the exercises suggested elsewhere for developing an awareness of phonemes, these activities must actually be done to be effective. It is impossible to realize their usefulness and importance in developing a keener perception of phonemes simply by reading about them.

1. Say the words *beet, bit, bait, bet, bat*, and *bought* in this order. Now say *beet-bought*. Hold your hand under your chin as you say them. You will feel your lower jaw drop wider open. Thus we know that different vowel sounds are related to the openness of the jaw. Notice, too, the so-called "long" vowel /ā/ in the midst of the above series. This demonstrates the nondescriptive nature of the terminology "long" or "short."

2. Pronounce the series *beet, Bert, boot*. You will feel your tongue moving progressively backward in your mouth. This exercise should give you a better idea of what phoneticians call *front, central*, and *back* vowels.

3. Say the pair of words *see-sue*. Notice that the lips are unround or relaxed for *see*, and round or pursed for *sue*. This illustrates the role lips play in producing phonemes.

4. Say the last sound of *sing* as represented by *ng*. Hold your nose as you say it. It can no longer be said. This shows why the phonemes /ng/, /m/, and /n/ are called nasal sounds.

5. Say these pairs of words: *sap-zap; fat-vat; pat-bat; tip-dip; chum-jum; shot-zhot; thigh-thy*. The first sound in each word in each pair we recognize as a consonant phoneme, although alert readers know that no English word begins with the sound /zh/. But if you say these pairs of words several times, you will sense that the second word in each pair feels as if it is said farther back in the mouth or throat. These second sounds are called *voiced* sounds because they are always accompanied by greater vibrations of the vocal cords. The first sound of each pair is *voiceless*, that is, said without this vibration.

REFERENCES

Berg, Frederick S., and Fletcher, Samuel G. *The Hard of Hearing Child.* New York: Grune & Stratton, 1970.

Bronstein, Arthur J. *The Pronunciation of American English.* New York: Appleton-Century-Crofts, 1960.

Carrell, James, and Tiffany, William R. *Phonetics.* New York: McGraw-Hill, 1960.

Crowell, Thomas L. *NBC Handbook of Pronunciation.* Thomas Y. Crowell, 1964.

Groff, Patrick. "Phoneticians, Reading Experts, and More." Unpublished manuscript.

Hanna, Paul R., et al. *Phoneme-Grapheme Correspondences as Cues to Spelling Improvement.* Washington, D.C.: U.S. Office of Education, 1966.

Kantner, Claude E., and West, Robert. *Phonetics.* New York: Harper & Row, 1960.

Kurath, Hans. *A Phonology and Prosody of Modern English.* Ann Arbor: University of Michigan Press, 1964.

Templin, Mildred C. *Certain Language Skills in Children.* Minneapolis: University of Minnesota Press, 1957.

4

GRAPHEMES AND
SPELLING PATTERNS

Writing is a secondary or derived system for symbolizing language [Smith, 1967, pp. 1–12]. Giving oral language its rightful precedence over written language does not mean, however, that writing should be considered as little more than a crude or misleading picture of speech. English writing may not be the ultimate representation of speech, but it is systematic in its own right. However, no spelling system, including English, can simply be the transcription of language sounds. Obviously there cannot be a one-to-one match in spelling between the number of phonemes in English—forty-one for the dialect used in this book—and these twenty-six letters. It is partly because of this mismatch that the teaching of phonics to children is so critical, and becomes so difficult at times.

In its attempts to get out of this dilemma, English spelling uses combinations of letters to represent sounds. It is obvious that there are more than twenty-six functional units in our alphabet. The units *gh, th, ch, ph, rh, sh, oi, oo,* etc., are as functional and basic as *a, b,* or *t.* However, it is most important that the teacher of phonics understands the fact that English does not consistently use *one* and *only one* letter to spell each phoneme. In written English we do not use in all words a single, unique letter to represent each sound in a word. One letter *or more* than one letter can represent a single sound.

231623

The Grapheme

To help explain this relationship of sound and spelling, we use the idea of a *grapheme*. A grapheme is a letter or cluster or combination of letters used to represent a single phoneme. A grapheme can be a single letter, for example, *a* in *a* ball, or *h* and *e* in *he*. A grapheme can also be more than one letter. Sometimes graphemes are not adjoined letters. For example, the vowel grapheme of *ate* is *a-e*. Some words in English have several letters in a single grapheme. In *though*, a two-phoneme word, *ough* is a four-letter grapheme representing the sound /ō/. When the term *grapheme* is used in this book, the phonics teacher should be reminded of these facts:

1. Graphemes in words are not always the same in number as letters in words. A grapheme may consist of one letter, or more than one letter. We add enough graphemes in English to make up the deficit between the forty-one sounds and the twenty-six letters in two ways: by combining letters, as in *ch, th, sh*, or by using a single letter as a grapheme for more than one sound, as in *pan* and *all* in which the grapheme *a* represents two different phonemes. And we complicate matters by sometimes using more than two letters for a grapheme, for example, *igh* in *high*. In a few cases we even have vowel letters in words that represent no vowel sound. Note the first *i* in *aspirin*.

2. A single phoneme may be represented by many different graphemes. For example, the /ī/ phoneme in *bite* can be represented by the following graphemes: *i-e* (bite); *igh* (nigh); *I* (I); *eye* (eye); *y* (my); *ye* (lye); *ai* (Cairo); *ay* (bayou); *aye* (aye); *ei* (Eiffel); *ie* (tie); *ui* (guise); *oy* (coyote); *uy* (buy); and *y-e* (style).

3. With very few exceptions each phoneme is represented by a grapheme. There is almost always a grapheme for each phoneme in a word. The exceptions to this are seen in words like *x-ray*, where the *x* is a grapheme for three sounds /ekz/ or /eks/; in *extra* where the *x* represents two sounds /ks/; in *expect* where the *x* represents the two sounds /ks/ or /gs/; or in *exists* /gz/. Other examples of exceptions to the one sound-one grapheme rule can be noticed with diphthong spellings, but these are not discussed in detail in this book because they present too complicated a problem in phonemics to teach children.

4. The sounds /yo͞o/, which we call a single phoneme, but are actually /y/ plus /o͞o/, generally are represented by two graphemes—but not *y* and *oo*. This is also true for /yûr/. To understand these statements, first recall the differences between /yo͞o/—/yûr/ and other vowel sounds in words. The /yo͞o/ sound is similar to the /o͞o/ sound, and the /yûr/ sound can be confused with /ûr/.

Listen carefully to words that have the /yo͞o/ and the /yûr/ sounds in order to detect them from other vowel sounds. Here are some often-used words [Greene 1955] on which to practice for this purpose. Say these pairs of words aloud. Listen for the indicated sounds.

be*au*ty /yo͞o/	b*oo*ty /o͞o/
m*u*seum /yo͞o/	m*u*scle /u/
resc*u*e /yo͞o/	iss*ue* /o͞o/
f*ew* /yo͞o/	fl*ew* /o͞o/
rep*u*tation /yo͞o/	rep*u*blican /u/
gen*u*ine /yo͞o/	fr*ui*t /o͞o/
f*ue*l /yo͞o/	cr*ue*l /o͞o/
b*u*reau /yûr/	cult*u*re /ûr/
m*u*sic /yo͞o/	m*u*ster /u/
vol*u*me /yu/	res*u*me /o͞o/
p*u*re /yûr/	p*u*rse /ûr/
c*u*rious /yûr/	c*u*rtain /ûr/

Note, on the other hand, that the following words are *not* ones with /yo͞o/ or /yûr/ sounds: *assure, rude, balloon, blue, boot, canoe, flu, conclude, knew, do, due, duty, eventual, junior, curtain, creature.*

It can be seen that (1) *ur* following /ch/ is not given the /yûr/ sound (crea*ture*), (2) *ur* following other sounds is given the /yûr/ sound (pro*cure, sure, bu*reau), and (3) *ue* at the end of words is generally given the /yo͞o/ sound (contin*ue*).

5. There are more different graphemes used to represent each *vowel* phoneme than are used for each *consonant* phoneme. John Malone [1962] has calculated that there are an average of 8.5 different graphemes per vowel sound and an average of 3.6 different graphemes per consonant sound.

6. Although the common marks of punctuation can also properly be called graphemes, we will not deal with them since the more frequently used marks are readily picked up by children in an incidental way and therefore pose no great problem for them in learning phonics. The more difficult marks, which include : ; , ( ) ", are rarely understood in the elementary school, in any case, and consequently they also are outside the purview of this book.

7. The speech sounds, as they are produced from individual to individual, year to year, and generation to generation, vary more *in their production* than do the corresponding letters of the alphabet. The reason for this is largely a matter of the relative permanence of the two types

of symbols. It is evident that the auditory symbols, that is to say, the sound waves themselves, have no permanency. They are gone the instant they are produced. Until the invention of a sound recording apparatus, they could be retained only in memory. The visual symbols, on the other hand, are as permanent as the materials out of which, and on which, they are recorded. This explains in part why "the spoken language has changed so radically since the sixth century that we would be unable to understand the language of that time if we heard it, whereas the alphabet used to record the language, even though changed in many respects, is still essentially the same" [Kantner & West 1960, p. 6].

Do We Need a Changed Alphabet to Teach Phonics?

Among the languages that approach the standard of each sound represented by one, and only one, letter are German, Russian, Spanish, and the Scandanavian languages. One of the unique features of English is that it is said to be one of the least predictably spelled languages, a fact for which there are many reasons. For one thing, English is a potpourri of many other languages. Furthermore, neither the science of language nor the power of literary societies has succeeded in exercising any control over the English spelling system. Efforts at "reforming" spelling by such people as Godfrey Dewey, George Bernard Shaw, Andrew Carnegie, Theodore Roosevelt, and Thorstein Veblen have been unsuccessful too [but see Wijk 1959].

Still another obstacle to proposed changes in spellings is the fact that there has been very little change in the spelling of certain common, high-frequency words. James Pitman and John St. John have shown that for fifty common words found in early English Bibles, the spellings established in a 1380 Bible were the same as those in the Authorized Bible of 1611. And they are still in use today [Pitman & St. John 1969, p. 72]. The consistency in the spelling of these very common words obviously reflects a profound aversion to spelling change [Groff 1976].

Arguments For and Against Spelling Reform

It has been argued [Chomsky & Halle 1968], moreover, that anyone who is a native speaker of English does not need a spelling system or orthography that is more phonemic. A phonemic spelling system is a system in which each letter (grapheme) in a word is so written that it tells the reader exactly how to pronounce the word. Obviously, this is not altogether the case at present. Note that *o* in *come* and *home* do not tell the reader to give the same pronunciation for this letter in both words.

Noam Chomsky and Morris Halle claim, nevertheless: "It is therefore noteworthy, but not too surprising, that English orthography, despite its often cited inconsistencies, comes remarkably close to being an optimal orthographic system for English" [1968, p. 49].

For example, from an intensive study of speech sounds Chomsky and Halle would say it is better to have the similar spellings of cour*a*ge–cour*a*geous, s*a*ne–s*a*nity, or r*e*lax–r*e*laxation even though the italicized vowel letter in them is read differently from word to word. Chomsky and Halle believe the reader who is mature in the knowledge of English vocabulary will read the two words correctly as an effect of the automatic processes of a deeper or unconscious linguistic knowledge. Chomsky, however, admits this may not be likely for the child [1970].

Pitman contends that "no one is likely to dispute the fact that English spelling is difficult and illogical" [1969, p. 41]. But, since others argue that "suggested reforms in spelling and other aspects of the writing system are usually based on impressionistic or superficial knowledge" [Francis 1958, p. 450], a serious consideration of Chomsky and Halle's argument seems worthwhile.

As a matter of fact, a look at the evidence pro and con shows that those (such as Pitman) who would change English orthography have provided no evidence to counter Chomsky and Halle's point that the present spelling system does not need drastic reform. Neither do the spelling reformers face up to such criticism as that of Gerd Fraenkel, who has observed that "every attempt to preserve one state of language in written form (no matter how exact) will be outdated after a short while. Only an extremely flexible spelling system would be able to keep pace with the spoken word" [1965, p. 110]. Henry Gleason, who believes it impossible to represent unambiguously in writing everything that could be said, notes that "it is doubtful that an alphabet which did accurately record speech would be practical" [1961, p. 119]. I. J. Gelb contends that "it may generally be admitted that the revision of national writings in the direction of Simplified Spellings is inadequate and not worth the effort" [1952, p. 244].

But, one must ask (again referring to Chomsky and Halle), for young children who are *not yet readers* is it "quite pointless for the orthography to indicate these predictable variants [stress and vowel sounds]?" [Chomsky & Halle 1968, p. 49]. We would accept the notion that it is beyond the scope of any spelling system to indicate all the pitch, stress, junctures, allophones, and the sound contours of spoken language. English orthography would be a cluttered spelling system, indeed, with printed words overrun with pitch, stress, juncture, allophonic, and contour symbols in addition to symbols indicating aspects of syntax and meaning. This would truly bring about the "orthographic chaos" that Thomas Edwards [1966, p. 350] mistakenly thinks is now the situation in the spelling system.

On the other hand, we would argue it is not pointless to try to control the degree of spelling unpredictabilities presented to children learning to read and spell. Although they know how to speak the language, children still need a system of instruction that attempts to make the relationships between speech and spelling predictable. We insist that a form of spelling "reform" must be given during such instruction so children, for a time at least, are led to believe that the spelling-to-speech system in English is neither inconsistent nor unpredictable. That is, children should be shown by the words given in reading that if they make one speech response to a given closed syllable, *an,* for example, they can make the same response whenever they see *an* in print—with good success with word recognition. We believe, then, that the spellings presented to beginning readers should be so selected that they can discover, first, that there is predictability in the sound-spelling system; and only second, that inconsistencies exist.

This does not mean that in the early stage of instruction in spelling and reading that children can be entirely protected from the fact that about 80 percent of the common words in English are not spelled entirely predictably [Groff 1961]. They should learn, instead, that a high percent of the *letters in words* do represent sounds predictably. Obviously children eventually will be required to discover the unpredictable nature of the relations of speech and print. Hopefully, though, this will come after they have gained some confidence in themselves as decoders of print or as recorders of sounds, and therefore will be able to tolerate and adjust to the exceptions to the sound-spelling correspondences learned up to that time. In short, we agree with Chomsky and Halle's implications that an elaboration or augmentation (reform) of our spelling system would introduce as many disadvantages for mature readers as it might overcome.

We do say, nonetheless, that children who are beginning to learn to read and to spell must be taught in a way that begins with predictably spelled words. Later, the students may be systematically introduced to ever-increasing numbers of unpredictably spelled words. We shall describe later how recurrent spelling patterns (e.g., *an, en, in, on, un*) and a recognition of function words (parts of speech other than nouns, verbs, adjectives, and adverbs) act to complete this program. We see no need, accordingly, for either an augmented alphabet such as the Initial Teaching Alphabet (ITA), or for a diacritical marking system, to teach phonics successfully to children.

The ITA system, as can be seen from Table 6, adds to, or augments, the traditional orthography of English to make a total of forty-four characters or "letters." As Table 6 shows, some of the ITA characters are traditional letters. In addition, fourteen of the augmentations are a combination of two or more orthodox letters, for example, æ, œ, ue, wh, ʧh, and au. Only

TABLE 6. INITIAL TEACHING ALPHABET

Number	Character	Name	Example	Number	Character	Name	Example
1.	æ	ain	æbl	23.	y	yay	yellœ
2.	b	bee	but	24.	z	zed or	zω
3.	c	kee	cat			zee	
	d			25.	ʒ	zess	aʒ
4.	d	did	dog	26.	wh	whee	whie
5.	೮	een	೮ch	27.	ʧh	chay	ʧhuɼʧh
6.	f	ef	fun	28.	th	ith	thin
7.	g	gay	gæt	29.	ťh	thee	ťhen
8.	h	hay	hay	30.	ʃh	ish	ʃhip
9.	ie	ide	ies	31.	ʒ	zhee	meʒuer
10.	j	jay	jam	32.	ŋ	ing	siŋ
11.	k	kay	kiŋ	33.	ɹ	er	her
12.	l	el	lip	34.	ɑ	ahd	faťher
13.	m	em	man		ɑ	ask	
14.	n	en	not	35.	a	at	at
15.	œ	ode	œpen	36.	au	aud	autumn
16.	p	pee	pæ	37.	e	et	egg
	q			38.	i	it	it
17.	r	ray	rat	39.	o	og	on
18.	s	ess	sit	40.	u	ug	up
19.	t	tee	top	41.	ω	oot	bωok
20.	ue	une	ueʒ	42.	ω	ood	mωωn
21.	v	vee	vois	43.	ou	oun	out
22.	w	way	wet	44.	oi	oin	oil
	x						

lower-case letters are used in ITA since the child meets these more frequently in print. It is also felt that the exclusive presence of lower-case characters that go below the line (capital letters do not) gives words a more distinctive shape and outline [Pitman & St. John 1969, p. 123].

Pitman's arguments for the advantages of his system do not involve evidence from analysis of the phonological components of language, however, which leads us to believe that Pitman argues for ITA largely from unproved assumptions. He claims:

By being temporarily protected [by ITA] from the illogical conundrums of orthodox spelling every child, and the one-thing-at-a-time-child in particular, feels secure and also therefore seeks out meaning and comprehension from the secondary clues offered by the context. They are not bogged down by excessive memorizing and, as the syllabic relationships develop, they quickly solve the unfamiliar word by a syllable attack which replaces the per-*character* analysis and phonic synthesizing which, incidentally, can very easily become a bad phonic habit, leading later on to slow reading speeds that are difficult to eradicate [pp. 123–124].

We believe the sequences of phonics given in *Phonics: Why and How* will protect children from the "illogical conundrums of orthodox spelling" without involving the use of an artificial alphabet. As for "syllable attack," Chapter 5 demonstrates how a word-structure analysis program based on "phonogram attack" has all the advantages claimed by Pitman for his augmented alphabet, but can be accomplished without the change of orthography he calls for.

Nor do we need to accept the opinions of Edward Fry [1964], the major contemporary advocate of a "diacritical marking system" (DMS). His is a system for putting added marks over, under, or through orthodox letters to indicate what sounds should be made, and/or which letters do not represent sounds. Fry claims that his diacritical marking system has over 99 percent phoneme-grapheme predictability. It aims to achieve essentially the same goals as ITA without distortion in word form or change in spelling, he says.

It is true that changes in spelling are not made in Fry's DMS, but it is difficult to see how he can contend that letter form is not changed. As can be seen from the list of examples of Fry's basic rules for his system, the surface appearances of words are changed:

(a)   Letters for "regular" consonants and "short" vowels are left unchanged, including *y* in *funny*.

(b)   "Silent" letters are "slashed" (w̸rite̸, rig̸t).

(c)   "Long" vowels are indicated by a bar over the letter: mād̸e̸, māi̸d, mȳ.

(d)   Unstressed vowels, schwa vowels, carry an overhead dot: ȧgo, lemȯn.

(e)   Other "consistent" sounds are indicated by a bar underneath: i̱s, a̱u̸to, y̱es, c̱ity, g̱em.

(f)   A bar beneath two letters together signals a digraph (s̱hut, c̱hat).

(g)   Exceptions to these rules are given an asterisk above the letter (ȯnce̸, o̊f).

(h)   The letter *r* is "temporarily" *r*aised to a vowel: fi̸r, fu̸r, he̸r, acre̸; a̱rm; vāry [1964].

The Predictability of Spellings

If we cannot advocate the changes to the spelling system offered by all the many would-be reformers of spelling, it behooves us to understand just how predictable our spelling system is. That is, to what extent can English be matched up, one grapheme—one phoneme?

TABLE 7. ONE-LETTER CONSONANT GRAPHEMES

Grapheme	As Seen in	Percent Occurrence [*]
b	bet	97
	all others (comb)	3
c	cube	76
	cell	23
	all others (ocean)	1
d	day	99
	all others (soldier)	1
f	fan	100
g	get	69
	gem	28
	all others (gnaw)	3
h	hat	91
	all others (hour)	9
j	just	100
k	kite	93
	all others (know)	7
l	late	98
	all others (colonel)	2
m	man	100
n	not	92
	all others (bank)	8
p	pen	99
	all others (pneumonia)	1
r	rat	100
s	sat	84
	runs	12
	all others (sure, measure)	4
t	talk	98
	all others (question, nation, equation)	2
v	van	100
w	want	83
	all others (wrong)	17
x	fox	91
	all others (exact, xylophone, luxury, luxurious, anxiety)	9
y	yet	100
z	zone	98
	all others (azure)	2

[*] Each percent (here and in Tables 8, 9, 10) refers to the percent of all occurrences of the given letter in "speech-comprehension" words of primary grade children (one- and two-syllable words only) that are given the indicated sound [Berdiansky, Cronnell, & Koehler 1969]. For example, b occurred in these "speech-comprehension" words 698 times. In 97 percent of these occurrences, the letter b is pronounced /b/.

Note well: This table shows that single-letter consonant graphemes can represent more than one sound each. For instance, x can represent six different sounds or sets of sounds, c can represent five different sounds, and so on.

TABLE 8. ONE-LETTER AND MARKER *e* VOWEL GRAPHEMES

Grapheme	As Seen in	Percent Occurrence
a, a-*e*	sat, saddle	38
	above	21
	n*a*m*e*, p*a*st*e*	14
	cart, ball, wad	12
	acre, baby	5
	war	2
	vary, any	1
	all others (was, cottage, sep*a*rate, pillar)	7
e, e-*e*	herd, father	26
	hidden	20
	set, cl*e*ver	18
	*e*dg*e*	16
	m*e*ter, we, cr*e*ate, zebra	11
	diff*e*rence	2
	scen*e*	2
	all others (cafe, pretty, silent, s*e*rgeant, reb*e*l)	5
i, i-*e*	sit, hidden, civic	64
	fin*e*	15
	title, pilot, find, liar, migrate	8
	off*i*ce	3
	fir	3
	onion	1
	all others (meringue, asp*i*rin)	6
o, o-*e*	lot, hockey, off, novel	29
	notice, only, horn, roll, go, poem	27
	cott*o*n	17
	h*o*m*e*	12
	won, l*o*v*e*°	5
	word	1
	all others (woman, who, col*o*r, licorice)	9
u, u-*e*	gum, sudden	74
	*u*s*e*	8
	put	7
	bug*le*, unit	5
	fluid	1
	lett*u*ce	1
	all others (rumor, busy, hurt, bury, medium)	4
y, y-*e*	baby	85
	deny, rh*y*m*e*°	9
	myth	3
	all others	3

Except where indicated, °, the data in Tables 8 and 10 are recalculated from Berdiansky, Cronnell, and Koehler [1969] to indicate marker *e*, and to delete the *ed* and *es* words analyzed there (*wives, named*). The source of the data for Tables 8 and 10 did not recognize the marker *e* grapheme.

GRAPHEMES AND SPELLING PATTERNS

Tables 7, 8, 9, and 10 are principally intended to illustrate t.
to which the speech sound in a word can be predicted from the gr
used to spell it. An inspection of these tables shows that some let.
words predict accurately and consistently the speech sound that shou.
given the word if it is to be read aloud correctly. Or vice versa, when a ʸ
word is said aloud, these letters consistently spell these words correctly.

TABLE 9. TWO-LETTER CONSONANT GRAPHEMES

Grapheme	As Seen in	Percent Occurrence	Grapheme	As Seen in	Percent Occurrence
bb	rubber	100	ng	sing	97
bt	debt	—	nn	runner	100
cc	hiccup	100	ph	phone	100
ch	machine, chest,		pn	pneumonia	—
	chorus,	82 /ch/	pp	happy	100
cq	lacquer	—	ps	psychology	—
ck	pack	100	pt	receipt	—
cz	czar	—	qu	quick	85
dd	daddy	100	rh	rhyme	—
dg	edge	—	rr	hurry	100
ed	baked, rubbed	—	rt	mortgage	—
ff	ruff	100	sc	science, discern	—
gg	egg	100	se	false, case,	
gh	ghost, cough	89		nauseous	—
gn	sign, gnaw	—	si	business	—
gu	vague	—	sh	shop	100
kn	knob	—	sl	island	—
ld	would	—	sp	raspberry	—
le	handle	100	ss	glass, issue,	
lf	half	—		scissors	96 /s/
lk	walk	—	sw	answer	—
ll	holly	100	th	Thomas, the,	73 /th/
lm	psalm	—		thin	22 /th/
lv	salve	—	tt	letter	100
mb	lamb	—	vv	flivver	—
mm	hammer	100	wh	who	84
mn	hymn, mnemonic	—	wr	write	—
mp	glimpse	—	zz	buzz	93
nd	handsome,				
	handkerchief	—			

All data in this table are from Berdiansky, Cronnell, and Koehler [1969].

Note well: Table 9 should be read as follows. The grapheme *bb*, for example, represents the phoneme /b/, as in *rubber*, 100 percent of the time for this spelling.

Where no data was available, as for *bt* (de*bt*), this signifies that such spellings occur relatively infrequently. That is, the spellings for which the data of occurrence ("percent occurrence") are available are the ones that should be taught in phonics.

TABLE 10. TWO-LETTER VOWEL GRAPHEMES

Grapheme	As Seen in	Percent Occurrence
ae	aesthetic, Caesar	—
ah	bah	—
ai	stain	90
	captain	6
	all others (plaid, said, Cairo, carriage)	4
au	sauce	82
	all others (laugh, chauffer, restaurant)	18
aw	law	100
ay	stray	99
	all others (quay, bayou, says)	1
ea	steam	69
	feather	20
	heard	5
	all others (steak, fear, ocean, hearth)	6
ee	seem	99
	all others (matinee, deer, been)	1
ei	seize°, ceiling	39
	reign	37
	all others (weird, heifer, their)	24
eo	people, leopard, yeoman	—
et	valet	—
eu	feud, neutral, amateur	—
ew	grew	95
	all others (sew, mew)	5
ey	key	56
	they	19
	all others	25
ez	rendezvous	—
ho	honest	—
ia	social	—
ie	field	78
	die	13
	all others (friend, sieve, soldier)	9
io	nation	—
oa	foam	93
	all others (broad, board)	7

TABLE 10 (continued)

Grapheme	As Seen in	Percent Occurrence
oh	oh	—
oi	boil	90
	all others (choir)	10
oo	food	66
	foot	27
	all others (flood, door)	7
os	appropos	—
ot	depot	—
ou	out	57
	tough	16
	soul	12
	soup	8
	fought	5
	all others (court, would, journal)	2
ow	low	55
	cow	45
	all others (knowledge)	5
oy	boy	96
	all others (coyote)	4
ua	guard, guarantee	—
ue	due	81
	all others (guess)	19
ui	juice°, fruit	59
	build	41
	(very infrequent: guise, circuit)	
uo	buoy, liquor	—
uu	vacuum	—
uy	buy	—
wo	two	—
ye	lye	—

Blanks indicate that the spelling did not occur frequently enough to be studied in the source used for these percents [Berdiansky, Cronnell, & Koehler 1969].

° Indicates data could not be recalculated to indicate marker *e*.

Quite as obviously, these four tables demonstrate that other letters are not too reliable for these purposes.

Some Generalities about Sounds and Spellings

Beyond the specific information as to the predictability of the correspondences between graphemes and phonemes of English given by the tables in this chapter, these tables suggest certain more general conclusions about this relationship a phonics teacher should keep in mind. For example:

1. It can be seen that some letters in words appear to represent no sound. Note the "silent" letters in *k*now and com*b*. This is less apparent in other words. For example, *g* seems to represent no sound when one says *strong*, but does in *stronger*.

2. Some phonemes are almost always represented by the same, single grapheme. It is useful for the phonics teacher to be aware of such predictable graphemes as /th/, /v/, and /h/.

3. Some graphemes appear to be purely arbitrary spellings of sounds. Notice *eau* in *beau* and *beauty*, and *ight* in *night*.

4. The English spelling system makes extensive use of doubled-letter graphemes, especially in the middle of words (*butter*). Sometimes these are useful in reading: *hiss-his, diner-dinner, unnamed-unaimed*. Sometimes they are not: *holy-wholly*. English phonology does not allow two same consonant sounds in a row in words except across morpheme boundaries. Note how this occurs in *bookcase* and *unknown* (two morphemes—doubled sounds allowed), but not in *butter* or *rubber* (one morpheme—single sound for *tt* and *bb*).

5. Certain graphemes are never doubled: *j, k, q, w, x,* and *v* (except in *flivver*).

6. Some vowel graphemes are useful in reading (m*ea*t-m*ee*t), but obviously cause trouble in spelling.

7. Many of the distinctions in writing depend on the letter ("marker") *e* (hat*e*). Many sound variants in reading are signalled by *e: hate-hat*.

8. Homophones are helpful in reading since their spellings sometimes make distinctions in the writing system that are not apparent in spoken language: *right-rite; to-two-too*.

9. The influence of foreign languages is apparent in the graphemes used in English spellings, such as the graphemes *qu* and *th* from Latin-French, *ou* and *ch* from French, and *ps* from Greek.

Practice with Graphemes

The phonics teacher can become sensitive to graphemes by practicing their identification in the following words. Identify each grapheme by putting it in a box or block. Note how *e-e* is boxed in:

g   r   a   ph   e   m   e

tub	bowl	ideal	fluff	pick
from	coop	noise	valve	length
mad	two	allow	wither	trust
laugh	soot	boat	exit	think
pep	church	weak	fence	angel
fate	better	whirl	beige	angle
mint	cradle	yawl	ration	tenth
feet	basket	huge	hobby	switch
talk	hook	rare	asked	tests
not	able	lark	traded	prolong

Rewrite the following words using the "key" letter for each sound given in this chart:

a—a̱t	i—i̱t	u—up	ou—o̱u̱t
ā—ā̱ngel	ī—fi̱nd	yo͞o—u̱nion	oi—o̱i̱l
e—be̱d, va̱ry	o—o̱dd, a̱rm	o͝o—fo̱o̱t	ûr—he̱r, afte̱r
ē—be̱	ō—o̱ld, co̱rd	o͞o—bo̱o̱t	ə—carto̱n
	ôr—co̱rd		

does	city	gone	fur	aid	why
loll	hear	veto	anger	waif	know
shaft	creek	stood	bubble	foist	when
says	pause	noon	curling	sour	because
bear	what	broom	soda	brow	toward
locate	soft	hoof	human	quit	fine

Read the following words written with "key" letters. Write these words as they are regularly spelled.

wuz	gon	əgrē
laf	dənōt	ād
sed	pətātō	fir
peûr	wo͝olf	oistər
lōcāt	wûri	toun
him	oltər	bōt
crēk	fo͞old	fer
stok	trubəl	fōrən

REFERENCES

Berdiansky, Betty, Cronnell, Bruce, and Koehler, John. *Spelling-Sound Relations and Primary Form-Class Descriptions for Speech-Comprehension Vocabularies of 6-9 Year-Olds.* Los Alamitos, Calif.: Southwest Regional Laboratory for Educational Research and Development, 1969.

Chomsky, Noam. "Phonology and Reading," *Basic Studies on Reading,* eds. Harry Levin and Joanna P. Williams. New York: Basic Books, 1970.

Chomsky, Noam, and Halle, Morris. *The Sound Pattern of English.* New York: Harper & Row, 1968.

Dechant, Emerald. *Linguistics, Phonics, and the Teaching of Reading.* Springfield, Ill.: Charles C. Thomas, 1969.

Edwards, Thomas J. "Teaching Reading: A Critique," *The Disabled Reader,* ed. John Money. Baltimore: Johns Hopkins University Press, 1966.

Fraenkel, Gerd. *Writing Systems.* Boston: Ginn, 1965.

Francis, W. Nelson. *The Structure of American English.* New York: The Ronald Press, 1958.

Fry, Edward. "A Diacritical Marking System to Aid Beginning Reading Instruction." *Elementary English,* 41(1964):526–529.

Gelb, I.J. *A Study of Writing.* Chicago: University of Chicago Press, 1952.

Gleason, Henry A. *An Introduction to Descriptive Linguistics.* New York: Holt, Rinehart and Winston, 1961.

Greene, Harry. *New Iowa Spelling Scale.* Iowa City: University of Iowa Press, 1955.

Groff, Patrick. "The New Iowa Spelling Scale: How Phonetic Is It?" *Elementary School Journal,* 62(1961):46–49.

Groff, Patrick. "Why There Has Been No Spelling Reform." *Elementary School Journal,* 76(1976):331–337.

Kantner, Claude E., and West, Robert. *Phonetics.* New York: Harper & Row, 1960.

Malone, John R. "The Larger Aspects of Spelling Reform." *Elementary English,* 36(1962):435–445.

Pitman, James, and St. John, John. *Alphabets and Reading.* New York: Pitman, 1969.

Smith, Henry Lee. "Cultural Anthropology, Linguistics and Literacy," *Imprints of Culture*, ed. Malcolm P. Douglass. Claremont, Calif.: Claremont Graduate School, 1967.

Wijk, Axel. *Regularized English: An Investigation into the English Spelling Reform Problem with a New, Detailed Plan for a Possible Solution.* Stockholm: Almqvist and Wiskell, 1959.

5

THE STRUCTURE
OF SYLLABLES

Over the years teachers have received frequent and abundant advice from phonics experts about the usefulness of dictionary syllabication. To give proper instruction to children in reading and spelling, this advice contends, the teacher should base the program in word-structure analysis on the ways the dictionary syllabicates words. Typical of the kind of advice given on this matter is that of Carl Wallen [1969]. He believes there are three "syllabic signals," which are illustrated by the way these words are divided (v = vowel letter; c = consonant letter):

1. *hap-pen*	VC-CV	2. *ho-tel*	V-CV	3. *mar-ble*	VC-CV
pen-cil	VC-CV	*ma-rine*	V-CV	*bu-gle*	V-CV
					(the *le* "rule")

Wallen insists that "the reader can become both a rapid and an independent reader only if he learns to perform the third procedure [the application of his three syllabic signals] successfully" [p. 94].

A few other experts in phonics disagree with these statements, and as we shall see, so do the experts in linguistics who write on this subject. This minority of dissidents insists that the teaching of dictionary rules of syllabication is misleading and futile and therefore a waste of children's time in school. One main purpose of this chapter is to describe the thinking of those who have rightly objected to the teaching of dictionary syllabication. We shall attempt to demonstrate that little that Wallen says about syllabication has any merit. We shall show, to the contrary, that his ideas on this matter are not supported by either the science of linguistics or by experimental research. We agree that "most of the rules for syllable division commonly given out in the schools are nothing more than guides to the use of the hyphen; they have no relevance to either rules for spelling or rules for pronunciation" [Brengelman 1970, p. 95].

We will demonstrate, too, the uselessness of some of the advice commonly offered as to what to *teach* about syllabication. One would rightly expect that any such teaching must help children identify the sounds to give to an unknown printed word, that is, to relate its printed and oral forms. The usual suggestions for teaching syllabication do not do this, however. Notice how the following purportedly important and "most commonly taught syllabication generalizations" *do not* in fact help children identify a word. It is obvious that to apply the following generalizations children must *first* be able to read correctly the word in question aloud. Why, then, would they need to know such generalizations?

> When a consonant comes between two vowels, the consonant is part of the first syllable if the first vowel is short, e.g., palace.
> When a consonant comes between two vowels, the consonant is part of the second syllable if the first vowel is long, e.g., hotel [Otto et al. 1974, p. 140].

The Advocates of Dictionary Syllabication

It has been shown [Groff 1971a] that somewhere between the publication of Edmund Burke Huey's *The Psychology and Pedagogy of Reading* in 1908, which did not refer to dictionary syllabication, and W. A. Cook and M. V. O'Shea's widely used *The Child and Spelling* in 1914, there apparently came into being a belief that dividing a word into syllables[1] may act as a prevention of spelling error, as Cook and O'Shea put it. Three other prominent experts in spelling instruction—Willard Tidyman, James Fitzgerald, and Gertrude Hildreth—in their turns, endorsed the idea of dividing words according to dictionary rules in their writings [Groff 1971b].

A most enthusiastic advocate of using dictionary syllabication for the teaching of reading in the 1930s was Edward Dolch [Groff 1971b]. In the 1940s the leading advocate of this school of thought was William S. Gray. For some reason, the publication of Gray's *On Their Own in Reading* [1948] acted to dispel almost all remaining doubts about the usefulness of dictionary syllabication in reading instruction. Apparently without examining the linguistic legitimacy of Gray's many complex rules of syllabication, or, as we shall see, the experimental examinations of their usefulness, later writers of phonics for teachers echoed his proposals on this matter.

---

[1] Unless otherwise noted syllable division or syllabication refers to *dictionary syllabication*, that is, the rules or practices for this found in the traditional dictionary.

A roll call of today's well-known writers on phonics indicates that almost all of them defend Gray's earlier notions about syllabication and reading [see Groff 1971b]. There appears to be almost unanimous agreement among these experts as to the value of dictionary syllabication in teaching reading and spelling. The collective influence of these prominent experts on the use of dictionary syllabication by classroom teachers has been massive. Thus, the basal materials most teachers use to teach reading and spelling have strongly reflected their favorable views on dictionary syllabication.

The Adversaries of Dictionary Syllabication

Other experts in reading give only conditional assent to the notion of the value of dictionary syllabication. A number of them react with outright rejection of the idea. In the former group we find John DeBoer and Martha Dallmann, Donald Durrell, Albert Harris, David Russell, George Spache, and Russell Stauffer [see Groff 1971b]. Stauffer's remarks are typical of this position: "No pupil has learned to be on his own in reading by memorizing the hundreds of rules supplied in *On Their Own in Reading* by Gray." Yet, he feels that "syllable rules are of some value in spelling, and it is in spelling class that they are frequently taught" [1969, pp. 358–359]. Thus, Stauffer would reject dictionary syllabication for reading but finds some value for it with spelling.

At least two well-known writers on word recognition (in the group made up of educationalists) totally reject the notion of dictionary syllabication. In one of his discussions of "cue systems" in reading, Kenneth Goodman obviously appears to question any usefulness of dictionary syllabication. He notes:

Within words there are these cue systems:

Letter-sound relationships (phonic generalizations)

Shape, or word configuration

Known little words in new words

Affixes

Recurrent spelling patterns

Whole known words [Smith, Goodman, & Meridith 1970, pp. 251–252].

It is apparent from this list of cue systems to word recognition that in Goodman's judgment any reference to dictionary syllabication is superfluous.

It is Paul McKee who rejects the use of dictionary syllabication in an even more outright and forceful manner. McKee says:

> Rarely . . . has he found that any pupil who has learned to use together context and letter-sound associations for consonants and a few other items needs to use a knowledge of rules of syllabication in order to call to mind the familiar spoken word for which a given strange printed word stands. Consequently this volume [McKee's book on teaching reading] does not recommend that the pupil be taught to use syllabication rules as aids in unlocking words which are strange only in print [1966, p. 114].

Linguists' Opinions of Syllabication

Linguists who have written about the uses of dictionary syllabication in the teaching of reading also have taken a strong stand against this practice. For Carl Lefevre, generalizations about syllabication should be made by the child "for himself inductively, and with a minimum of help from teachers, in the course of learning to read and write" [1964, pp. 178–179]. Ronald Wardhaugh is as severe in his rejection of teaching dictionary syllabication as McKee. He notes:

> Reading teachers are asked to teach their children to divide words as follows: *but-ter, mon-key, rob-in, ro-bot,* even though, as has been pointed out elsewhere. . . , such rules are often quite circular, have almost nothing to do with the actual sound patterns of English and almost everything to do with line-breaking conventions, and have hardly any possible application beyond the typesetter's domain. They certainly do not make sense as a systematic statement about the syllables of the spoken language, nor are they entirely consistent with one another. . . . if children can use them, they do not really need them, because their use requires that children have the very knowledge the rules are supposed to be teaching [1969, p. 9].

Wardhaugh continues by agreeing with many, however, that "statements about units such as prefixes, roots, and suffixes and for compounding do have some value" [p. 9].

In regard to this last point, Roger Shuy [1969], another linguist, suggests that the boundaries of syllables should be marked (1) between compound words, *ink-well;* (2) to separate affixes, *love-ly;* (3) between certain clusters, for example, *sil-ver,* where morphemes are not involved; (4) to follow rules for open syllables, *ti-ger,* and for closed syllables, *shad-ow;* and (5) to separate syllabic consonants, /l, r, m, n/, as in *pood-le.* It can be seen that these divisions, in certain respects, do not follow dictionary syllabication.

Resolving the Dispute over Syllabication

These are the stands taken in the controversy over syllabication. The majority of reading experts are able to give almost unqualified support for the teaching of dictionary syllabication. A very small group is committed to a contrary view of the matter. All linguists reject it.

Where does the phonics teacher turn for a resolution to this dispute? Two sources of evidence are available to help settle it. The first of these is the writing in the field of linguistics, especially phonetics and phonemics, that discusses the nature of the syllable as the science of language has studied it. The second is the result of classroom experiments as to the effects of teaching syllabication on the reading and spelling skills of children.

Linguistics and Dictionary Syllabication

As much as one searches for information on the nature of the syllable from linguistics, one cannot uncover evidence that supports the idea of dictionary syllabication [Groff 1971b]. Nowhere in phonetics or phonemics does one learn that dictionary syllabication is based on true or defensible descriptions, or theories of the boundaries of the syllable. This lack of support by scholars in linguistics for dictionary syllabication as an accurate picture of this phenomenon conflicts sharply, of course, with the advice given to teachers by almost all the writers on traditional phonics.

Research on Teaching Syllabication

It is an established fact that no description or theory of the syllable in linguistics supports the validity of dictionary syllabication as a true picture of this speech phenomenon [Groff 1971b]. But should dictionary syllabication be taught as a matter of expediency? That is, despite the fact that it does not truly describe the syllable, does the teaching of this syllabication help children learn to read and spell? Does the research evidence from classroom experiments on the value of teaching dictionary syllabication support this? The answer is *no*. A thoroughgoing review of the research evidence [Groff 1971b] indicates that the use of dictionary syllabication as a means of teaching children to learn to recognize words has no special value.

The disappointing results of teaching dictionary syllabication as an aid to spelling and the negative or inconclusive evidence as to its effect on reading leads us to reject the position of the advocates of dictionary syllabication. Furthermore, the relentless rejection of dictionary syllabication by linguists adds force to our view that the teaching of dictionary syllabication is neither necessary nor useful [Groff 1971a].

The Anomaly of Dictionary Syllabication Research

The results of studies on the utility of phonics generalizations based on dictionary syllabication of words, such as that by Theodore Clymer [1963], are unsatisfactory as information on which to base a method for teaching word analysis. The artificiality of dictionary syllabication, the fact that it does not truly describe the syllable, suggests that some of the findings in such studies are inaccurate and misleading.

Clymer, for example, studied which of several so-called phonics generalizations are "stated specifically enough so that it can be said to aid or hinder in the pronunciation of a particular word" [1963, p. 254]. One generalization that was studied for its usefulness according to this criterion was: "If the first vowel sound in a word is followed by two consonants, the first syllable usually ends with the first of the two consonants" [p. 257]. However, this was not deemed a useful generalization because the dictionary made this division with only 72 percent of the primary-grade words so described (for example, *bul-let*). Twenty-eight percent of these words had a dictionary syllabication in which the consonants were not divided, as in *sing-er*.

These results, we insist, are irrelevant to phonics teaching since they are based on the faulty premise that dictionary syllabication is the authentic one. Linguists would say that the true syllabication of *bullet* is *bull-et;* all theories of syllabication would agree that there are three phonemes in the first syllable of this word.

What we know of graphemics (cf. Chapter 3) would also lead us to reject the syllabication *bul-let*. *Bullet*, according to its graphemes, has to be divided either *bu-llet* or *bull-et*. It cannot be divided *bul-let* since this would split the grapheme *ll*, leaving the erroneous impression that the first *l* is a grapheme representing one sound, and that the second *l* is a grapheme of a second sound.

The dictionary division of bullet (*bul-let*) is also wrong for the practical purposes of teaching reading and spelling. For reading, it would wrongly suggest that bullet is given two /l/ sounds. For spelling, it is wrong since it does not give children the proper visual image of *bullet* that they need. Children learning to spell *bullet* need the visual image of *bull-et*, since they cannot depend on an *auditory* example of *bullet*, /bŏolət/, as a complete guide to its spelling. If we amended the above rule to read: "If the first vowel sound (to include a diphthong) in a word is followed by two consonants, the first syllable usually ends with the *second* of these consonants," we would have a worthwhile rule to teach.

A Revised Approach to Syllabication

The evidence from both the science of phonetics and the research on teaching dictionary syllabication compels us to adopt a new attitude and, in turn, a different set of procedures for teaching word-structure analysis.

We recommend a return to the teaching of word families or phonograms (or "graphonemes" as Virginia Jones [1970] calls them). These are frequently occurring vowel-consonant patterns, checked and free vowel-consonant combinations. These closed syllables as they also may be called are shown in *es, an, en, in, on, un*. The use of these closed syllables or phonograms for phonics is the best alternative to dictionary syllabication plans for several reasons. (1) The phonogram form of syllabication is equally adaptable to any system of reading: the basal reader, language experience or individualized reading, the "linguistic" approach, programmed readers, and so on. It requires no changes in spelling or any special material for children. (2) It is important to note that phonograms act to mark the boundaries of separate syllables in a more linguistically legitimate way than do the divisions ordinarily suggested, such as vc-cv (*but-ter*) and v-cv (*ma-nage*). (The terms *syllable* and *phonogram* are used interchangeably here, although phonograms generally are not syllables. For example, *get* is a syllable. Its phonogram is *et*.) (3) We calculated that only 65 percent of monosyllabic words seen in high-frequency polysyllabic words can be read with their autonomous pronunciation (as accented syllables), while not appreciably distorting the pronunciations of the bigger words. Thus, using closed syllables is a more useful practice than finding monosyllabic ("little") words in bigger words [Groff 1973]. (4) Closed syllables or phonograms are useful in teaching phonics because the sounds to give their vowel letters are relatively predictable. When children see a phonogram anywhere within a word, they can be fairly sure its vowel letter will be pronounced in a consistent fashion.

Recent research has attempted to indicate the extent of this predictability factor. Robert Emans [1967] found that when a vowel letter is in the middle of a one-syllable word, the vowel is "short" when read 73 percent of the time. Virginia Jones [1970] investigated the nature of spelling patterns by marking all the vowel-consonant (for example, *on, in, an*) and vowel-consonant-"silent" *e* (*ake, ime*) patterns in a large sample of words. These marked patterns, or, in her words, "graphonemes" served as a syllabication of the words she analyzed. (Jones did not use dictionary syllabication in her study.) Jones found that if all the graphonemes in words were treated as stressed syllables (no schwa sound given to any of them), they would be pronounced with either a "short" vowel or a "long" vowel sound much of the time. A recalculation of her data indicates that almost 80 percent of the closed syllables she identified could be given "short" or "long" vowel sounds ("short" = /a-e-i-o-u/; "long" = /ā-ē-ī-ō-yōō/).

This compares favorably with the evidence Lou Burmeister [1969] gives from her study of dictionary syllables. Burmeister's data can be calculated to indicate that when all dictionary syllables are spoken as closed syllables, that is, when they are all spoken as if they were individual words, they are given the "short" vowel sound most of the time. Her data shows that the indicated percent of vowel graphemes in dictionary syllables are given the "short" sound of the vowel shown here, when they are read as stressed syllables:

/a/: 85%   /e/: 85%   /i/: 87%   /o/: 77%   /u/: 78%

Richard Wylie and Donald Durrell also found that the closed syllables or phonograms in primary-grade words they studied were "stable," in that they were given either a "long" or "short" sound. They concluded that of the "phonograms which appear in primary grade words, 272 or 95% have stable sounds of vowels" [1970, p. 787]. Eleanor Gibson believes "that the smallest component units in written English are spelling patterns." By a spelling pattern she means "a cluster of graphemes in a given environment which has an invariant pronunciation according to the rules of English." This spelling pattern can be a "unit of one or more letters," its critical feature being that it has a "single, regular pronunciation" [1965, p. 1071]. Phonograms fit this definition.

Closed syllables also are useful in that they do not require any special teaching of vowels or vowel sounds. Vowel sounds are taught as part of the closed syllable sound. Thus, the decision as to which vowels to teach and whether they should be taught before consonants is avoided. The phonics teacher simply decides which phonograms to teach, and the decision about vowels comes as a result of this.

The uncertainty of what sound to give to a vowel letter(s) in a word is reduced when phonograms are taught. For instance, what pronunciation should be given to the vowel letter *o* when it follows *h* (*ho*) at the beginning of a word? This depends on the word in question, of course. This could be *hot, hoot, hook, hour, honest, house, hope, honey,* or *hoist.* It is apparent that to know which of the various sounds to give the letter *o* one must read from *right to left.* That is, it is critical here to know which letters *follow* the vowel letter in a word if one is to be able to give the vowel letter its appropriate sound. Awareness of the fact that they must read a word from right to left in order to identify vowel sounds is what phonogram teaching especially provides for children. The combination, vowel-consonant, in phonograms

TABLE 11. RANK ORDER DISTRIBUTION OF PHONOGRAMS

Rank	Times Occurred*	Phonogram	Example	Number of Exceptions
1	160	er	h*er*	12
2	78	in	w*in*	3
3	75	en	m*en*	3
4	71	or	f*or*	7
5	54	al	p*al*	3
6	51	an	m*an*	1
7	45	on	*on*	5
8	39	un	f*un*	2
9	37	ate	g*ate*	1
10	35	et	s*et*	0
11	37	it	s*it*	3
12	32	ess	gu*ess*	0
13	34	is	h*is*	4
13	30	ing	r*ing*	0
15	28	ent	s*ent*	0
16	33	ic	pan*ic*	7
17	27	om	T*om*	5
18	23	ab	c*ab*	2
18	22	ap	t*ap*	1
20	28	es	y*es*	8
21	24	ec	r*ec*ord	5
22	21	im	h*im*	3
22	20	id	h*id*	2
24	22	ed	r*ed*	5
25	16	ex	*ex*it	0
26	18	el	*el*evator	3
27	17	as	h*as*	3
27	15	if	*if*	1
27	16	il	civ*il*	2
27	20	ul	*ul*timate	6
31	16	am	h*am*	3
31	13	ish	d*ish*	0
31	16	ur	f*ur*	3
34	14	um	h*um*	2
34	14	us	b*us*	2
36	11	ant	pl*ant*	0
36	11	ill	w*ill*	0
36	11	ure	s*ure*	0
39	10	ef	ch*ef*	0
39	11	ig	d*ig*	1
39	10	ip	l*ip*	0
39	12	op	t*op*	2
43	17	ac	*ac*cent	8
43	13	ad	h*ad*	4
43	11	ep	st*ep*	2
46	13	ol	*ol*ive	7
47	10	ag	b*ag*	5
47	10	os	p*os*ing	5
49	33	at	c*at*	30
50	20	ar	c*ar*	19

constantly informs children that the consonants that follow a vowel act to signal both the pronunciation of the vowel and the vowel(s) and consonant(s) that follow.

High-Frequency Phonograms

Table 11 presents a list of high-frequency phonograms based on a study of these by Jones [1970]. Given here is a ranked distribution of these phonograms as analyzed from a random sample of over 1,400 words taken from a beginning dictionary for children. The 50 phonograms in Table 11 are ranked in the order of frequency of their occurrence in this sample. For example, *er* occurred in 160 phonograms of the total in the sample, so it is ranked number 1. At the other extreme, *ar* as in *car* occurred in only 20 phonograms. It is ranked last, or number 50. Also note that in 19 other phonograms with the *ar* spelling the vowel sound /r/ heard in *car* did not prevail.

This list of phonograms is important to the teacher of phonics since it gives the specific spelling patterns that children are likely to see in the reading materials they use. The list alerts the teacher to those patterns that will occur over and over, the patterns children will be required to read with relatively great frequency, and the patterns that have highly predictable spellings. The implication for the teacher of phonics from this data is clear. In teaching phonics make sure your pupils have much practice in the recognition of the words in these high-frequency phonograms so that they will learn to perceive them quickly wherever they appear in a word.

We further analyzed the most frequently occurring marker *e* phonograms that appear at the ends of high-frequency words. The phonics teacher can see from Table 12 that the marker *e* phonograms, with the exception of *ate* and *ure*, occur relatively infrequently. Many of these phonograms have two or more sound-spelling correspondences. Often the correspondence varies between that found for monosyllabic words and for polysyllabic words. This is seen and heard in *late* /lāt/ and *senate* /sen it/. Children must learn to be ready to apply more than one vowel sound to the marker *e* phonograms in polysyllabic words.

Table 11 Footnotes

Adapted from Jones [1970], pp. 34–36.

° "Times occurred" refers to the incidence of the sound-spelling correspondence indicated in the "Example" column. For instance, *er* occurred with the sound as in *her* 160 times. In addition, *er* occurred 12 times in words in which the /ûr/ sound, as in *her*, was not heard. The "Rank" of these phonograms is based on their predictability. That is, in determining the rank order of the phonograms, the number of exceptions was subtracted from the "times occurred" number. All phonograms are treated as if they were accented syllables. Thus, civil is interpreted as /siv-il/ and not as /siv-əl/ or /siv-l/.

The vowel sounds given to marker *e* phonograms in monosyllabic words is regular. Generally, monosyllabic marker *e* spellings, V*Ce*, are given the sounds /ā, ē, ī, ō, yo͞o/, as in *tame, theme, time, hole, mule*. From our analysis of the high-frequency monosyllabic words [Groff 1972] we found that only 9 percent of these spellings (phonograms) were given vowel sounds other than /ā, ē, ī, ō, yo͞o/.

The relative occurrence or distribution of the marker *e* phonograms is shown in Table 12. These are the marker *e* phonograms that occur at the ends of high-frequency words. Examples of the variant sound-spelling correspondences of some of these phonograms are also given in Table 12.

Phonograms Versus "Sight Words"

The phonics teacher should not think that phonograms are some variety of "sight words," or that phonograms are learned by "sight" or by recall of their total outline or configuration. The idea of "sight words" appears to be popular, but there is no research evidence to support the notion that beginning readers learn words first by "sight" or by "wholes" [Groff 1974].

With phonograms children are *not* directed to look at the total forms of phonograms (for example, the *a*-phonograms *al, an, ate, ab, ap, as, am, ant, ad, ag, at, ar*) as separate visual forms, as advocates of "sight word" reading claim should be done. In this book's phonics system children have learned to associate the sound and the spelling of the final consonant letter in a given phonogram before reading a complete phonogram. For instance, for the *al* in *pal* they already know that the sound /l/ is represented by the letter *l*. In a phonogram children hear and see another sound and letter combination. The generalization students now make is that *a* represents /a/. And, *most importantly,* in the phonogram they hear the actual sound of /a/. The true sound of this vowel cannot be given if it is isolated. After practice with *al* as /al/ in both words and sentences, children proceed to another phonogram, for example, *an*. At this stage students carry with them the knowledge that *a* represents /a/. They have, as we saw, previously learned that *n* represents /n/. With teaching done in this order, children soon are reading many *a*-phonograms in words, including those with the "marker e" (at*e*).

Even at this early stage in reading the teacher writes sentences that contain words with *a*-phonograms and reads for children the words in the sentence that they do not yet know. In this manner all the cues to word recognition are activated.

Research Evidence on the Phonogram Approach

Results from earlier experiments with her system led Jones to conclude "that the experimental method, the Phonogram Method, can be successfully

TABLE 12. RANK ORDER DISTRIBUTION
OF MARKER *e* PHONOGRAMS

Rank	Times Occurred	Phonogram	Examples
1	51	*ate*	*late, senate*
2	37	*ure*	*sure*
3	31	*age*	*page, average*
4	30	*ence*	*fence, silence*
5	29	*ine*	*pine, genuine*
6	27	*ance*	*glance, attendance*
6	27	*ive*	*alive, give*
8	17	*ose*	*hose*
8	17	*one*	*one, gone, phone*
10	16	*ite*	*bite*
10	16	*are*	*are, square*
10	16	*ide*	*side*
13	15	*ace*	*face, preface*
13	15	*ake*	*take*
15	14	*ore*	*more*
16	13	*ise*	*rise*
16	13	*ire*	*fire*
16	13	*ere*	*where, severe*
16	13	*ice*	*nice*
20	11	*ame*	*came*
20	11	*ove*	*love, move, drove*
22	10	*ute*	*cute*
23	8	*ale*	*male*
23	8	*ome*	*home, come*
23	8	*ade*	*fade*
23	8	*ile*	*while*
27	7	*ease*	*please, lease*
27	7	*oke*	*woke*
27	7	*ize*	*size*
27	7	*ave*	*have, save*
27	7	*ike*	*like*
32	6	*erve*	*serve*
32	6	*use*	*accuse*
32	6	*ole*	*whole*
32	6	*ote*	*vote*
32	6	*ange*	*range, orange*
32	6	*ime*	*time*
38	5	*ense*	*sense*
38	5	*ume*	*costume*
38	5	*ude*	*rude*
38	5	*ase*	*case*
38	5	*uce*	*reduce*

Adapted from Jones [1970].

employed as an approach to teaching beginning reading" [Groff 1971b, p. 86]. As to her more recent studies of the effectiveness of "graphonemes" (phonograms), it has been found that "field test data from the [Jones] program indicate the Alaskan native students using the program are progressing in reading achievement, as measured by the Metropolitan Achievement Tests, at a rate greater than that predicted in the development strategy" [letter to Groff 1971].

Durrell's evidence for the phonogram approach is even stronger [1968]. He notes that the various studies he has been involved with that investigated the usefulness of this approach "indicate that the phonogram is the unit most children depend upon in recognizing words in beginning reading" [pp. 19–25].

This phonogram approach involves the question of whether certain systematic, high-frequency spelling patterns can be abstracted by learners who have been taught a learning set procedure aimed at accomplishing this end. The results of research by Project Literacy, which investigated this question with kindergarten and first-grade children, was reviewed by Aaron Carton:

> While only one in twelve participating kindergarteners completed the experiment, three out of five of the first graders did show evidence of forming learning sets by solving at least 80 percent of the problems at the end of the five-day study. The conclusion that these young pupils actively searched for an underlying pattern on principle, even if it was a wrong one, was substantiated by individual response patterns, by the remarks of the pupils, and by the fact that those who had not succeeded in abstracting the patterns scored consistently at *less* than chance levels [1969, p. 572].

If these abstractions of spelling patterns can be accomplished by some pupils with instruction of such a very short duration, it becomes credible that it could be accomplished for a great many more over the normally extended period of reading instruction used in schools.

Other recent evidence that lends support to the usefulness of teaching a recurrent spellings, or phonograms, approach of word analysis has been given by Wylie and Durrell [1970]. About 450 children "who showed normal intelligence and reading progress" were examined by Wylie at the end of the first grade. These children had been in a phonograms program of word recognition during the year. Wylie asked 230 of these children to identify (by circling) *"short"-vowel phonograms* after hearing them read aloud, and to do the same for single vowel letters after hearing *isolated vowel sounds.* The whole phonogram was found to be significantly easier to identify than the isolated vowel letter. He asked all the children in his study to identify in the same way 152 *phonograms with "long" versus "short"* vowels. There was found no significant difference in the pupils' abilities to do this. Using the same procedure, he found no significant differences in these pupils' abilities to identify *"silent e" phonograms (ate) versus vowel digraph phonograms* (e.g., *ear*). These pupils identified significantly larger numbers of *"short" or "long" vowel phonograms* than they did *phonograms with other vowel sounds.* The pupils identified significantly larger numbers of phonograms that ended with *single consonants* than those that ended in *two-consonant clusters.* Wylie found that *"high-frequency" phonograms* (those found in more than ten primary grade words) were identified significantly more times than *"low-frequency" phonograms* (those found in from five to ten primary words).

This research on the use of phonograms suggests that it is better to teach vowel sounds inside phonograms than as isolated sounds. It implies that one need not delay the teaching of phonograms with free vowel sounds. But it does note that "short" and "long" vowel sounds should precede the teaching of other vowel sounds, and that consonant clusters in phonograms are more difficult for children than single consonants.

Other studies indicate the usefulness of teaching syllables. In their study of teaching "graphonemes" in first grade reading, Speer and Lamb [1976] found that their pupils' ability to read these phonograms was highly correlated (r's from .77 to .92) with reading achievement. Gleitman and Rozin [1973] also reported that children they studied were successfully taught to read with the use of syllables. This was a method similar in certain respects to the phonogram approach advocated in this book. This study concluded that naive pre-readers are more capable of recognizing a meaningful word segmented syllabically rather than phonemically (sound-by-sound).

Then, Brown [1971] found that syllables were easier for young children to blend than were two phonemes. Glass and Burton [1973] noted that second graders did not look at each letter in words but saw letter clusters within whole words and instantly associated sounds with these letter clusters. This is the kind of word analysis that the training in phonograms described in this chapter will facilitate.

REFERENCES

Brengelman, Fred. *The English Language.* Englewood Cliffs, N.J.: Prentice-Hall, 1970.

Bronstein, Arthur J. *The Pronunciation of American English.* New York: Appleton-Century-Crofts, 1960.

Brown, D. L. "Some Linguistic Dimensions in Auditory Blending in Reading," *The Right to Participate,* ed. Frank P. Greene. Clemson, S.C.: Twentieth Yearbook of the National Reading Conference, 1971.

Burmeister, Lou E. "The Effect of Syllabic Position and Accent on the Phonemic Behavior of Single Vowel Graphemes," *Reading and Real-*

ism, ed. J. Allen Figurel. Newark, Del.: International Reading Association, 1969.

Carton, Aaron S. "Linguistics and Reading Instruction," *Reading and Realism,* ed. J. Allen Figurel. Newark, Del.: International Reading Association, 1969.

Clymer, Theodore. "The Utility of Phonic Generalizations in the Primary Grades." *Reading Teacher,* 16(1963):252–258.

Durrell, Donald D. "Phonics Programs in Beginning Reading," *Forging Ahead in Reading,* ed. J. Allen Figurel. Newark, Del.: International Reading Association, 1968.

Emans, Robert, "Usefulness of Phonic Generalizations Above the Primary Level." *Reading Teacher,* 20(1967):419–425.

Gibson, Eleanor J. "Learning to Read." *Science,* 148(1965):1066–1072.

Glass, Gerald G., and Burton, Elizabeth H. "How Do They Decode? Verbalizations and Observed Behaviors of Successful Decoders." *Education,* 94(1973):58–64.

Gleitman, Lila, and Rozin, Paul. "Teaching Reading by Use of a Syllabary." *Reading Research Quarterly,* 8(1973):447–483.

Gray, William S. *On Their Own in Reading.* Chicago: Scott, Foresman, 1948.

Groff, Patrick. "Dictionary Syllabication—How Useful?" *Elementary School Journal,* 72(1971a):107–117.

Groff, Patrick. "A Phonemic Analysis of Monosyllabic Words." *Reading World,* 12(1972):94–103.

Groff, Patrick. "Should Youngsters Find Little Words in Bigger Words?" *Reading Improvement,* 10(1973):12–16.

Groff, Patrick. *The Syllable: Its Nature and Pedagogical Usefulness.* Portland, Oreg.: Northwest Regional Educational Laboratory, 1971b.

Groff, Patrick. "The Topsy-Turvy World of Sight Words." *Reading Teacher,* 27(1974):572–578.

Jones, Virginia W. *Decoding and Learning to Read.* Portland, Oreg.: Northwest Regional Educational Laboratory, 1970.

Lefevre, Carl A. *Linguistics and the Teaching of Reading.* New York: McGraw-Hill, 1964.

McKee, Paul. *Reading.* Boston: Houghton Mifflin, 1966.

Otto, Wayne, et al. *Focused Reading Instruction.* Reading, Mass.: Addison-Wesley, 1974.

Shuy, Roger. "Some Language and Cultural Differences in a Theory of Reading," *Psycholinguistics and the Teaching of Reading,* eds. Kenneth S. Goodman and James T. Fleming. Newark, Del.: International Reading Association, 1969.

Smith, E. Brooks, Goodman, Kenneth S., and Meridith, Robert. *Language and Thinking in the Elementary School.* New York: Holt, Rinehart and Winston, 1970.

Speer, Olga B., and Lamb, George S. "First Grade Reading Ability and Fluency in Naming Verbal Symbols." *Reading Teacher,* 29(1976):572–576.

Stauffer, Russell G. *Teaching Reading as a Thinking Process.* New York: Harper & Row, 1969.

Wallen, Carl J. *Work Attack Skills in Reading.* Columbus: Charles E. Merrill, 1969.

Wardhaugh, Ronald. *Reading: A Linguistic Perspective.* New York: Harcourt Brace Jovanovich, 1969.

Wylie, Richard E., and Durrell, Donald D. "Teaching Vowels Through Phonograms." *Elementary English,* 47(1970):787–791.

6

THE PRINCIPLES
OF PHONICS TEACHING

The principles used to guide the teaching of phonics should be based on two sets of information: (1) the psychology of learning and perception, especially as it pertains to young children *who have not yet learned to read*, and (2) linguistics. (In previous chapters we have illustrated the linguistic data with which one must be concerned in teaching phonics.) Thus, the principles that govern the teaching of phonics skills can be called *psycholinguistic* principles. They are based on what we know of the psychological nature of children, their learning patterns, their potentials, and how they interrelate with the linguistic matters of phonemics and graphemics. The principles of phonics teaching that follow are stated in such a way that this interrelationship is constantly in view.

To begin with, it is important to stress that the principles that guide the learning of oral language are not the same as those that govern the learning of phonics. To learn the oral language, children proceed best on a *whole-task* basis. They need little or no formal instruction based on a sequencing of the component skills of oral language. Quite the reverse is true for reading. It seems learning to speak is a universal and a natural skill, whereas reading is a secondary and contrived one. All societies, however primitive, use spoken language. The need for written language is not universal to man, but speaking is. The need for written language emerges only when a society moves away from what is called its "natural" state of being.

In discussing the following principles for phonics teaching, we also have tried to keep in mind the admonition from Francis Johnson [1969] not to depend exclusively upon the findings from linguistics. Johnson says that in the past we have found good instruments or models for *explaining* good writing—rhetoric. But this does not mean, ipso facto, that we have discovered the models for *acquiring* good rhetoric. He further stated that just because we know that President Kennedy's political speeches were effective and could determine why they were does not mean that we have a vehicle for making Vice-President Agnew's political speeches equally effective [Johnson 1969]. It is as true for phonics teaching as for any other language teaching with children that even though we realize how dependent we are on the linguist to provide a primary source of raw material, we also realize our obligation to analyze that raw material and to use it together with that from other associated disciplines [Johnson 1969].

We would say, therefore, that the following twenty principles should govern the teaching of phonics:

1. The application of phonics skills is only *one* of the ways children use to recognize words. To believe otherwise, or to insist that in all cases the more phonics application the better, overestimates the value of phonics skills. The ultimate aim of any word-analysis program, therefore, is to teach children to displace a letter-analysis of unfamiliar words with a perception of the larger structures of these words (predictable spellings, closed and open syllables, morphemes, affixes), and with the use of the cues one can get from the structure of sentences. An overreliance on phonics in older pupils obviously is an uneconomical mode of reading. It can act to slow these readers down, and by so doing inculcate an idea of "word-calling" rather than the efficient reading of sentences. Phonics, then, should be taught as much as possible within sentence context. Children need to relate phonics cues to other cues within the reading material.

2. Research in reading has demonstrated that success in beginning reading cannot be accurately predicted from the chronological age of the pupil. Authorities disagree as to the minimal mental age necessary for successful reading instruction. Mental age requirements will vary with the instructional procedures used, as Gates demonstrated about forty years ago [1937].

Thus the decision as to when to begin phonics instruction depends more on the philosophy of the individual school or classroom than on children's mental or chronological ages. Traditional schools generally insist that children begin to learn to read in kindergarten or first grade. Phonics instruction, however, might be delayed for some children in schools committed to such concepts as the "open classroom" or the "integrated day," especially those in which children choose what they will learn and when. This is not because the children are unable to learn phonics, but because they are not as yet interested in learning to read.

Teachers (doubtless unwittingly) may contradict themselves about this.

According to one study [Bridges & Lessler 1972] only 32 percent of a group of teachers rank "reading skills" as the most important skill to be developed in the first grade. Yet, 85 percent of the teachers in the same study cited the lack of reading skills as their most important reason for not promoting children to second grade!

3. Almost all children when entering first grade have auditory perception adequate to learn phonics. The relationship between auditory perception or discrimination and phonics appears to be just as complex as the relationship between beginning reading and age. There is a lack of agreement in experimental data as to the relationship between learning to read and auditory discrimination. There is little doubt, however, that when normal children first come to school they have highly developed phonological and grammatical systems working for them. They comprehend all the sounds and intonations of the language. They use almost all the grammatical structures adults do. Ninety percent correctly produce all but seven of the phonemes, /s, sh, z, zh, th, ch, hw/ [Carroll 1960]. By age seven children reach a 90 percent level of correct articulation [Healey 1963]. While it may be that these very young children cannot be expected to have *all* the auditory skills necessary for a successful phonics program, surely they have developed *enough* of these skills to make this success very likely.

We cannot accept, then, the notion that "many children have not developed the degree of auditory discrimination necessary for learning to read" [Bond & Wagner 1960, p. 29]. By this is meant, for example, the ability "to isolate specific sound elements to the degree necessary to find the rhyming words in jingles or to isolate from a group of words those that begin with a specific sound" [p. 29]. We do not know of the research that says "many" six-year-old children cannot do these things, although this is a commonly stated belief in reading books for teachers. We doubt, too, that there is evidence that "many children with low intelligence find it almost impossible to remember phonemes from one day to the next" [Aukerman 1971, p. 10], or that many children cannot perceive speech sounds [Edwards 1966, p. 360]. If this were the case, how could these children have learned to talk? Some research shows that "by the fourth year, the child's phonological system closely approximates the [mature] model, and the remaining deviations are usually corrected by the time the child enters school" [Erwin & Miller 1963, p. 125].

The statistical evidence on the relationship of seven standardized tests of auditory discrimination and beginning reading achievement of over seven hundred children would also throw into question whether many children do not learn to read because of faulty powers of auditory discrimination. The correlations between these two factors were found generally to be low [Dykstra 1966]. The evidence of this relatively low correlation (median $r = 0.35$) between beginning reading and the measures used to test auditory discrimination is convincing. In addition, Anne Morency [1968] obtained a correlation of only .225 between the auditory discrimination scores of 174 first-grade children and their later reading scores in the third grade. This would suggest that there was only about 5 percent common elements between the two variables. These children as third graders scored an average of *only 3.5 items more* (out of a possible 40) on the test of auditory discrimination used than they did as first graders. Children's articulation of sounds, as Joseph Wepman [1960] found, is not significantly related to their growth in reading ability in the first grade.

Further evidence against the assumption that auditory perception relates directly to word perception is given by Donald Shankweiler and Isabelle Liberman [1972]. They found that the mistakes children make ("error patterns") as they repeat a word spoken to them are strikingly different from the errors the children make in reading these same words. "With auditory presentation, errors in oral repetition averaged 7 percent when tabulated by phoneme, as compared with 24 percent in reading, and were about equally distributed between initial and final position, rather than being markedly different. [There are several studies that show children make significantly more mistakes in reading the final parts of words than the initial parts.] Moreover, contrary to what occurred when the list was read, fewer errors occurred on vowels than on consonants" [p. 307]. (Studies also indicate children make many more mistakes in reading vowel letters than consonants.)

There is even some question as to whether auditory discrimination skills are developed in either structured or unstructured reading readiness programs. As a result of his study, Moe [1972] thinks they are not. He concluded that children in this study exhibited auditory discrimination skills that they developed independently of structured reading readiness instruction. It is important to remember, too, that standardized tests of auditory discrimination, as used in Moe's investigation, seemingly do not measure unique aspects of auditory discrimination among kindergarten children.

It is also important to realize the small influences the school years have on this matter. For example, Mildred Templin [1943] found that from grade two through grade six children improve in their ability to correctly match phonemes *by only 3 percent*. Another study shows that when seven-year-olds were asked to say whether initial consonants in spoken words and in nonsense syllables were the same or different, *only 2 percent* of the 432 responses they made were in error. These words and syllables represented "all possible pairings that could occur in English" [Tikofsky & McInish 1968, pp. 61–62]. Similarly, Eugene Gray [1963] found that after the age 7.0 and through age 8.5 children did not make any significant gains either in their abilities to say a word correctly after an adult says the serial order of its phonemes, e.g., /k/-/a/-/t/, *cat,* or their abilities to tell the number of sounds heard in a word an adult pronounces in a normal fashion.

There is some lesser evidence to the contrary, we must admit. For example, Helen Robinson found that the ability of children to make certain scores on the *Wepman Auditory Discrimination Test* significantly affected reading scores of both first and third graders [1972]. The relative weight of evidence appears to us to be against such a conclusion, however. (Wepman [1960], himself, found no such evidence for third graders.) And then the validity of the Wepman Test itself is open to question [Groff 1975b]. In sum, we agree with P. David Allen that our ideas about deficiency in verbal ability of normal six- or eight- or ten-year-olds can be disregarded, and we can build on the strengths that they bring to the task of reading [1972]. If the so-called auditory abilities are an influential force on children's reading abilities, this is probably so only for a very small percent of young children. There seems little doubt, therefore, that we need to maintain a cautious, skeptical outlook concerning the importance of auditory discrimination on reading ability [Groff 1975b].

Thus, instead of relying on scores from tests of auditory perception per se to indicate whether children will proceed satisfactorily in phonics, i.e., are ready for it, we suggest two other ways to determine readiness. *First,* find out if children can correctly recognize rhyming monosyllabic words. Do this first with pairs of words (*cat-rat; cat-come*) and then strings of words (*cat-rat-come-bat*). Can children repeat the words that rhyme or repeat the word in a string that does not rhyme with the others? *Second,* find out if the students can recognize alliteration. For example, can they say whether pairs (then strings) of monosyllabic words begin with the same sound? Can they repeat the word in a string that does not begin like the others? Harris Slavin believes there is one other good test of readiness for phonics instruction. This is to find out if children can learn monosyllabic Pig Latin, for example, if they can change the statement "Come home," to /umkā ōmhā/. Slavin observes that beginners in reading are delighted to try to learn this "secret" language and that those who cannot learn it obviously do not fail because they are simply not interested in trying [1972]. Trying to teach Pig Latin seems an intriguing way to attempt to determine if children can identify and isolate phonemes, or analyze syllables into phonemes.

4. Auditory blending, as a prerequisite to phonics, is needed only by a select group of pupils. Auditory blending is usually described as an activity in which the teacher supposedly says, in the order they appear in a word, each separate sound of the word. After this, children are asked to say the word in question as it would be normally pronounced. ("Try to guess what word I'm making.") For example, the three sounds in *mail,* /māl/ ostensibly can be isolated and said as /m/-/ā/-/l/, with an abnormal pause between each sound. After hearing these sounds, children are expected to say /māl/.

Otto and others call this blending ability "a prereading skill of high promise" [1974, p. 82]. George and Evelyn Spache say that "there is strong support in many studies for the use of tests of auditory discrimination and auditory blending" [1969, p. 386]. We cannot agree with these conclusions for several reasons.

First, the main assumption about auditory blending is that the teacher can in fact say English phonemes in isolation (not in a syllable). This notion is not a defensible one. Linguists are adamant in their contention that the sounds of our language cannot be said in such an isolated way, which does not mean a sound that somewhat resembles an English phoneme cannot be said. It does contend that having young children listen to English sounds allegedly made in isolation, in effect, has them listen to a phonology that is not English [Groff 1975c]. In short, this practice wrongly suggests that we teach children phonics with sounds that are not really in our language! Apparently realizing this objection from linguists, some advocates of auditory blending suggest that in this activity only vowel sounds be made in isolation [Durkin 1970, p. 275]. It is true that single vowel sounds can constitute an entire syllable, e.g., /hap-ē/, /u-long/, /bûr-ō/. This does not happen in monosyllabic words, however, (*a* as an article and *I* excepted). These short words we show below to be the proper ones with which to teach vowel sound-spelling correspondences. The effectiveness of teaching vowel sounds within phonograms (Chapter 5) also argues against the need to teach children to listen to isolated vowel sounds.

A second question about auditory blending is whether in learning to read children will ever need to go through this process: (1) identify a single letter, (2) try to attach an isolated, nonphonemic sound to it, (3) "blend" this facsimile English sound to another facsimile sound that has been identified, and (4) translate these two strange sounds into the pronunciation of a word. This criticism does not question the fact some children can be taught to make this translation, for example, of /āē/ + /po͝oh/ into /ăp/ (*ape*). It does question whether this is the way children decode words.

Third, does such skill predict the future reading ability of pupils? This is a controversial matter. Jeanne Chall, Florence Roswell, and Susan Blumenthal [1963] find evidence that there is a moderate statistical relationship between first-grade children's auditory blending ability and their reading ability. To the contrary, a larger study [Dykstra 1966] (that tested over ten times the number of pupils as did Chall and her colleagues) found no significant relationship between these two factors. This conflict between the findings of research studies on this subject is typical. That is, some studies find moderate relationships here; others discover there is no significant relationship between auditory blending ability and reading skill [Groff 1976].

In sum, the evidence about auditory blending should be interpreted to mean that activities for this purpose need not be a required part of a phonics program. This evidence does suggest, however, that certain children, those found to have retarded auditory abilities, may profit to some extent from such training. So, training in auditory blending should be given on a highly selective basis. On the other hand, it is quite appropriate to teach children to identify the true sound unit of English, the syllable, to say these syllables, and to blend or combine them into words. This approach is explained in Chapter 5.

   5. The so-called visual discrimination skills[1] need not be taught. They are "discovered by the child for himself by means of perceptual and cognitive skills common to many aspects of visual perception" [Smith 1971, p. 1]. As Frank Smith has said, "The main point about the visual aspect of reading is not that a child requires a special kind or degree of acuity to discriminate between two letters; probably any child who can distinguish between two faces at six feet has the ability to do that. The child's problem is to discover the critical differences between the two letters, which is not so much a matter of knowing how to look as knowing what to look for" [p. 1]. The "what" a beginning reader must look for are the features of letters and words that actually distinguish them from one another. In this book the letters are arranged for teaching so that these distinguishing features will be made apparent for the beginning reader (see Chapter 8).

   A review of the research on the relationships of visual perception and reading reveal, as Ruth Waugh and Zana Watson have reported, that children who receive instruction designed to increase visual perceptual performance demonstrate improvement on perceptual tests but do not show greater achievement in reading than those not receiving this instruction [1971]. Moreover, beyond the first grade level visual perception tests are not predictors of reading achievement and do not differentiate good from poor readers [1971]. Eve Malmquist [1960] obtained only the average low correlation of 0.31 between five visual perception test scores of first-grade pupils and their reading achievement. Helen Robinson's more recent study [1972b] also found no such relationship. From her review of the research on visual perceptual training, Robinson [1972a] is led to conclude that research is not conclusive on the question of the effectiveness of perceptual training designed to improve reading. It is true that the long-term effect of perceptual training to improve reading is uncertain, to say the least. Moreover, as Robinson discovered from her critique of this research, reading instruction may, in turn, provide crucial elements resulting in improved scores on perceptual tests.

---

[1]The skills include having children copy or select geometric shapes or forms, to give "eye pursuit" activities, to have them match designs using beads, pegboards, blocks, cutouts, or puzzles, to have them name the parts or details of pictures, and so on.

The most useful conclusion to draw from a critical analysis of research on perceptual training and reading is a rejection of the notion that most children need such training in order to develop reading skills. Stephen Klesius [1972] doubts that any positive influence on reading results from the use of perceptual-motor development programs for all children without consideration of their prior environmental experiences or needs. Georgia Pitcher-Baker's review of the research on perceptual training [1973] led her to the same conclusion. She explains that there may well be no one-to-one relationship between perceptual training and reading achievement.

Then, D. LaMont Johnson [1974] asserts that there is no possible justification for spending large amounts of time, energy, and money on perceptual training programs designed to improve reading, beyond the fact that such programs are offered for sale by publishers. Regretfully, these publishers did not first determine if there is a cause and effect relationship between perceptual training and reading, he notes, or even, for that matter, if visual perception is trainable.

Evidence that the available theories of language acquisition are largely irrelevant in helping us to decide issues in beginning reading instruction [Wardhaugh 1971b] further convinces us of the futility of trying to use so-called deficiencies in language acquisition as signals as to when to begin phonics. As Compton [1972] found, pupils chosen as "verbal" by their first-grade teachers learned to read as well as those classified as "nonverbal."

In fact, young children's abilities to apply inflections to words may be a better sign of their readiness for reading instruction than either their visual or auditory discrimination abilities (as these are presently measured). Mary Brittain [1970] compared children's abilities to change pseudowords such as *wog* to plurals, past tense, possessives, progressives (*ing*), comparatives, and superlatives, and to third-person singular, with their reading abilities in grades one and two. She found closer relationships to exist between these two variables than have been found between reading ability and either visual or auditory perception.

In summary, it is better simply to try phonics with children than to wait until they achieve some set age or IQ, or some score on tests of visual perception. Children's responses to actual phonics lessons will indicate if they are ready, and at what pace such lessons should proceed.

6. The teacher can make only limited use of the descriptions of how mature or able readers perceive words in deciding how to teach nonreaders phonics. Smith makes clear these differences between the beginning and the mature reader. As he correctly notes, not only does the beginner use different means for identifying words than the skilled reader but "the beginning reader has to acquire special skills that will be of very little use to him once he develops reading fluency" [1971, p. 3]. It has become increasingly clear that "whatever the definition of reading, the processes involved

for the proficient reader and for the beginner do not completely overlap"
[Williams 1970, p. 45]. As it becomes more apparent that we cannot use the
act of skilled reading as a model for what should be taught in phonics, it is
also clear that "we cannot afford to lose interest in fundamental investigations of the behavior of the beginning reader, investigations that focus on
the basic processes of word recognition that are clearly so crucial to the five
year old" [Williams, pp. 45–46]. These are the studies upon which *Phonics:
Why and How* depends most.

    7. **At the beginning of their reading instruction children should be
taught the letter cues to word recognition rather than a certain number of
whole ("sight") words.** As Joanna Williams rightly says, "It is most interesting to note the fact that the most widely used reading method over the past
thirty years (the look-say or whole word) has stressed identification of words
on the basis of overall shape and configuration. But it is adults and not
children who sometimes show this strategy in word recognition" [p. 42].
Accordingly, we believe that children who are learning to read must learn
to discriminate graphemes within words from the beginning of their instruction. The proposition that children learning to read somehow first
recognize "whole" or "sight" words as such has never been substantiated.
Therefore, we must agree with Gibson that "overall word shape is not a
sufficiently good differentiator, and children should not use it" because "not
only is differentiation [of words] poor without internal analysis, but transfer
to new words cannot occur" [1975, p. 300]. Peter Desberg and Betty
Berdiansky [1970] concluded on the basis of their review of the research that
letter cues, especially first and last letters in words, and *not* whole-word
shape cues are the most used means by which beginning readers recognize
words. More recently, both Knafle [1972] and Mason and Woodcock [1973]
have found that word shape is not an effective cue to word recognition. The
research shows, then, that training in making grapheme-phoneme associations has more transfer value for beginning readers than does whole-word
training.

    Indeed, there are those who consider the whole-word recognition idea
to be downright dangerous, such as David Reed who sees the "whole word
fallacy" as being more ridiculous and dangerous than the phonic fallacy .
[1970]. (The phonic fallacy is the notion that there is *a set* of spelling-
to-sound correspondences rules that can tell us how to pronounce *all*
graphemes.) "It is more dangerous," Reed says, "because it has been used for
a longer period as one of the methods of the basal readers, which have been
employed in the vast majority of instances in teaching American school
children to read" [1970, p. 222]. For a good summary of the evidence
against "sight" words, the notion that word recognition is a unitary phenomenon, or that the beginning reader perceives a word instantaneously
and its parts simultaneously (the whole-word recognition idea), see Geyer
[1970] or Groff [1974].

There is little doubt, however, that less than the total number of graphemic (letter) cues available in a word need to be perceived in order for a mature reader to read it. Unquestionably, as children mature in their reading skills, they reduce both the *time* needed to discriminate graphemic cues and the *number* of graphemic cues they require to recognize a word. They need to see only part of a word, or a sentence, in order to make a "closure" and guess the remainder of it. "There is plenty of evidence to show that the adult reader does not read a word by identifying each letter, one at a time, decoding it to a separate response in a left-to-right sequence" [Gibson 1969, p. 438]. There is nothing, then, to support the views of phonics advocates who claim that fast readers quickly process each letter, one-by-one, as they read, much as would an expert typist who can type 150 words per minute [Washburn 1964].

8. **Children recognize words by their letters, but as well, by spelling units larger than letters.** An issue that is raised repeatedly regarding phonics is: "Should beginning reading instruction start with teaching whole words as units—or with teaching the sounds letters make in words?" [Heilman 1964, p. 11]. We believe that this issue on the use of phonics versus a "sight-word" method to be a false one, not because we deny the idea that anything less than a word is meaningless to children. (Actually, anything less than a sentence is.) We regard the issue as false because it sets up an unsubstantiated dichotomy between how children perceive parts and wholes. As Eleanor Gibson concludes, "The very notion of parts and wholes in perception is mistaken; objects are differentiated by distinctive features which must be discriminated, and objects are also characterized by structure" [1969, p. 447]. The evidence that Gibson has reviewed to reach this conclusion is impressive.

This information requires us to conclude that children recognize words by a combination of the perception of their letters and by certain structures in words that yield larger units than the single letter. One aspect of this structure of words is the probability that one letter will follow another in words. For example, we come to expect to see *cr* only at the beginning of words, never at the end. For *ck*, we learn to expect the opposite. This expectation of letter order starts early in a child's learning-to-read history. In one experiment, first-grade children read pronounceable pseudowords (e.g. NAR) significantly better than unpronounceable pseudowords (e.g., RNA). By third grade children were able to read four- and five-letter pseudowords (GLURCK) significantly better than their unpronounceable counterparts. "These results suggest that a child in the early stages of development of reading skill reads in short units,[2] but is already beginning to generalize certain regularities of spelling and spelling-to-sound

---

[2] Also shown by the evidence of eye-voice span research. This span is the distance the eye gets ahead of the voice when one reads aloud.

correspondences" [Gibson 1969, p. 439]. There appears to be little doubt children use word structure and the sequential order of letters as meaning cues in order to recognize words.

By accepting this proposition, the phonics teacher can avoid the fruitless debate as to whether a certain number of "sight" words should be recognized by children *before* they are taught phonics. The evidence suggests that whether or not teachers think they are teaching "sight" words, children are responding to certain letter cues in these words.

9. As nearly as possible teach children phonics with the words they actually speak. Along with the relative mastery of the phonological and grammatical system that pupils bring with them as they enter first grade, children also show that they comprehend and utilize a large number of words. By this we mean that children speak these words in intelligible sentences and respond to them when others say them. Each child because of his or her peculiar environment out of school and life-style has accumulated a vocabulary that reflects these factors.

These words offer a special potential for the phonics teacher since children have shown they understand these words by using them. Thus, when these words are used in phonics no problems of syntax or word meaning are involved. While the evidence is incomplete, children should learn phonics faster with such words and sentences than they would with words and sentences from prewritten texts that inevitably involve difficulties with syntax and meaning. It is recommended, therefore, that as nearly as possible the teacher use a child's own words and sentences to teach phonics. (Make sure, however, that a word chosen here for phonics study is not an exception to a phonics generalization that is being taught at the time.) Research also suggests that words for which children may more easily form mental images (such as *den* vs. *not*) will be easier for them to learn to read. Edward Wolpert concluded from his study that more high imagery words were learned by first-grade children than low imagery words. His findings agree with most other recent literature dealing with verbal learning [1972]. Phonics programs that use sentences like *The fat rat sat on the mat* [Fries 1963] thus are open to serious question.

Basal readers also have often failed to take children's language into consideration. As Evelyn Hatch notes, "it must be clear that the language of the child is not exactly parallel to that of his reading textbooks. While all four of the reading books investigated seemed to be moving away from 'unnatural' sounding sentences . . . toward more realistic forms, many still used sentences which would be difficult for the child because they are not forms which he customarily uses" [1971, p. 30].

Obviously, the phonics teacher generally wants to use familiar, true words. There is, however, a place for pseudowords or nonwords in the testing phase of phonics instruction. For example, if a teacher gives children the pseudoword *glurch* to read aloud, he or she gains a clear insight into whether children understand the sound-spelling relationships of /g/-*g*, /l/-*l*, /ur/-*ûr*, /ch/-*ch*.

10. **It is mandatory that the teacher adapt** *Phonics: Why and How* **to the dialect of the pupils.** For example, teachers in any locality must compare the speech sounds of their pupils with the ones used here and not hesitate to add, subtract, or exchange the sounds that they hear in their pupils' dialect which differ from "Western" dialect given in this book. Bruce Cronnell regards the absence of such advice in six major spelling texts as "a major failure" of these books [1971, p. 50]. We agree and note that the same thing can be said about the major basal reading texts. However, the *spelling* of any dialect should be standard, e.g., *going* for either /gō-ing/ or for /gō-in/.

It follows that "It is unreasonable to expect disadvantaged black children to read a variety of English they do not speak." If this is one of the reasons, as Kenneth Johnson insists, that "many of these children don't learn to read well," it suggests that one should "teach disadvantaged black children to read in their dialect first, then transfer them at a later date into reading standard English" [1970, p. 27].

Moreover, there is no evidence to show that trying to change children's dialects to improve their spelling or reading has been successful. Although one can find recent recommendations for teachers to do so for spelling [Boyd & Talbert 1971], there is no basis for this recommendation in the research [Groff 1973]. Richard Rystrom, for example, found that attempts to change the dialect of first-grade black children did not significantly increase their reading achievement [1970].

In sum, we would agree with Ronald Wardhaugh that "the task in phonics is one of systematically relating the two systems [phonological and writing] for the child, not trying to change the first system, a doubtful goal, or making it like the second system, an impossible goal" [1971a, p. 64].

We must disagree, therefore, with the notion that "with older children, careless habits of pronunciation such as 'gimme' for 'give me,' 'negstor' for 'next door' or 'put nearly' for 'pretty nearly,' must be corrected before phonics knowledge can function in spelling" [Anderson 1972, p. 235]. The author confesses that he says "gimme" for "give me," and "negstor" for "next door." In fact, so do all my educated friends! Since we insist that one need not violate the normal junctures of spoken language to teach or use phonics, we would quarrel, too, with Constance McCullough's notion that "we have to add spoken book English to the child's speech patterns and sounds *before* we can expect the child to read and understand book English" [1968, p. 181, emphasis added]. Consider the number of children who would *never* be taught to read if we followed this advice![3]

---

[3] For a devastating, and at times satirical, castigation of the "arrogance and hypocrisy" of those who think it mandatory that low-income children learn to speak a dialect other than their native dialect, see James Sledd [1972]. Instead, Sledd maintains, and we agree, that instruction in English should aim at reducing the stigma attached to the nonstandard dialect of low-income children.

11. **As nearly as possible, the teaching of phonics should adhere to the factual data that one can gather from the science of linguistics.** But, admittedly, the usefulness of some of these data is limited in teaching children. Wherever *Phonics: Why and How* violates the linguistic data (e.g., in a nonreference to children of the /ə/ sound or a description only of a "Western" dialect), it is done knowingly with the abilities of children and teachers to accommodate to these data clearly in mind. In short, children's ability to understand linguistic data is held to be more important in the decision to teach such data than is the authenticity of any particular datum itself.

12. **The total number of phonics generalizations to be taught depends on several factors, (e.g., pupils' needs and abilities and the level of phonics being taught).** In general, nevertheless, we can say that the larger the number of letter-sound relationships children can learn the better. Emery Bliesmer and Betty Yarborough [1965] make this clear from their study, which found 74 percent of comparisons of reading scores to favor programs using deliberate, systematic ("synthetic") phonics over those using non-systematic or incidental phonics. They conclude that "the order of instruction of letter-sound elements and/or relationships may not be as important in the success of synthetic programs as that the number of letter-sound relationships taught be sufficient to equip pupils with means for independent decoding of words" [1965, p. 504].

It remains for one to say, of course, what that "sufficient" number of rules is. Since this has not been determined theoretically or empirically, any decision of the number of rules must be a pragmatic one. That is, the teacher should teach the number of rules given in the different levels of *Phonics: Why and How* that are sufficient for the particular group of pupils being taught. This text provides a rational sequence of phonics skills. It cannot advise as to the absolute number of these required by any given group of children, however. The individual phonics teacher must make this decision.

13. **Learning dictionary rules of syllabication (which traditionally has been required of children learning phonics) is wrong both linguistically and psychologically (cf. Chapter 5).** Dictionary rules of syllabication violate the notion of a psycholinguistic approach to the teaching of phonics.

14. **A phonics lesson should be conducted largely with predictably spelled words.** What we know of research in perceptual learning substantiates our belief that as children learn to read they "learn to attend to distinctive features of things, to invariants that lead to perceptual constancy and permanence. . ." [Gibson 1969, p. 445]. These invariants help children to deduce higher order structures and rules about reading. This finding implies that unless invariant spellings of sounds are used in the phonics program children's natural mode of perception may be thwarted. As a consequence, their later ability to deduce rules may be retarded. A sequence

of word analysis that is begun with invariant spellings of sounds, and moves to variant spellings, is a critical necessity. We agree with William Gilhooly [1973] on the importance of beginning phonics with a writing system faithfully encoding speech sounds.

Research that supports this thesis is readily available. Calfee, Venezky and Chapman [1969] found that better readers were more able to pronounce pseudowords made up of predictable spelling patterns (e.g., *chung, dag*) than were poor readers. Gibson, Osser, and Pick [1963] discovered that pronounceable pseudowords (e.g., *tup*) are read by first-grade readers more easily than are unpronounceable ones. Olson [1970] also found that regularly spelled genuine words were more readily pronounced than were less regularly spelled ones. Chapman, Venezky and Calfee [1970] determined that children's knowledge of predictable letter-sound correspondences allows for more broad and independent reading than does the lack of such knowledge. Then, it has been found that beginning readers learn significantly better to recognize words [McCutcheon & McDowell 1969; Otto & Pizillo 1970] and to make generalizations about these words [McCutcheon & McDowell 1969] when they are trained on words of high spelling similarity rather than on words of low similarity. Samuels and Jeffrey [1966] are among those who found that very young children learn to recognize words with letters in common better than they can words with no letters in common. Richardson [1966] discovered that the use of words with letter similarities with first graders resulted in more prolonged memory of these words for these pupils than did the use of words with letter dissimilarities. The findings of Vandever [1973] and of Hartley [1970] concur with the idea that words with phoneme-letter consistency are remembered better by first graders than are those with unpredictable spellings. It is clear from Hartley [1970] that a beginning reader has less difficulty learning words that have minimal spelling contrasts than those with maximal contrasts. As she concludes, when words with maximal spelling contrasts are used, the student needs more information such as a context cue to aid learning. There is evidence [Rosinski & Wheeler 1972], too, that young children soon begin to extract the actual spelling structure of words. For instance, they say that *tup* and *dink* are more like "real" words than are *nda* or *xogl*.

On the other hand, it is difficult to locate research findings to support Smith's idea [1971] that the readability of a word for beginning readers is not facilitated when the word is written so that its graphemes are systematically related to the speech sounds these graphemes represent. In one study, Levin and Watson [1963a] concluded that if children are presented words that have a variety of spelling-sound correspondences they are more likely to develop a useful problem-solving approach to word recognition than if these presented words are spelled predictably. The notable weaknesses in the design of this study have been pointed out [Desberg and

Berdiansky 1970]. In a second study of teaching children more than one sound per grapheme at one time, Levin and Watson [1963b] found the task of making varying associations to a single word is more difficult here for the child than when a single phoneme-to-grapheme association is taught. It appears Otto and Pizillo [1970] are alone in finding that transfer of training to a generalized list of words is best accomplished by beginning readers when they are trained on words that have no spelling similarity.

Our stand on this matter is also supported by the evidence of the relative ineffectiveness of presenting variable correspondences in one lesson (the *o* in *come home, Tom*) as is found in the traditional basal reader. In the *First Grade Reading Studies,* significant differences were found several times between the results of the basal reader and phonics approaches that stressed teaching one spelling-sound correspondence at a time. The basal reader approach generally was found *less effective* in these comparisons [Stauffer 1967] than were phonics methods.

While we agree that children should be given a single spelling pattern to learn in a given phonics lesson in order to make the lesson teachable, we see no error in pupils "sampling" words, as Sarah Gudschinsky calls it, that involve other "kinds of complexities and contrasts for which the pupil needs recoding [oral reading] strategies" [1972, p. 104]. In fact, it is not possible to use natural and interesting written sentences to teach phonics unless this is done. (The full explanation of how phonics and the use of context cues are combined for word recognition is given in Chapters 18 and 19.)

This leaves us with the problem of deciding what is an "unpredictably spelled" word in lessons for phonics. Of late, the propriety of calling some words "regularly spelled" and others "irregularly spelled" has been questioned. These two terms usually are used to mean, for example, that a word like *raft* is "regularly spelled" and a word like *laughed* is not. This decision generally is made by determining the percent of times in a total number of high-frequency words the phonemes in these individual words (*raft-laughed*) are spelled as they are in the individual words. For example, these percents are now easily obtained [Hanna et al. 1966].

/r/ is spelled *r* 97% of the time,
                                    while /1/ is spelled *l* 91% of the time
/a/ is spelled *a* 97% of the time,
                                    while /a/ is spelled *au* 0.1 of 1% of the time
/f/ is spelled *f* 78% of the time,
                                    while /f/ is spelled *gh* 0.4 of 1% of the time
/t/ is spelled *t* 97% of the time,
                                    while /t/ is spelled *ed* 0.4 of 1% of the time

It is therefore obvious that some sound-spelling correspondences occur more frequently than others in high-frequency words (in this case the 17,000 most-used words), for example, /t/-*t* as versus /t/-*ed*. Now suppose we had in English a word pronounced /zaft/. How would this be spelled? Obviously, it is much more likely that it would be spelled *zaft* than *zaughed*.

There still remains the problem, however, of deciding what percent of times a certain phoneme-grapheme correspondence must occur before it is called a "regular" one. Should this be 90, 70, 50 percent, or what? Thus, to Richard Venezky and Ruth Weir "regular and irregular" are not appropriate descriptions of spelling-sound correspondences since "a correspondence that is (by some definition) irregular from a phonemic standpoint may be regular from a morphemic standpoint" [1966, p. 3]. They say, notice the *b* in *bomb* is "silent" but the *b* in *bombard* is not. Which sound-spelling correspondence here is "irregular?" they ask. (See item 16 in this chapter.) And, they continue, "low frequency correspondences, though classified as irregular, may still represent describable [spelling] patterns" [p. 3]. For example, note how the so-called "silent" letters of *sign* and *bomb* represent sounds when another morpheme (*al, ard*) is added: *sign-signal, bomb-bombard*. There are many other patterns in spelling that cannot be accounted for if one attempts to relate spelling directly to sound, or sound directly to spelling.

For these reasons we do not use the terms "regular" or irregular" for spellings in *Phonics: Why and How*. We refer, instead, to words whose spellings or sounds are predictable from the basis of the child's knowledge of their sound-spelling correspondences. *In* Phonics: Why and How *the spelling of a word is called unpredictable if it does not fall at the time into one of the categories of spellings being taught (in Levels 1 through 10).*

15. At the earlier levels of phonics instruction only one-syllable words should be used. The exclusive use of one-syllable words for these stages of phonics has a profound importance. The use of one-syllable words excludes the need for children to recognize long words in this instruction. The number of syllables in long words doubtless acts to inhibit the learning of phonics. A recent study has calculated the total number of spelling-to-sound correspondence "rules" necessary to read one-syllable words versus the number needed to read two-syllable words. From this we found thirty-eight more rules (for a total of seventy-three) are needed to read the latter words [Berdiansky, Cronnell, & Koehler 1969]. Then, we calculated from twelve studies of commonly used words that on the average only 16 percent of these high-frequency words were polysyllabic words. A similar finding came from our survey of the first-grade sections of several prominent standardized reading tests [Groff 1975]. Only 20 percent of the words in these sections were found to be polysyllabic. This also seems striking evidence that long words are harder to read than one-syllable words.

There are other matters that suggest the use of one-syllable words in phonics instruction. In one-syllable words children do not have to deal with less-accented syllables. The schwa sound /ə/ in less-accented syllables has twenty-two different spellings, by one count [Hanna et al. 1966]. The large majority of one-syllable words that have a one-letter vowel grapheme (e.g., cat), on the other hand, will be spoken with just the checked vowel sounds, plus /o/. The vowel sound-spelling patterns for these one-syllable words thus are more stable than for the /ə/ sound-spelling correspondences. Through the teaching of one-syllable words children also more easily learn the structures of syllables and phonograms, which they then can readily transfer to the analysis of polysyllabic words, when ready for this.

16. **Spelling-to-sound correspondences do not account for all spelling patterns, such as nation-national.** Venezky and Weir [1966], Carol Chomsky [1970], and Noam Chomsky and Morris Halle [1968] are right in noting that another kind or level of correspondences, beyond grapheme to phoneme, is involved here.

Venezky and Weir call this other kind of correspondence "morphophonemic." In *nation* and *national* for example, the position of the first *a* does not tell what sound this letter should be given. Instead, the first *a* in *national* is conditioned by the fact that the morpheme *al* has been added to the morpheme *nation*. In other words, morpheme boundaries must be known in order to predict what certain spelling-sound correspondences will be. Notice how one's knowledge as to whether a word consists of one or two morphemes controls the sounds given to certain words:

1 morpheme	2 morphemes
le*tt*er	mi*dd*ay
co*n*gress	i*n*grain
s*a*ne	s*a*nity

Venezky and Weir imply that these morphophonemic correspondences should be taught from the beginning of any phonics program. Such information is not taught in *Phonics: Why and How*, however, for two reasons: (1) Many of the morphophonemic correspondences involve only a few high-frequency words. We do not know from Venezky and Weir which of such correspondences involve a relatively high percent of high-frequency words. (2) We are convinced from the research that monosyllabic words are easier for beginners to read and spell than are polysyllabic words and therefore are preferable for early phonics lessons. Most morphophonemic correspondences involve polysyllabic words.

Doubtless, as Frederick Brengelman [1970] demonstrates, "the rules for spelling polysyllables are much more complicated" than those for spelling monosyllables. This is principally due to two facts: (1) polysyllables normally contain only one strongly stressed syllable; the others are given a weaker stress, notably the schwa sound /ə/, and (2) most polysyllables are made up of more than one morpheme. The spellings given to morphemes tend to be the same, however, regardless of changes to their sound when they are heard in more weakly stressed syllables of polysyllabic words, for example *reform-reformation*. However, "it is clear that the spelling of polysyllables requires more than the sound of the words themselves; it requires recognition of the morphemes that make up the word and knowledge of how these morphemes are spelled under their strongest stress" [Brengelman, p. 91]. This explains the *ed* spelling of words such as *slapped* and *hummed*.

We will indicate at Level 10 examples for teaching the spelling of polysyllabic words that agree with Carol Chomsky's conclusion that "good spellers, children and adults alike, recognize that related words (*president-preside*) are spelled alike even though they are pronounced differently. They seem to rely on an underlying picture of the word that is independent of its varying pronunciation" [1970, p. 303].

17. Vowel sound-spelling correspondences are more variant and therefore present more teaching problems than do consonant sound-spelling relationships. There is little disagreement that consonant sound-spellings are relatively easy to teach, but this is not the case for vowels. As Paul McKee remarks, "The question of what to do about teaching letter-sound associations for vowels as part of instruction in beginning reading is unsettled and highly arguable, awaiting the results of conclusive research on the validity of such teaching. . ." [1966, p. 103]. McKee is more optimistic about such teaching, nonetheless, than most writers on phonics. He reports that he "has repeatedly found that, in unlocking in helpful context a strange word containing several vowels, pupils who know how to use consonant sounds with the context switch easily from a first-thought wrong sound for each vowel to the sounds the vowels have in the familiar word to be called to mind." Thus, he believes that "pupils who are told to think first for each vowel the short *u* sound as in *until* switched quickly to the vowel sounds in *automobile*" [p. 105]. McKee claims to have gained evidence for this simple switching from an unpublished study he made of six hundred first-grade children at the end of their school year. These pupils, who had been "taught during the year letter-sound associations for consonants only," were given a test that "checked each pupil three times" on twenty-four vowel letter-sound associations. Out of the twenty-four given the students, "more than half of the pupils responded correctly three times for seventeen associations" [p. 106].

We believe that these pupils learned, incidentally, that the vowel sound to be given a vowel letter in a word depends on the consonant letter(s) that follow this vowel letter. Cavoures [1966] found that for second-graders it was harder to identify vowels in isolation than to identify them in phonograms. Accordingly, it is likely that by teaching vowel phoneme-grapheme relationships directly *in phonograms*, it is logical to assume an even higher degree of success than McKee reports will result. And, as we describe in Chapter 5, the teaching of phonograms to first-grade children is indeed feasible.

18. All parts of speech used in phonics do not pose the same problem for the learner. For one thing, at least 20 percent of the 250 words of highest frequency of use by children are function words. (These 250 words comprise 70 to 75 percent of all the words children choose to write [Rinsland 1945].) Function words are not nouns, verbs, adjectives, or adverbs. "The essential difference that sets off 'function' words from those of the four large form-classes or parts-of-speech lies in the fact that *one must know the function words as items* in order to respond to certain structural signals" [Fries 1963, p. 107]. This can be shown in these contrasting sentences:

1. The *boys* ran away.	1. Have the *boys* run away?
2. *Who* ran away?	2. *Have* the boys run away?

It is easy to see that many content words can be substituted for the italicized words in the first sentences (e.g., *girls, cows*). But try to substitute a function word for the italicized words in the second sentences. This is difficult to do if one wishes to maintain the original quality and structure of the sentence. It is likely, therefore, that function words, although they total a relatively small number of different words, are more difficult to recognize by means of context cues than are the other parts of speech.

Second, the research on miscues [Allen 1972] indicates, too, that beginning readers have difficulty reading nouns that are used as modifiers. They do not have trouble, he says, reading *river* as a noun, but may have difficulty reading *river*boat. This illustrates in another way the effect parts of speech may have on word recognition.

Much more research is needed on the role parts of speech play in word recognition, however. We have noted above that Edward Wolpert [1972] found that first graders learned to read "high imagery" words better than "low imagery" words. Yet, Chester [1972] found it was as easy for pre-reading first graders to learn to read function words as to learn to read content words, whether these were taught in isolation or in a sentence context.

19. The teaching of phonics for use in reading and in spelling (and therefore handwriting) can proceed hand in hand. Many of the phonics skills useful for recognizing words are also useful for spelling words, although, as we have shown elsewhere, phonics is decidedly less useful for spelling than for reading. We do not agree, however, that this limitation is as extensive as claimed by McKee. He insists, for example, that "it is almost impossible to teach about vowels what might be profitable for purposes of spelling without doing serious damage to the teaching of reading itself" [1966, p. 109]. We know of no evidence to support this contention.

We must also disagree with Jeanette Veatch who contends that "word analysis is best taught during the writing time—in the first grade—and in the formal spelling time from that point on. . . . To teach word analysis during reading violates the whole operation of reading, which is flash-type recognition" [1966, p. 52]. It appears to us, however, that it is wrong to limit the number of phonics skills only to those that are applicable to spelling. As we have shown, there are many phonics skills used to read that do not function for spelling. The phonics skills that can be taught for spelling are only partially those that children can use for reading. Accordingly, we would argue for a reversal of Veatch's belief that phonics skills learned for spelling "are transferred to the particular reading situation requiring their use" [p. 52]. We would say, instead, that phonics teaching be done for reading, and then these skills be transferred to the particular spelling situation for which they can be useful.

20. Oral reading is an important part of phonics instruction since phonics is inherently a process whereby children recognize that their speech sounds are represented by letters. The question arises, nonetheless, is there any danger to silent reading skills of saying a word aloud? Particularly, should lip movements, whispering of words, or even saying words aloud be discouraged after a certain point in phonics instruction? The evidence on the relationship of vocalization or implicit speech (as this can be called) and reading would say no. Earlier, there were attempts made to teach children to read without the teacher or the pupil saying words aloud [Buswell 1945]. The *nonoral* teaching method was based on the theory that a reader can and should go directly from the printed word to comprehension of it without any implicit speech between. We have learned that this is an impossibility, which explains why the children in the early nonoral experiments used as much implicit speech as did children who learned to read by reading aloud. As Gibson [1975, p. 302] rightly concludes, "For a child who is learning, subvocal speech may be essential for getting the message."

Modern research shows that good readers do use less implicit speech than do poor readers. This should *not* be interpreted to mean, however, that the teacher should make aggressive efforts to eliminate children's vocalizing as they read. The research indicates that the use or disuse of vocalization is a developmental matter. Its use proceeds through the stage at which all words are said aloud or whispered to the final stage of silent speech in reading, where implicit speech is hidden (except to an electronic device attached to the reader's throat) [Edfeldt 1960]. In sum, the research advises us that implicit speech is necessary as a developmental learning reinforcement activity and it should *not* be prematurely eliminated [Davies 1972].

REFERENCES

Allen, P. David. "Cue Systems Available During the Reading Process: A Psycholinguistic Viewpoint." *Elementary School Journal,* 72(1972):258–264.

Anderson, Paul S. *Language Skills in Elementary Education.* New York: Macmillan, 1972.

Aukerman, Robert C. *Approaches to Beginning Reading.* New York: John Wiley & Sons, 1971.

Berdiansky, Betty, Cronnell, Bruce, and Koehler, John. *Spelling-Sound Relations and Primary Form-Class Descriptions for Speech-Comprehension Vocabularies of 6–9 Year-Olds.* Los Alamitos, Calif.: Southwest Regional Laboratory for Educational Research and Development, 1969.

Bliesmer, Emery P., and Yarborough, Betty H. "Comparison of Ten Different Beginning Reading Programs in First Grade." *Phi Delta Kappa,* 47(1965):500–504.

Bond, Guy L., and Wagner, Eva Bond. *Teaching the Child to Read.* New York: Macmillan, 1960.

Boyd, Gertrude A., and Talbert, E. Gene. *Spelling in the Elementary School.* Columbus: Charles E. Merrill, 1971.

Brengelman, Frederick. *The English Language.* Englewood Cliffs, N.J.: Prentice-Hall, 1970.

Bridges, Judith S., and Lessler, Ken. "Goals of First Grade." *Reading Teacher,* 25(1972):763–767.

Brittain, Mary M. "Inflectional Performance and Early Reading Achievement." *Reading Research Quarterly,* 6(1970):34–50.

Buswell, Guy T. *Non-Oral Reading: A Study of Its Use in the Chicago Public Schools.* Supplementary Educational Monographs, No. 60. Chicago: University of Chicago Press, 1945.

Calfee, Robert C., Venezky, Richard L., and Chapman, Robin S. *Pronunciation of Synthetic Words with Predictable and Unpredictable Letter-Sound Correspondences.* Technical Report No. 71. Madison: University of Wisconsin Research and Development Center for Cognitive Learning, 1969.

Carroll, John B. "Language Development," *Encyclopaedia of Educational Research,* ed. Chester W. Harris. New York: Macmillan, 1960.

Cavoures, Dorothy G. "Phoneme Identification in Primary Reading and Spelling." *Dissertation Abstracts,* 26(1966):5905–5906.

Chall, Jeanne, Roswell, Florence G., and Blumenthal, Susan H. "Auditory Blending Ability: A Factor in Success in Beginning Reading." *Reading Teacher,* 17(1963):113–118.

Chapman, Robin S., Venezky, Richard L., and Calfee, Robert C. "Use of Simple and Conditional Letter-Sound Correspondences in Children's Pronunciations of Synthetic Words." Paper presented at the annual convention of the American Educational Research Association, Minneapolis, 1970.

Chester, Robert D. "Differences in Learnability of Content and Function Words Presented in Isolation and Oral Context When Taught to High and Low Socioeconomic Students." *Dissertation Abstracts International*, 32(1972):3833A.

Chomsky, Carol. "Reading, Writing and Phonology." *Harvard Educational Review*, 40(1970):287–309.

Chomsky, Noam, and Halle, Morris. *The Sound Pattern of English*. New York: Harper & Row, 1968.

Compton, Mary E. "A Study of the Relationship Between Oral Language Facility and Reading Achievement of Selected First-Grade Children." *Dissertation Abstracts International*, 32(1972):6448A–6449A.

Cronnell, Bruce. *Beginning Spelling: A Linguistic Review of Six Spelling Series*. Inglewood, Calif.: Southwest Regional Laboratory for Educational Research and Development, 1971.

Davies, William C. "Implicit Speech—Some Conclusions Drawn from Research," *Some Persistent Questions on Beginning Reading*, ed. Robert C. Aukerman. Newark, Del.: International Reading Association, 1972.

Desberg, Peter, and Berdiansky, Betty. *Word Attack Skills: Review of Literature*. Los Alamitos, Calif.: Southwest Regional Laboratory for Educational Research and Development, 1970.

Durkin, Dolores. *Teaching Them to Read*. Boston: Allyn & Bacon, 1970.

Dykstra, Robert. "Auditory Discrimination Abilities and Beginning Reading Achievement." *Reading Research Quarterly*, 1(1966):5–34.

Edfeldt, Ake W. *Silent Speech and Silent Reading*. Chicago: University of Chicago Press, 1960.

Edwards, Thomas J. "Teaching Reading: A Critique," *The Disabled Reader*, ed. John Money, Baltimore: Johns Hopkins University Press, 1966.

Erwin, Susan M., and Miller, Wick R. "Language Development," *Child Psychology*. 62nd Yearbook, National Society for the Study of Education. Chicago: University of Chicago Press, 1963.

Fries, Charles C. *Linguistics and Reading*. New York: Holt, Rinehart and Winston, 1963.

Gates, Arthur I. "The Necessary Mental Age for Beginning Reading." *Elementary School Journal*, 37(1937):497–508.

Geyer, John J. "Models of Perceptual Processes in Reading," *Theoretical Models and Processes of Reading*, eds. Harry Singer and Robert B. Ruddell. Newark, Del.: International Reading Association, 1970.

Gibson, Eleanor J. *Principles of Perceptual Learning and Development*. New York: Appleton-Century-Crofts, 1969.

Gibson, Eleanor J. "Theory-Based Research on Reading and Its Implications for Instruction," *Toward a Literate Society*, eds. John B. Carroll and Jeanne S. Chall. New York: McGraw-Hill, 1975.

Gibson, Eleanor J., Osser, Harry, and Pick, Anne D. "A Study of the Development of Grapheme-Phoneme Correspondence in the Perception of Words." *Journal of Verbal Learning and Verbal Behavior*, 2(1963):142–146.

Gilhooly, William B. "The Influence of Writing-System Characteristics on Learning to Read." *Reading Research Quarterly*, 8(1973):167–199.

Goodman, Kenneth S. "Analysis of Oral Reading Miscues: Applied Psycholinguistics." *Reading Research Quarterly*, 5(1969):9–30.

Gray, Eugene T. *A Study of the Vocal Phonic Ability of Children Six to Eight and One-Half Years*. Ph.D. Dissertation, University of Oklahoma, 1963.

Groff, Patrick. "Blending: Basic Process or Beside the Point?" *Reading World*, 15(1976):161–166.

Groff, Patrick. "Children's Speech Errors and Their Spelling." *Elementary School Journal*, 74(1973):88–96.

Groff, Patrick. "Long Versus Short Words in Beginning Reading." *Reading World*, 14(1975a):277–289.

Groff, Patrick. "Reading Ability and Auditory Discrimination: Are They Related?" *Reading Teacher*, 28(1975b):742–747.

Groff, Patrick. "Should Sounds in Phonics Be Isolated?" *Minnesota Reading Quarterly*, 20(1975c):57–59.

Groff, Patrick. "The Topsy Turvy World of 'Sight' Words." *Reading Teacher*, 27(1974):572–578.

Gudschinsky, Sarah C. "The Nature of the Writing System: Pedagogical Implications," *Language and Learning to Read,* eds. Richard E. Hodges and E. Hugh Rudorf. Boston: Houghton Mifflin, 1972.

Hanna, Paul R., et al. *Phoneme-Grapheme Correspondences as Cues to Spelling Improvement.* Washington, D.C.: U.S. Office of Education, 1966.

Hartley, Ruth N. "Effects of List Types and Cues on the Learning of Word Lists." *Reading Research Quarterly,* 6(1970):97–121.

Hatch, Evelyn. *The Syntax of Four Reading Programs Compared with Language Development of Children.* Inglewood, Calif.: Southwest Regional Laboratory for Educational Research and Development, 1971.

Healey, William C. *A Study of the Articulatory Skills of Children from Six to Nine Years of Age.* Ph.D. Dissertation, University of Missouri, 1963.

Heilman, Arthur W. *Phonics in Proper Perspective.* Columbus: Charles E. Merrill, 1964.

Johnson, D. LaMont. "Does Perceptual Training Improve Reading?— Another View." *Academic Therapy,* 10(1974):65–68.

Johnson, Francis C. "The Failure of the Discipline of Linguistics in Language Teaching." *Language Learning,* 19(1969):235–244.

Johnson, Kenneth R. "When Should Standard English Be Taught to Speakers of Nonstandard Negro Dialect?" *Language Learning,* 22(1970):19–30.

Klesius, Stephen E. "Perceptual-Motor Development and Reading— A Closer Look," *Some Persistent Questions on Beginning Reading,* ed. Robert C. Aukerman. Newark, Del.: International Reading Association, 1972.

Knafle, June D. "Word Perception: An Experiment with Cues in the Development of Unit-Forming Principles." *Dissertation Abstracts International,* 32(1972):4424A.

Levin, Harry, and Watson, John. "The Learning of Variable Grapheme-to-Phoneme Correspondences," *A Basic Research Program on Reading,* ed. Harry Levin. Ithaca: Cornell University Press, 1963a.

Levin, Harry, and Watson, John. "The Learning of Variable Grapheme-to-Phoneme Correspondences: Variations in the Initial Consonant Position," *A Basic Research Program on Reading,* ed. Harry Levin. Ithaca: Cornell University Press, 1963b.

McCullough, Constance M. "Vital Principles in Need of Application," *A Decade of Innovations: Approaches to Beginning Reading*, ed. Elaine C. Vilscek. Newark, Del.: International Reading Association, 1968.

McCutcheon, Beth A., and McDowell, Eugene E. "Intralist Similarity and Acquisition and Generalization of Work Recognition." *Reading Teacher*, 23(1969):103–107.

McKee, Paul. *Reading*. Boston: Houghton Mifflin, 1966.

Malmquist, Eve. *Factors Related to Reading Disabilities in the First Grade of the Elementary School*. Stockholm: Almqvist and Wiksell, 1960.

Mason, George E., and Woodcock, Carrol. "First Grader's Peformance on a Visual Memory for Words Task." *Elementary English*, 50(1973):865–870.

Moe, Alden J. "An Investigation of the Uniqueness of Selected Auditory Discrimination Skills Among Kindergarten Children Enrolled in Two Types of Reading Readiness Programs." *Dissertation Abstracts*, 32(1972):6295A.

Morency, Anne. "Auditory Modality—Research and Practice," *Perception and Reading*, ed. Helen K. Smith. Newark, Del.: International Reading Association, 1968.

Olson, James H. "A Study of the Performance of Second Grade Children on 'Taught' and 'Untaught' Words Having Regular and Less Regular Spelling Patterns." *Dissertation Abstracts International*, 31(1970):1147A.

Otto, Wayne, et al. *Focused Reading Instruction*. Reading, Mass.: Addison-Wesley, 1974.

Otto, Wayne, and Pizillo, Carole. "Effect of Intralist Similarity on Kindergarten Pupils' Rate of Word Acquisition and Transfer." *Journal of Reading Behavior*, 3(1970–1971):14–19.

Pitcher-Baker, Georgia. "Does Perceptual Training Improve Reading?" *Academic Therapy*, 9(1973):41–45.

Reed, David W. "A Theory of Language, Speech, and Writing," *Theoretical Models and Processes of Reading*, eds. Harry Singer and Robert B. Ruddell. Newark, Del.: International Reading Association, 1970.

Richardson, Norma S. "A Study of Three Methods of Teaching Word Recognition Skills." *Dissertation Abstracts*, 27(1966):998–999A.

Rinsland, Henry D. *A Basic Vocabulary of Elementary School Children*. New York: Macmillan, 1945.

Robinson, Helen M. "Perceptual Training—Does It Result in Reading Improvement?" *Some Persistent Questions on Beginning Reading*, ed. Robert C. Aukerman. Newark, Del.: International Reading Association, 1972a.

Robinson, Helen M. "Visual and Auditory Modalities Related to Methods for Beginning Reading." *Reading Research Quarterly*, 8(1972b):7–39.

Rosinski, Richard R., and Wheeler, Kirk E. "Children's Use of Orthographic Structure in Word Discrimination." *Psychonomic Science*, 26(1972):97–98.

Rystrom, Richard. "Dialect Training and Reading." *Reading Research Quarterly*, 5(1970):581–599.

Samuels, S. J., and Jeffrey, W. E. "Discriminability of Words, and Letter Cues Used in Learning to Read." *Journal of Educational Psychology*, 57(1966):337–340.

Shankweiler, Donald, and Liberman, Isabelle Y. "Misreading: A Search for Causes," *Language by Ear and by Eye*, eds. James F. Kavanagh and Ignatius C. Mattingly. Cambridge: MIT Press, 1972.

Slavin, Harris B. "What the Child Knows about Speech When He Starts to Learn to Read," *Language by Ear and by Eye*, eds. James F. Kavanagh and Ignatius B. Mattingly. Cambridge: MIT Press, 1972.

Sledd, James. "Doublespeak: Dialectology in the Service of Big Brother." *College English*, 33(1972):439–456.

Smith, Frank. *Understanding Reading*. New York: Holt, Rinehart and Winston, 1971.

Spache, George D., and Spache, Evelyn B. *Reading in the Elementary School*. Boston: Allyn & Bacon, 1969.

Stauffer, Russell G., ed. *The First Grade Reading Studies*. Newark, Del.: International Reading Association, 1967.

Templin, Mildred. "A Study of Sound Discrimination Ability of Elementary School Pupils." *Journal of Speech and Hearing Disorders*, 8(1943):127–132.

Tikofsky, Ronald S., and McInish, James R. "Consonant Discrimination by Seven-Year-Olds: A Pilot Study." *Psychonomic Science*, 10(1968):61–62.

Vandever, Thomas R. "Phoneme-Grapheme Consistency, Cue Emphasis, and Decoding." *Journal of Experimental Education*, 42(1973):81–84.

Veatch, Jeannette. *Reading in the Elementary School*. New York: Ronald Press, 1966.

Venezky, Richard L., and Weir, Ruth A. *A Study of Selected Spelling to Sound Correspondence Patterns*. Cooperative Research Project No. 3090. Washington, D.C.: U.S. Office of Education, 1966.

Wardhaugh, Ronald. "A Linguist Looks at Reading." *Elementary English*, 48(1971a):61–66.

Wardhaugh, Ronald. "Theories of Language Acquisition in Relation to Beginning Reading Instruction." *Language Learning*, 21(1971b):1–26.

Washburn, Watson. "Phonics: The Essential Foundation for Reading Instruction," *Children Can Learn to Read—But How?* ed. Coleman Morrison. Providence: Rhode Island College Press, 1964.

Waugh, Ruth, and Watson, Zana. "Visual Perception and Reading." *Education*, 91(1971):266–269.

Wepman, Joseph M. "Auditory Discrimination, Speech, and Reading." *Elementary School Journal*, 60(1960):325–333.

Williams, Joanna P. "Reactions to Modes of Word Recognition." *Theoretical Models and Processes of Reading*, eds. Harry Singer and Robert Ruddell. Newark, Del.: International Reading Association, 1970.

Wolpert, Edward M. "Length, Imagery Values, and Word Recognition." *Reading Teacher*, 26(1972):180–186.

II

The "How" of Phonics: Teaching Monosyllabic Words

7

CLASSROOM PRACTICES IN PHONICS TEACHING

The teaching of phonics is no different in many respects from good teaching in general. Obviously, good teaching calls for a humane, enthusiastic, and well-informed teacher who spends adequate time in preparation for lessons. For this chapter we have chosen to discuss five problems that are especially critical to successful phonics teaching.

1. How much practice, and of what kind, is needed to develop phonics skills? To answer this question we should keep in mind that if a child participates in a logical sequence of phonics activities, rather than in random practice, this is likely to result in greater knowledge of phonics. It is also axiomatic that small group instruction is essential if children are to be stimulated to learn phonics at a pace that is commensurate with their abilities and potentials.

As with other forms of associative learning, phonics requires, by its very nature, a goodly amount of practice, exercise, or repetition. There is nothing inherently distasteful about practice or drill, although most of us have experienced bad forms of it. Practice in phonics, if it takes the forms described in the following chapters, need not be resented by children. In fact, most children seem to take pleasure in perfecting the skill of fluent word recognition. Not only are most conscious of the social implications of such skill, but they also derive pleasure from learning phonics to recognize words since it pleases the adults whom they admire.

However, phonics exercises with inattentive pupils are worse than no exercises at all. There are children who are persistently inattentive in phonics lessons, even when their classmates are interested. Forcing such a child to attend to phonics generally fails. In our view, the best idea is to excuse this child from group phonics lessons temporarily on the basis he or she is not emotionally "ready" for phonics. An attempt should be made to get a mother, an older pupil, a student teacher, or a teacher's aide to give the child some one-to-one tutoring, which generally proves more effective at this point. Return this child to the phonics group at a later time.

The nature of phonics skills makes it important that these skills not only be given in a logical sequence, but that eleven other conditions also prevail.

1. Phonics lessons should be relatively short.

2. Lessons should be frequent, daily in most cases.

3. Lessons should be fast-paced and not linger on any matter, such as a fact that a single pupil in a group seems to misunderstand.

4. Lessons should cover only a very small segment of phonics at a time.

5. The lesson should start with an item that children know.

6. The pupils should repeat items from lesson to lesson until the teacher feels almost all children in a group can respond correctly.

7. No absolute deadline should be set for how much will be covered in a given time. Only the pupils' responses can determine this.

8. The teacher should be constantly on the alert to regroup children on the basis of their growth in phonics, hence, the need for several small groups.

9. Some phonics game (see the Appendix) should be played or explained in almost every lesson. The children can be directed to play these games in pairs after they leave the group activity.

10. Keep charts of children's progress to reinforce their efforts to learn by knowing they are making progress.

11. There should be some individual work, especially in spelling.

It should be noted that spelling instruction can be given, to a great extent, to pupils working alone (or at least in pairs). As soon as children can read words, they should be able to work on spelling individually, at their own speed. The teacher can tape record word lists, or instructions to be followed. Easy-to-follow work sheets arranged sequentially can be used by the pupil. These resemble the exercises in the spelling text but are easier to read and set no time limit on the learner. The pupil can proceed through them self-paced.

The pace at which group lessons in phonics are conducted is a problem that deserves special comment. The question here is whether the pace of a lesson should be set by the goal of (1) trying to learn with as few errors as possible, or (2) trying to learn as fast as possible. There is evidence that pupils instructed to learn concepts as rapidly as possible do learn concepts faster than pupils instructed to learn concepts with as few errors as possible [Frayer & Klausmeier 1971]. This evidence suggests phonics lessons be conducted at a brisk pace with more reward given for how fast a pupil tries to learn something than for errorless responses. Giving positive reinforcement for quick responses in phonics lessons will likely bring out wrong responses that might otherwise be hidden, foster intelligent guessing, and generally act to reduce the pupil's reluctance to respond, or the tension of the learning situation.

2. **What forms should phonics lessons take?** We have noted that in some unusual cases children who are restless and inattentive during the phonics lesson may truly not be emotionally "ready" for phonics. However, the large majority of children who exhibit inattentiveness, we feel, do so for other reasons. The causes for their lack of empathy for the phonics activities probably lie in the form of the lesson itself.

Phonics lessons will frustrate and repel children if they have these four insidious aspects: (1) children must wait for turns, (2) children do not understand what they are being asked to perceive and how to respond, (3) they are not given immediate "right" or "wrong" feedback for responses to phonics activities, and (4) they are not told by the teacher at all times which words are exceptions to the rules being learned.

The first of these instructional faults—requiring children to wait for turns—can be avoided easily through the use of *response cards*. These are cards containing the answers the phonics teacher hopes to elicit. Each child is given a few. The teacher asks for a response. *Each child responds each time by raising a card.* The happy result: no child has to wait for a turn.

The second major fault of phonics lessons is more difficult to remedy. Part of the problem is solved, nonetheless, by the use of response cards. If children are active at all times, they are more likely to be attentive. And, if they are more attentive, it follows that they will miss less of the lesson, and therefore what is being taught will become more meaningful. It is helpful, too, if the teacher makes quite sure whether a child understands a question *before* assuming the child cannot respond correctly. Unless proved otherwise, the teacher should assume the question is phrased wrongly rather than that the child cannot answer. It is remarkable how many times unresponsive children will answer when a question is asked a different way.

The third major fault of phonics lessons—the lack of feedback—is partially overcome by the use of the response cards. The phonics teacher also should be alert at all times to mistakes children make in the phonics lessons and be quick to tell them "right" or "wrong." To be able to respond to children in this way means, of course, that the teacher cannot teach large groups of children. Groups for phonics instruction must be small enough so that the teacher is aware of and can respond to each child.

The need for feedback carries with it a necessary evil. This is the matter of telling children when they are wrong. Unless children are told which of their responses are wrong, it is likely they cannot learn which responses are correct and usable in the future [Frayer & Klausmeier 1971]. Some sensitive children who make wrong responses will become anxious in this situation, nonetheless, and rather than run the risk of being punished (in their eyes) for a wrong response, will not hazard any responses. Children who develop such anxieties display their fear of the situation by finding other things to do during the lesson, such as talking to or hitting classmates, conveniently losing the place, finding all sorts of objects to play with, daydreaming, talking to themselves, asking irrelevant questions, and so on. In either case, with introverted or extroverted behavior, children signal that they are overwhelmed by the negative feedback received. To help relieve this trauma the teacher must put such children into a phonics group at a lower level of accomplishment where negative feedback for them will be less likely. Hopefully, the confidence these children can build in their ability at this level will condition them for a greater tolerance of negative feedback in the future.

Feedback should often take the form of asking, "Did that sound right or make sense?" This helps children develop a strategy for correcting their miscues, especially those that are syntactically acceptable—for example, the substitution of a different noun for the actual noun in a sentence.

Evidence of the dangers of erroneous or misinformative feedback by the teacher is now available. A serious hazard to learning is created when children are told by the teacher that their responses are wrong when actually the responses are correct. Less well-known (or understood) research findings suggest that misinformative feedback to children on one task situation may even inhibit their performance on a later task [Frayer & Klausmeier 1971]. The clear implication here is that the effective teacher of phonics is one who is well informed. Clearly, teachers who "stay one page ahead of the child" in teaching reading are a genuine handicap to the child's learning, since the probability of providing misinformative feedback is so high.

To overcome the fourth major fault—words that contain untaught rules—these words must be viewed by pupil and teacher alike as exceptions. There should be a low frequency of such words presented, of course. Above all, children must be reminded that it is not their fault if they respond wrongly to exceptional words. Children also should be complimented for their good thinking when they apply a spelling-sound rule to a likely exceptional word to which it does *not* apply.

There are ten other ways the teacher can shape successful phonics lessons.

1. The teacher can be sure to utilize children's personal meaning vocabularies. Familiar words imbedded in familiar sentence patterns help pupils understand.

2. The teacher should consciously endeavor to talk in uncomplicated sentences. Instructions, directions, or questions given in complex syntax invite misunderstandings.

3. A quick shift or "branching" to something children have previously demonstrated knowledge of is appropriate when they appear confused.

4. Rephrasing of directions and questions sometimes helps.

5. Giving the activity a game-like format convinces some children that the effort to understand will be worthwhile, that is, it will be rewarded with something that is fun to do.

6. Reduce the number of difficult concepts to an absolute minimum and teach these by using examples rather than rules.

7. Encourage the children to say aloud the words involved in the lesson. A reinforcement to the written word of its spoken equivalent, even when done in a stage whisper, often makes a relationship clear. Phonics lessons are not "Be quiet and listen" activities.

8. Be persistent and repeat something that was previously misunderstood. Remember, children may be grasping a phonics concept even though at a given point they cannot produce a proper response.

9. Let a child who does understand what is being taught explain it to the others. Somehow such explanations are often effective when the teacher's are not.

10. Practice the general rules of teaching effectiveness. For example, make sure children have settled down before beginning; remove distracting influences; appear enthusiastic and positive about the planned activity; make many rewarding remarks about responses; work off muscular discomfort by having children stand to respond and by alternating activities (board work, response cards, talking); begin by doing something everyone knows how to do; utilize innocuous competition to see who gets a privilege; attach humorous names to difficult concepts (e.g., "bossy" r); and have children repeat something the teacher says to find how well they understand it.

3. Is it an effective and economical way to teach phonics to work systematically with small groups of children? In such small-group teaching, the teacher can make it possible for all children in the group to respond regularly to the phonics activities being conducted. Thus, the teacher can secure the evidence of the different rates at which these children can learn phonics so that new, small groups can be continuously formed. Continuing the reformation of these groups is critical to such small-group teaching.

Even the advocates of individualized reading support the idea of small-group teaching of phonics. As Jeannette Veatch says, "The major point of grouping children is that it saves classroom time. It saves wear and tear on teacher energy. It teaches much to many in a short space of time" [1966, p. 178]. Advocates of individualized reading generally believe that "the knowledge of when to organize a group usually comes, as can be seen, from the individual conference" [p. 178]. These short conferences (necessarily so since they must be held on a regular basis with each child in the class) are intensive sessions on a one-to-one basis with individual pupils. Here the teacher supposedly analyzes all the reading performance of the children since their last conference, including phonics skills, and decides what group instruction in phonics (and all the other reading skills) are needed.

We do not believe it humanly possible for the teacher to gain an understanding of a child's word recognition problems and abilities and reform them in such short, once- or twice-a-week sessions. We recommend, instead, that the teacher set up small groups of pupils in phonics and change the membership of these groups as often as dictated by the differing rates of learning of individual children. This belief is supported by teachers of individualized reading whom we asked to criticize the statement that phonics teaching suffers in individualized reading. In general, they suggested that a more systematic and structured program in phonics was needed to improve this heterodox approach to reading instruction [Groff 1964].

A valid criticism of trying to teach phonics individually in conferences is that this doubtless wastes the teacher's time and effort. One advocate of individualized reading insists on the necessity of conducting the following activity with only one child at a time.

Working with Tommy as he is beginning to read, the teacher may write his name on the chalkboard, identifying the first letter as a *t*. She may then ask Tommy to think of other words that begin with the same sound. As he says the words, she writes them on the board so that he can see *t* in the initial position. Tommy might suggest the word cat. In this case, he would be asked, "Where do you see the letter *t*—at the beginning of the word? Where do you hear the sound *t*?" [Wilsberg 1965, p. 34].

It appears to us that it is reasonable to ask, "Why only with one child?" Surely many beginning readers need to understand and practice the details of phonics. To teach each of them to thirty children separately as if there were no such common need involves a misappropriation of the teacher's time and efforts.

The lack of sequence and persistence of teacher effort that appears in this example of individualized phonics teaching in a conference is dismaying. For example, after Tommy had learned something about the /t/-t correspondences, the purpose of Tommy's next conference might be to discuss the selection of a new book to read. When one realizes that these two short individual conferences will probably be all the individualized instruction Tommy would get in reading from this teacher—*for a week*—it is proper to wonder if phonics can be successfully taught with such a haphazard schedule. We believe, instead, that phonics should be taught *systematically*. Generally, this means moving through an arranged sequence of activities (since everything cannot be taught at once), and persisting with the teaching of any phonics element until the child indicates an understanding of it. Common sense should prevail here, of course. If the children appear to be frustrated at any point, try to break off a particular activity and branch off into another phonics item.

4. What is the optimal kind of writing of letters for phonics instruction? It seems a truism that if the material of a phonics lesson is written by a phonics teacher in a legible manner this will facilitate pupils' learning of phonics [Groff 1975]. The degree to which the teacher can approximate the models of letters found in handwriting manuals doubtless does help pupils perceive differences in letter forms. While it is more difficult to isolate other factors that affect the readability of letters offered the phonics learner, there is some relevant evidence, nevertheless.

For example, for some time we have known that manuscript handwriting is more readable for pupils and therefore is read by them faster than is cursive handwriting. Olive Turner's finding to this effect in 1930 has been confirmed by several other researchers. But with adults, Hugh Bell [1939] found that manuscript handwriting was not as readable as was typewritten material. There is some doubt whether this is true with children, however. Bror Zachrisson [1965] has found, for instance, that both first- and fourth-grade pupils read materials in sans serif print just as well as that in serif print. He also found no significant difference of opinions among these pupils as to the readability of these two kinds of print. (In serif a smaller line is used to finish off a main stroke of a letter, as you can see at the top and bottom of l and x. In sans serif these letters would appear as I and x.) The manuscript letters written by the phonics teacher are sans (without) serif, of course. Keller's research [1974] also suggests there is no disadvantage to the phonics learner in having to read the teacher's manuscript handwriting rather than printed materials.

The size of the writing used in phonics lessons should also be of concern to the teacher. From their survey of printed type sizes Matthew Luckiesh and Frank Moss [1942, p. 374] believe the type size for optimum readability for adults with normal vision (reading at fourteen inches) is at least 12-point and perhaps somewhat larger. Remember that 12-point type is often that found in a pica typewriter, and it is about three sixteenths of an inch tall. For children through age eight, however, one of the recommendations is for the use of 18- or 20-point type (one fourth of an inch or a little over) [Zachrisson 1965, p. 40]. It appears reasonable, therefore, to call for the use of the larger type "primary" typewriter for making up phonics worksheets. Moreover, such sheets probably should be double-spaced, since the space between lines, the leading, "has an important effect on the legibility of type" [Tinker 1963, p. 106]. As Zachrisson [1965, p. 139] points out, by the time the child is a fourth grader "there is no reason to claim that a larger type size should be used than is normally used for adult reading." For beginning readers, however, he concedes it is "a questionable assumption" to contend "that there is no interaction between size of type face and reading skill" [p. 136].

Then, if a child reads the teacher's writing, say four feet from the chalkboard, should the size of the writing by the teacher be increased at least four times (to approximately one inch)? If "obviously a 6-point type focused at a distance of 7 inches from the eye is approximately equivalent to 12-point type at a distance of 14 inches" [Luckiesh & Moss 1942, p. 374], would not the reverse obtain for distance viewing? No doubt the answer is yes. The teacher accordingly should plan to write letters of a size to equal at least one fourth of an inch times the number of feet the pupil is sitting from the chalkboard.

It has also been noted that "several experiments have shown that lower case is more legible than capitals" [Zachrisson 1965, p. 43]. More than this, we know that lower-case letters are about as easy for the beginning reader to learn to recognize as are upper-case letters [Smythe, et al. 1971]. Considering these facts it makes good sense for the teacher to use lower-case letters exclusively in phonics instruction.

The length of the line of type or handwriting children are asked to read is also of importance. As Miles Tinker [1963, p. 211] concluded, "there was a slight and rather consistent tendency for the shorter lines [in this case 3.5 inches] to be read faster" by mature readers. The study of Luckiesh and Moss [1942, p. 203] leads them to more stringent conclusions that lines of just slightly more than two inches in length are the most readable. Somewhere between two inches and three and one-half inches, then, should become the standard length of lines on the phonics worksheet.

Finally, we would all agree that when the letters in a word appear crowded together that each letter in this word seems especially difficult to identify. It is likely that when letters are crowded together in a word, the middle letters of the word are difficult to see because they are "masked." Arthur Linksz reports evidence that shows that if letters "are separated from one another by about 120 percent of their own width, there is no more masking effect, and that the masking effect is most pronounced when this separation is around 30 percent of the letter's width" [1973, p. 164]. A careful separation of letters appears to reduce the "masking" effect that the series of letters in the word has upon middle letters of the word. This masking effect explains, to a degree, why children see the beginning and ending letters of a word more readily than those in the middle of a word. The former letters are the ones not masked or visually inhibited by any other letter. All this suggests that when writing words for beginning readers the phonics teacher should be careful to leave generous spaces between the letters of words. Typewritten material does not allow for such generous spaces between letters, which may mean that children can read well-spaced manuscript handwriting as well as they can read typewritten material.

5. How does one evaluate children's achievement of phonics knowledge? Generally, the evaluation of children's growth in phonics should be based on the principles of phonics teaching given in Chapter 6. That is, the teacher should look to several sources of children's reading for such evidence. Testing should be done on language the children actually use. The adult model of reading performance should not be held as the standard to measure pupil progress. The testing of pupils' phonics skills should first be with one-syllable, predictably spelled words, and so on.

More specifically, a good system of phonics evaluation is indicated by the following items:

1. An insistence that children read for meaning. With the exception of the use of pseudowords (*glurch*) to test phonics knowledge, children's ability to tell the meaning of what they read should not be overlooked.

2. Evidence that evaluation is ongoing with few, if any, formal tests. Each instructional period should allow for a few minutes for the teacher to review what children have learned.

3. Teachers' awareness that some children cannot always produce evidence of their comprehension of what is being taught. In these cases attentiveness is a good sign of learning.

4. The testing of children's knowledge of function words always within familiar syntax.

5. Finding out regularly whether children can apply phonic generaliza-

tions they learned at previous levels or times of instruction. Backtracking or recapitulation may be required.

6. An emphasis upon the analysis of words, and yet the encouragement of reading speed. "How fast can you read this word?" should be a common challenge.

7. The absence of requirements that children repeat phonics rules in a verbalized, verbatim fashion. The teacher's basic concern rather should be whether children actually can read certain kinds of words in sentences that follow various spelling patterns and structures.

8. An awareness that children's use of nonstandard dialect may make it appear they have made a reading error when this is not the case. Children's oral reading may be a translation of the standard English of the written page into the sounds and words of their own dialect (including intonation), which may not be a standard dialect.

9. A consideration of whether the mistake children make is similar, grammatically and phonemically, to the words they attempt to read. If the miscue is the *same part of speech* as the word on the page, it indicates that children are using the sentence structure as an aid to word recognition. If the sounds of the miscue made by children are similar to the sounds of the word on the page (if they were correctly read aloud), this indicates children are trying to use phonics (to relate the sounds of language with their spellings). The teacher should notice precisely the nature of these attempts to use phonics, and where they went astray, in order to correct the misinterpretation.

10. A patient attitude toward children, which permits enough time for them to make corrections of their mistakes. Too often, teachers correct children at the moment they make errors. It is better, instead, to allow a reasonable amount of time for children to correct themselves. If children return to the word or passage on the page that was involved in the miscue and correctly read it, this should be considered a good sign. These regressions in reading, which traditionally were thought to be a bad practice, are to be seen as normal and can be encouraged.

We feel that this type of evaluation of oral reading miscues has more value than the counting of oral reading "errors" with a second plan for testing, the so-called *informal reading inventory* (IRI) [McCracken 1968]. The IRI directs the teacher simply to count all the repetitions, substitutions, additions, omissions, mispronunciations, the times an unknown word is supplied to the child, and the times the child ignores the punctuation. The simplistic counting system of the IRI gives the teacher little insight, however, as to how the child is trying to process printed material. Its main purpose seems to be to place the child at what are supposed to be definitive levels of word-recognition ability: *frustration* (1 error per each 10 words on the average), *instructional* (1 error per each 20 to 39 words), *independent* (1 error per 40 words or more). The credibility of this placement is severely weakened, however, when one learns that the existence of these supposed levels cannot be verified. William Powell and Colin Dunkeld concluded from their study that the criteria used in the IRI need verification [1971].

Worse yet, IRI insists on a precise identification by children of each word they read aloud, while it ignores many of the important interpretive items that should be involved in evaluation [Burke & Goodman 1971]. As a result the IRI can have the undesired effect, for example, of causing children to stop using grammatical (context) cues, and thereby can stifle their commonsense notions of what word(s) may logically be read aloud. This could lead children to try the impossible task of "sounding out" every word they read aloud.

Standardized tests are yet another means used to evaluate pupils' growth in phonics. Unfortunately, children apparently have difficulty in following the directions in the standardized diagnostic tests in reading. When such standardized tests are administered to groups of children, it is good to prepare children to do their best on these tests. For this preparation the teacher should have children practice completing the types of exercises found in phonics tests. Carol Winkley's analysis [1971] of nine major phonics tests shows that they ask children to

1. Give the names of letters.

2. Select a letter from a group of letters so as to mark the one(s) that correspond to a sound heard in a spoken word. This is done at the beginning, middle, and end of words.

3. Select a printed word in which a letter appears that stands for a particular phoneme in another word (no spoken word given).

4. Select a pseudoword, e.g., *spiness*, from others after hearing its pronunciation.

5. Find and mark the letter representing the sound heard in the name of a pictured object.

6. Mark a word for the same purpose. Beginning, middle, and ending errors should appear in the words used as foils.

7. Recall the grapheme representing a phoneme heard in a word and write it. (Phonics tests have spelling items as well as reading items.)

8. Select a word spelled phonetically to match a regular spelling, e.g., *spays-space.*

Winkley rightly says that most of the so-called diagnostic reading tests cannot be used to determine the specific area of skill deficiency in children [1971]. If the results such tests give are dubious, it is important that children be familiar with them so as not to be penalized for supposedly doing poorly on them.

This knowledge of the weaknesses of diagnostic tests, coupled with Howard Livingston's recent evaluation that even some popular general reading tests also do not measure (or do not measure well) the skills that are inherent in the process of reading [1972], suggests one thing. *The responsibility for the evaluation of children's learning of phonics continues to rest with the teacher* rather than with some standardized test. Moreover, this will continue to be the case until the standardized tests more adequately measure what it is in reading that teachers actually teach. As of now these tests have been judged as not being fair teacher-assessment tools [Klein and Alkin 1972]. Some experts say that children's scores on such tests should *not* be used to evaluate the quality of the efforts of phonics teachers.

From all this evidence we sense it is impossible to give specific advice as to how to decide at what point children have learned enough of any particular topic in phonics to move on to the next item. Some argue that a certain criterion, a percent of correct responses such as 80 percent, should be set that children would have to meet [Otto, et al. 1974]. Some teachers may opt for this rather arbitrary system. Others advise that the teacher have children read aloud selections from graded basal readers at one grade level, then move to the next higher, and so on, until they miss a certain number of words. We have already described the shortcomings of this method. It is said that scores from standardized tests (given at some indeterminant point) should be used, or that "all sources of information" (whatever this is) should be utilized. We are struck here, however, with the unsupported claims for the use of standardized tests, and with the vagueness of such recommendations.

Despite the fact all these aspects of evaluation can be negatively criticized, it is likely that they all have some merit. Phonics teachers, therefore, might use evidence gathered from all of these methods of evaluation in their efforts to determine when pupils are ready for the next level in phonics. Overall, the best guide we can offer as to when a teacher should discontinue the teaching of a certain phonics item in order to branch off into a previously taught one, or to advance to the one at the next higher level, is evidence of children's attitudes toward learning the phonics item in question. That is, we must place confidence in the phonics teacher's judgment as to when pupil frustration begins to set in, so that a slowing down, a reteaching, or a shift to a new phonics item is called for. We admit that experience with phonics teaching is the best and perhaps the only way to develop such judgments. Since no one has yet come up with a satisfactorily practical method to evaluate the teaching of phonics, this is something every phonics teacher must learn to do.

REFERENCES

Bell, Hugh M. "The Comparative Legibility of Typewriting, Manuscript and Cursive Script: 1. Easy Prose, Letters and Syllables." *Journal of Psychology*, 8(1939):295–309.

Burke, Carolyn L., and Goodman, Yetta M. *Reading Miscue Inventory: Teachers Manual.* New York: Collier-Macmillan, 1971.

Frayer, Dorothy A., and Klausmeier, Herbert J. *Variables in Concept Learning: Task Variables.* Madison: University of Wisconsin Research and Development Center for Cognitive Learning, 1971.

Groff, Patrick. "Can Pupils Read What Teachers Write?" *Elementary School Journal*, 76(1975):32–39.

Groff, Patrick. "A Check on Individualized Reading." *Education*, 84(1964):397–401.

Keller, Nancy B. "An Investigation into the Problems of Word Recognition as Affected by Different Kinds of Print." *Dissertation Abstracts International*, 34(1974):6518A.

Klein, Stephen P., and Alkin, Marvin C. "Evaluating Teachers for Outcome Accountability." *Evaluation Comment*, 3(1972):5–11.

Linksz, Arthur. *On Writing, Reading, and Dyslexia.* New York: Grune & Stratton, 1973.

Livingston, Howard F. "What the Reading Test Doesn't Test—Reading." *Journal of Reading*, 15(1972):402–410.

Luckiesh, Matthew, and Moss, Frank K. *Reading as a Visual Task.* New York: D. Van Nostrand, 1942.

McCracken, Robert A. "The Informal Reading Inventory as a Method of Improving Instruction," *The Evaluation of Children's Reading Achievement*, ed. Thomas C. Barrett. Newark, Del.: International Reading Association, 1968.

Otto, Wayne, et al. *Focused Reading Instruction.* Reading, Mass.: Addison-Wesley, 1974.

Powell, William R., and Dunkeld, Colin G. "Validity of the IRI Reading Levels." *Elementary English*, 48(1971):637–642.

Smythe, P. C., et al. "Developmental Factors in Elemental Skills: Knowledge of Upper-Case and Lower-Case Letter Names." *Journal of Reading Behavior*, 3(1971):24–33.

Tinker, Miles A. *Legibility of Print*. Ames: Iowa State University Press, 1963.

Turner, Olive G. "The Comparative Legibility and Speed of Manuscript and Cursive Handwriting." *Elementary School Journal*, 30(1930):780–786.

Veatch, Jeannette. *Reading in the Elementary School*. New York: The Ronald Press, 1966.

Wilsberg, Mary E. "The Place of Skill Development," *Making Sure of Skill Development in Individualized Reading*, ed. Esther E. Schatz. Columbus: Ohio State University Press, 1965.

Winkley, Carol. "What Do Diagnostic Tests Really Diagnose?" *Diagnostic Viewpoints in Reading*, ed. Robert E. Liebert. Newark, Del.: International Reading Association, 1971.

Zachrisson, Bror. *Studies in the Legibility of Printed Text*. Stockholm: Almqvist and Wiksell, 1965.

8

TEACHING PHONICS:
LEVEL 1

Phonics instruction begins with the development of children's abilities to recognize letters. This is the first step in phonics instruction for a number of good reasons. Since the 1920s, at least, it has been found that children's abilities to recognize letters is the single best predictor of first-grade reading achievement [Smith 1963]. Several research studies reinforce the conclusion that learning letters is of great value to the beginning reader [Brown 1967; Dreyer 1969; Roger Johnson 1969; King 1964; Lowell 1970; Myers 1967; Schoolcraft 1973; Silvaroli 1965; Speer and Lamb 1976]. This evidence strongly implies that children will learn the phoneme-grapheme correspondences that are taught in phonics best if they are first taught to identify letters. Doubtless the evidence as cited here led Richard Rystrom to observe that the ability to recognize letters must precede the ability to perform more complex tasks such as decoding and word analysis [1969]. Yet, much to his surprise, Rystrom found that the third graders he studied scored only 49 percent on his letter discrimination test.

Although we agree with S. Jay Samuels, who says that the most valuable aspect of learning letters probably is the development of the pupils' "ability to visually discriminate one letter from another and not . . . knowledge of the letter names" [1970, p. 31], the children's fluent knowledge of letter names does give both the phonics teacher and pupils a vocabulary they can understand and use. Much time is saved when children are not confused by the teacher's references to letters by their names.

A reasonable objection has been made, however, to teaching the names of letters. Some research evidence shows that it helps the child little in learning to read. From his two studies Samuels concludes that knowing the names of the letters does not facilitate learning to read words made up of the same letters [1971]. In each of his studies twenty-five first-grade pupils were taught to name the letters and an equal number were taught an irrelevant task. Samuels found no significant differences between the abilities of these two groups in their ability to recognize four words by the look-say method. This finding was confirmed by Ronald Johnson [n.d.].

Therefore, the phonics teacher should first be sure that children can distinguish letters as being alike or different from each other before expecting children to remember their names. We know that beginners' knowledge of letter names is predictive of their later success in reading. This success does not relate so much to their having learned letter names, however, as it does to the fact that in learning these names they have accomplished a more fundamental task, that of identifying the distinguishing features of letter shapes.

Opposition to Teaching Letters

Those who disagree with the idea that children should learn letters as an aid to their learning to read usually base their opposition on one of two points. Advocates of "isolated" phonics are opposed to teaching letters because they believe that children should be taught to relate single, isolated phonemes with graphemes, and then to blend these sounds into pronounceable words. They contend that this kind of practice makes the knowledge of letters superfluous since the sounds of the letters can be used in place of their names. But this argument cannot be supported. The teaching of phonics with phonemes spoken in isolation is wrong since phonemes cannot be given their sounds this way. We agree, instead, with linguists who insist that the *syllable* is the irreducible unit of speech. Phonemes come to life only when spoken in syllables.

For example, Lila Gleitman and Paul Rozin [1973] rightly conclude, "One cannot physically separate the word *go* into 2 sound segments, one a pure 'g' and the other a pure 'o.' A simple way to show this is to record a syllable on tape and replay it over and over again, cutting a little bit off the end of the tape each time." When this is done the consonant sound /g/ "cannot be isolated. Rather, it is recognizable only in the context of a vowel" [p. 458]. Frank Smith also reports that "if the two words [*dim* and *doom*] are recorded, it is impossible to cut the tape in order to separate the /im/ or /oom/ from the /d/. Either one is left with a distinct /di/ or /doo/ sound, or else the /d/ sound disappears altogether" [1971, p. 33]. There is little doubt, then, that for phonemes to be distinctive, they must be produced with other sounds, in syllables.

A second group opposing the teaching of letters do so because they downgrade phonics in general. Some educators question any analysis of words. These advocates of a pure "look-say," total-word configuration approach to word recognition believe that children can best learn to read by learning to recognize each word *in toto* as if each word were a separate learning task. We believe that this theory of the learning of reading is also weak on several counts. First, there is no research evidence to support its claims [Groff 1974]. Second, it flies in the face of logic to assume that in learning to read the time-saving acquisition of generalizations about spelling-sound correspondences is improper and less than useful.

The best method of all is to teach the letters and their names *plus* the sounds they represent *concurrently.* As Dorothy Ohnmacht found in her study [n.d.], "initial instruction [for first graders] in letter names and sounds produced significantly greater reading achievement than did instruction in letter names alone." The findings of Nevins [1973] and of Jenkins, Bausell, and Jenkins [1972] agree with those of Ohnmacht. This means that after a couple of letters have been learned the teacher should proceed to Level 2 (see the next chapter) for activities with words involving these letters. *Repeat this cycle until all the letters are learned.*

We want to stress that the system of letter learning suggested here is not an activity isolated in time from teaching pupils how the sounds in words are represented by letters. Words and letters are almost immediately seen together (as are words in sentences). It should be emphasized that pupils learn very few letters before beginning to learn the relationships of these letters to the sounds in words they represent. As often as possible these words also should be presented to pupils in sentences *so that they are taught from the beginning to recognize words* (1) *through the use of phonics cues,* and (2) *from context and semantics cues.* This practice helps keep another all-important principle before pupils—that reading is a meaning-getting activity and not an isolated and formalistic exercise in letter or word identification.

Teaching Letters and Their Names

We suggest the development of children's abilities to recognize and name letters be carried out in this way.

1. Be sure to have letter cards for each child. By using these response cards the children do not have to wait to take turns. Each can respond at every step of the lesson. When the children hold up their letter cards, the teacher can easily see who has made an incorrect response and can help correct it.

2. Be careful of the language used. Although it is not necessary to follow
    the directions in the following steps word for word, the teacher should
    be sure that directions he or she uses are easy to follow. If there is any
    chance a child may not be able to follow a longer sentence, break up
    the directions into two sentences.

3. The use of at least two letters in all lessons has a distinct advantage.
    The use of two different letter cards requires that the child make many
    discriminations that would not be otherwise necessary. When begin-
    ning to work with letters, ask children to just say if the two letters
    shown them are "the same" or "different." This will be relatively easy
    for them [Gibson 1963]. Then increase the level of difficulty by having
    the pupils match a given letter with a multiple-choice set of two
    letters, then three, then four, and so on. After two letters are learned,
    it is wise in teaching slower learners to introduce only one new letter
    in the next lesson.

4. Use lower-case letters first since children will need to read these much
    more often than they will upper-case letters. Lower-case letters are
    only slightly more difficult to learn to name than are upper-case
    letters; 84 percent of seven-year-olds can name the former, 86 percent
    the latter [Smythe et al. 1971].

5. Remember that Level 1 is not concerned with developing auditory
    discrimination of the sounds that the letters can represent. In all
    activities on this level the children should respond with the *names of
    the letters* ("tee" and "are"; /ō/ and /ī/; etc.).

6. It is not advisable at Level 1 to direct children's attention to letters at
    the ends of words. This kind of discrimination is reserved for a later
    level.

7. The use of colored chalk is recommended as a means of helping
    children to see isolated letters and letters at the beginnings of one-
    vowel words. One study [Jones 1965] has found that young children
    did significantly better on matching tests of words and letters when
    these were in color instead of black and white. In his review of such
    research Wayne Otto saw the implication of these studies to be "that
    children's paired-associate learning should be enhanced by the addi-
    tion of color cues for any or all of the following reasons: aided
    perception and increased differentiation, the opportunity for cue
    selection, and greater motivation. Furthermore, there is the possibility
    that color may serve as a vehicle for mediation" [1967, p. 40]. This use
    of colored chalk seems particularly pertinent for vowel-letter recog-
    nition. Each of the vowel letters can be given a different color
    representing the sound it stands for.

8. As children begin reading, they should learn the *allographs* of a grapheme (the different forms of the same letter, e.g., a-A-*a*). *After* children can distinguish and name the lower-case allograph of a grapheme they should be taught to identify the others [Rystrom 1969]. Do not teach different allographs of a grapheme at the same time.

9. The letters need not be taught in alphabetical order since children learning to read have no need for knowledge of this ordering. It is not necessary to use such activities as singing games to learn the alphabet because this has little if anything to do with the central task here, which is learning to make the correct association of letter names and forms.

10. The learning of letters depends on learning the distinctive features of the letters to be discriminated. These are the differences in form that allow children to distinguish one letter from another. While logical to assume, it has also been verified experimentally that it is easier for children to learn highly similar letters (*b-d*) if these are not presented to the child together. On the contrary, the child learns dissimilar letters (*s-b*) better if these are presented together [Williams 1970]. Each letter in a pair being taught should differ from the other letter in more than one feature if possible. As Eleanor Gibson has explained [1968], a letter that differs in only one feature from another letter is more often confused than one differing in two or more features. Probably the features of letters that are used to recognize them are

> curved (*o, c, p*) or straight (*k, l*)
> closed (*o, p*) or open (*c, k*)
> descending (*g, y*) or ascending (*l, f*)
> symmetrical (*v, m*) or nonsymmetrical (*r, f*)
> intersected (*t, p*) or nonintersected (*l, c*)
> diagonal (*w, z*) or nondiagonal (*g, h*)
> vertical (*l, i*) or nonvertical (*e, w*)
> horizontal-vertical (*t*) or horizontal-diagonal (*z*)
> diagonal-vertical (*k*) or diagonal-horizontal (*z*), etc.

11. It is probably wise to avoid teaching letters which represent certain sounds too close together. The plosives /p/ and /b/ (and thus *p* and *d*) probably should not be taught together. We cannot agree, then, that "it would seem advisable to follow a sequence similar to the following: /t/, /m/, /d/, /p/, /n/, /b/, /l/, /s/, /g/, etc." [Hanna, Hodges, & Hanna 1971, p. 132]. If one followed this advice, the two plosives /d/ and /p/ (and *d* and *p*) would be taught together. This is to be avoided. A consonant phoneme from one classification of sounds (and the letter that represents it) should be contrasted with another. This would

apply for *plosives:* /p/, /b/, etc.; *nasals:* /m/, /n/, /ng/; *fricatives:* /f/, /v/, etc., as well as for *laterals:* /l/, /r/; and *semivowels:* /w/, /y/.

12. Teach the letters in an order that corresponds as nearly as possible with the relative degree of difficulty children have in naming and writing them, as well as the frequency with which a letter is used in words.

Evidence of this difficulty is obtained from three sources: the first is children's ability to match letters. When seven-year-old children were asked to match capital letters, Eleanor Gibson found that a high degree of distinction was made by these children between capital letters that had straight features (E) and those that had curved features (B). None of these children ever mismatched G-M or G-N. The high-confusion pairs of capital letters were E-F, M-N, C-G, M-W. "Diagonals [A, K, M, N, V, W, X, Y, Z, R, Q] are low in discriminability for children, even at seven years when they have learned the alphabet" [1969, p. 90]. We can infer from this study that the straight letters (*i*, *l*, *t*) should, as taught, be contrasted with the letters with curved features (*a*, *b*, *c*, *d*, etc.). This evidence also suggests that the diagonal letters be taught last.

A second source for understanding which letters present difficulties is the study by Helen Popp [1964] as to how well kindergarten children can match a given lower-case letter. Popp found that these children most often confuse the letters that have reversible parts: *p-d-q-b*, *h-u*, and *i-l*. The next largest number of confusions they make is with letters that have similar parts: *k-y*, *c-e*, *d-h*, *h-n*, *h-y*. The third most confusable group were the letters that have similar sizes: *s-e*, *u-e*, *q-f*, *k-h*, *u-m*, etc. As Popp rightly concludes, her results "seem to substantiate" those found by Gibson.

A third source of information on this topic is the number of times letters appear in the initial position in words and syllables. It is easier for children to identify the initial letter in words than those in other positions. Consequently, the frequency of letters in this position should be considered when teaching the letters.

In our analysis of high-frequency monosyllabic words [Groff 1972], we found that single consonant letters occur in the initial position of these words in the rank order given in Rank 1 of Table 13. Rank 2 of this table shows the rankings found in a similar analysis of "simple words" (all of the consonant-vowel-consonant spellings) of the *Oxford Universal Dictionary* [1963]. Rank 3 of Table 13 represents the rank order in which single consonant letters occur in the initial position of all the syllables of the most frequently used 17,000 words [Hanna et al. 1966]. Rank 4 of Table 13 represents the rank order in which first graders correctly write in manuscript handwriting the lower-case consonant letters [Lewis & Lewis 1964].

TABLE 13. THE DIFFERING RANK ORDERS OF LETTER OCCURRENCE IN EIGHT STUDIES

Letter	(Groff) Rank 1	(Dolby-Resnikoff) Rank 2	(Hanna et al.) Rank 3	(Lewis and Lewis) Rank 4	(Coleman) Rank 5	(Smythe et al.) Rank 6	(Durrell) Rank 7	(Coleman) Rank 8
b	1	2	7	12	11	17	17	8
s	2	11	2	13	6	2	2	1
h	3	1	14	5	16	7	15	16
l	4	4	8	1	1	19	19	11
f	5	10	10	7	3	7	13	5
r	6	12	9	11	2	2	10	10
p	7	7	4	19	13	7	4	7
w	7	13	15	6	21	7	9	14
t	9	9	1	8	4	5	5	17
m	10	3	6	16	10	5	6	3
d	11	5	5	14	20	20	18	15
c as /k/°	12	6	2	3	15	2	3	—
n	13	14	12	9	7	13	14	13
g as /g/°	14	10	11	20	12	15	20	12
j	15	16	16	17	8	7	11	9
v	16	17	13	2	9	17	16	6
k	17	15	18	15	14	7	7	4
y	18	no data	21	18	18	16	12	18
q	19	18	17	21·	17	21	21	—
z	20	19	20	10	19	13	8	2
x	21	20	19	4	5	1	1	—

° Rank 1 only.

Rank 5 gives the order in which preschool children learn to copy these letters [Coleman 1970]. Ranks 6 and 7 give the rank orders in which seven-year-olds [Smythe et al. 1971] and first graders [Durrell 1956] correctly name the lower-case letters. Rank 8 indicates the order in which preschool children learn to pronounce a sound when shown a letter [Coleman 1970].

To decide on the order in which to teach vowel letters, we turned to Dunn-Rankin's [1968] study of the "general visual ambiguity" of letters. He found the vowel letters to be visually distinguishable in this rank order: *a-o-e-i-u.* We suggest that this is the order in which they should be taught.

A Sequence for Teaching Letters

A preferred sequence for teaching consonant and vowel letters can be arranged based on the principle that as nearly as possible phonics should be taught with high-frequency monosyllabic words. The suggested sequence for teaching consonant letters is based on (1) the difficulty of writing and naming these letters, (2) the need to contrast letters with different graphic features, (3) the frequency with which consonant letters appear initially in high-frequency words, and (4) the classifications of consonant sounds (plosives, fricatives, nasals, laterals, and semivowels) that the letters represent.

On the basis of these four considerations and the data from Table 13 and Dunn-Rankin [1968], the following order of teaching letter names emerges:

t-s	l-c	f-m	b-r	h-w
a-t	o-l	e-f	i-b	u-h

At this point the identification and naming of letters in phonograms can be begun. See Step 3 below. The other consonant letters can be taught in these pairs:

p-v   d-n   k-g   j-z   q-x   y-any letter

Some teachers [Connell 1968] have believed that "circle" letters should be taught in this order: (1) in groups where the circle is made counterclockwise (*a, c, e, d, f, g, o, q, s, u*); and (2) in groups where they are written clockwise (*b, h, j, m, n, p, r*). Does the research support this assumption? The study by Edward and Hilda Lewis [1964] that investigated which manuscript letters are hard for first graders to write indicates that letters involving circles are harder for young children to write than straight-line letters (*k, t, z, w, x, v, i, l*). There seems little doubt about this since of the straight-line letters only *y* and *k* are among the fifteen most difficult letters for young children to write. The Lewis' data also show that among the fifteen most difficult letters, six have counterclockwise circles and six, clockwise circles. Thus, one must be skeptical of claims given with no statistics that assert reversals in writing (*b* for *p*) will be "almost completely eliminated" if teachers will just teach letters with clockwise circle strokes before those with counterclockwise strokes [Connell 1968].

A Special Problem: Teaching Vowel Letters

The vowel letters *a, e, i, o, u* may be more difficult to learn than consonant letters since so few high-frequency monosyllabic words begin with vowel letters. In addition, the number of different sounds a vowel letter can represent is larger than the number for a consonant letter. It is recommended that the words beginning with the sounds /a, e, i, o, u/ and /ā, ē, ī, ō, yōō/ be used to teach the names of the vowel letters. A list of high-frequency words of this nature follows. The words in the last column are not to be used because they do not begin with /a, e, i, o, u/ or /ā, ē, ī, ō, yōō/.

/ā/	/a/	Do not use
ache	act	air
age	add	all
aid	am	any
aim	an	arch
ape	and	are
ate	ant	arm
	as	art
	ask	
	at	
	aunt	
	ax	

/ē/	/e/	
each	edge	ear
ease	egg	earn
east	else	earth
eat	end	eight
eve		eighth
		eye

/ī/	/i/	
ice	if	—
	ill	

/ī/	/i/	Do not use (con't)
	in	
	inch	
	ink	
	inn	
	is	
	it	
	its	
/ō/	/o/	
oak	odd	of
oats	off	oil
oh	on	once
old	ought	one
or	ox	ounce
owe		our
own		out
		owl
/yo͞o/	/u/	
use	up	urge
	us	

Should teachers tell their pupils that *a, e, i, o,* and *u* are called vowel letters and that the remainder of the alphabet is made up of consonant letters? Perhaps a better way to pose the question is, "What purpose would be served by doing so?" We find no purpose served by it at this level and therefore suggest that such instruction is unneeded at this point.

We doubt, for example, the value of such advice given by McKee: "Very early in the first grade—certainly in connection with the reading of the first preprimer—the pupil should be told that the letters *a, e, i, o,* and *u* are called vowels, that each vowel stands for many different sounds, *but that for the time being he does not need to be concerned about knowing what those sounds are"* [1966, p. 110, emphasis added]. How can the teacher talk meaningfully with young pupils about "sounds" when these beginning readers do not yet understand the concept of phonemes or even of words as such? In fact, this is precisely what instruction in phonics will do—it will give the child an awareness of the individual sounds in the language. It may also be asked, what purpose could be served by giving six-year-old children the information McKee recommends (if this actually were possible, of course) and then telling them to forget about it "for the time being"? Quite to the contrary, the phonics teacher should never enter into any explanation of a spelling-sound correspondence without being prepared to develop it to the level of conscious awareness in the pupils. The dropping of little hints during periods of instruction about such correspondences does little to help children learn phonics.

Useful Activities in Teaching
the Three Steps of Level 1

Step 1: Identifying and Naming Initial Consonant Letters. The objective of these activities is to teach children to identify initial consonant letters quickly by name.

1. Write two letters, for example, *t* and *s*, on the chalkboard. Children are given two cards, one with a *t*, one with an *s*. (Clip two corners of the cards, left and right, to help the child hold it right side up.) Say: "This is *t*. This is *s*. Say the names with me, *t*, *s*." Point to the letters on the board.

2. Say: "Look at your cards. Hold up *t*. Hold up *s*." Be sure all the children in the group are holding up the right card. Alternate *t* and *s* a few times.

3. Say: "Let's see if I can fool you. Is this *t*?" (Write some other letter.) "Is this *t*?" Write a *t*. Repeat for *s*.

4. Say: "If I write *t*, hold up your *t* card. Hold up your *t* card only if I write *t*." About every third time write *t*. Repeat for *s*.

5. Say: "Now watch carefully. Does this word [write a one-vowel word such as *tag*] begin with *t*? Is *t* the first letter in this word? If it is, hold up your *t* card." Write a few words, half of which do not start with *t*. Repeat with *s*.

6. Say: "I will write an *s* word or a *t* word [a word beginning with *t*]. When I write an *s* word, hold up your *s* card. When I write a *t* word, hold up your *t* card." Write a few one-vowel words beginning with either *t* or *s*.

7. Say: "I will write a word with *s* in it." (Write *sat*.) Draw a block around the beginning letter. "What letter is this?" Do the same for *tar*. Then have children draw a block around the beginning consonant letter of several one-vowel words: $\boxed{s}$ ap, $\boxed{s}$ un, $\boxed{s}$ aw, and $\boxed{s}$ at. Stress drawing a block around the *beginning* letter. Do the same for *t*.

8. Say: "I will write a word with *t* in it." (Write *sat*.) Draw a block around the last letter. "What letter is this?" Do the same for *tar*. Then

have the children draw a block around the final consonant letter of several one-vowel words: ma$\boxed{t}$, sa$\boxed{t}$, pu$\boxed{t}$, etc. Stress drawing a block around the final consonant. Do the same for *s*.

9. Say: "See the *r*. Circle all the letters like the first letter." Give the children work to complete in this format, presenting several rows:

    ```
    s  —  s  s  t  s
    t  —  t  s  t  s
    ```

    Or say: "See the *r*. Circle all the letters in a row that are just like it. Let's do the first row together."

10. Say: "Circle the words that begin like the first letter in each row." Give the children work to complete in this format, presenting several rows:

    ```
    s  —  sag  run  tag  sat
    t  —  tag  sag  toy  top
    ```

    Or say: "See the *r*. Circle all the words in the row that start just like it. Let's do the first row together."

11. Say: "Mark the letter that is different from the others." Give a format like this one:

    ```
    t  t  t  s
    s  t  s  s
    t  t  s  t
    s  s  t  s
    t  s  t  t
    ```

12. Say: "Mark the word that is different from the others." Present a format such as this one:

    ```
    tag  sun  tag  tag
    tag  tag  sun  tag
    sun  sun  tag  sun
    tag  tag  tag  sun
    sun  tag  sun  sun
    ```

13. Say: "Put a line under the two letters if they are alike." Use a format like this one:

    ```
    s    s
    s    t
    s    t
    t    t
    t    s
    ```

14. Say: "Put a line under the two words if they are alike." Use a format like this one:

tag	tag
sag	sag
sag	tag
sag	sag
tag	sag

15. Say: "How many *s*'s can you find in this row? Count them. Show how many with your fingers."

s	s	s	s
s	t	t	s
r	t	s	t
t	t	t	s

Then, repeat the process for *t*.

16. Present pairs of words that are alike except that one contains the first letter (*t*) and the other the second letter (*s*), for example, *tag-sag, so-to,* etc. Say: "What part of this word [write *tag*] is different from this word [write *rag*]?" Write one word underneath the other one.

17. Say: "Look at these numbers [1 through 9]. Some numbers have *t* by them. Some have *s* by them. What numbers have *t* by them? Which ones have *s* by them?" Make up a worksheet using this format:

1	t	6	s
2	s	7	s
3	t	8	t
4	t	9	t
5	s		

(Obviously this activity is designed also to teach the numbers 1 through 9.)

18. Say: "Draw lines from a letter in one column to one like it in the second column." Use this format:

s	t
s	s
t	s
s	s
t	t
s	s
t	t

19.   Say: "Draw lines from a word in one column to the same word in the
      second column." Follow this format:

tag	tag
sun	sun
sun	tag
sun	sun
tag	tag
tag	sun

20.   Say: "Draw a line from a letter in one column to the word that begins
      with the same letter in the second column. Let's do the first one
      together." Try this format:

s	tag
t	tag
s	sun
s	tag
t	sun
s	sun
t	sun

21.   Say: "I will write a word. If *t* is at the beginning, hold up your fist
      [show them]. If *t* is at the *end,* hold up your fingers [show them]."
      Words to use: *bat-tub-rat-dot-tap,* etc. Also do this with *s: sat-has-
      tis-sap-sam,* etc.

22.   As each letter is taught and children have learned its name, associate
      the letter with a one-vowel word that begins with one consonant. Do
      not use clusters *br, cr, sn, tr,* etc. Instead use words that have three
      phonemes *c-v-c,* and that are spelled with three one-letter graphemes
      (*cat*). (Remember, this is not possible for *q.*)

23.   Cut and shape pipe cleaners into lower-case letter forms. Glue these
      letters on small cards with a strong adhesive. Play this game. Say:
      "Close your eyes. I will give you a card. On the card is a letter. Feel
      the letter. Don't look at it! Can you tell me what letter is on the card?"
      This game can also be played by pairs of pupils.

Step 2: Identifying and Naming the Vowel Letters. The objective here, as
with the Step 1 activities with consonant letters, is to teach children to
identify and name letters quickly.

1.   Write two letters, for example, *a* and *t,* on the chalkboard. Children
     are given two response cards, one with *a* and one with *t.* Cut corners
     of cards so children will hold them right side up.

2. Say: "This is *a*. What is this? [*t*] Say the names with me, *a-t*." Point to the letters on the board while saying their names.

3. Say: "Look at your cards. Hold up *a*. Hold up *t*." Be sure children have cards held up correctly. Alternate a few times.

4. Say: "Which letter is tall? Hold it up. Which is round? Hold it up."

5. Say: "Can I fool you? Is this *a*?" Write *a* or some other letter. Alternate a few times. Repeat for *t*.

6. Say: "I will write an *a* word or a *t* word. Watch. Does this word begin with an *a*? Hold up your *a* card if it does." (Write *an*, *age*, *add*, *aid*, or some one-vowel words beginning with *t*). "Does this word begin with a *t*?" (Write *tin*, *tag*, *tap*, *time*, *tis*, or some one-vowel words beginning with *a*). "Hold up your *t* card if it does."

7. Hold up a card. Say: "What is the name of this letter?" Do this several times during the learning of any letter.

8. Say: "How many *a*'s can you find in this row? Count them. Show with your fingers." (Repeat process for *t*.)

a	s	a	a
t	t	s	a
i	a	a	a
t	t	t	a

9. Say: "Circle all the letters that are like the first letter." Give children work to complete in this format, presenting several rows.

a	—	a	a	t	a
t	—	t	t	a	a

10. Say: "See this *a*? Circle all the letters in a row that are just like it. Let's do the first row together."

a	a	t	a
t	t	a	a

11. Say: "Circle the words that begin like the first letter." Give the children a work pattern to complete in this format, presenting several rows:

a	—	an	add	take	at
t	—	tell	task	act	ask

Or, say: "See this *a*? Circle all the words in a row that start just like it. Let's do the first row together." Do the same for *t*.

12. Say: "Circle the letter that is different from the others."

<pre>
a   a   a   t
t   a   t   t
a   a   t   a
t   t   a   t
</pre>

13. Say: "Circle the word that is different from the others."

<pre>
an   an   an   tin
tin an   tin tin
an   an   tin an
tin tin an   tin
</pre>

14. Say: "Put a line under the two letters if they are the same."

<pre>
a   a
a   t
t   a
a   a
t   t
</pre>

15. Say: "Put a line under the two words if they are alike."

<pre>
an   tin
an   an
tin   an
tin   tin
an   an
</pre>

16. Say: "Look at these numbers [1 through 9]. Some numbers have *a* by them. Some have *t* by them. Which numbers have *a* by them? Which have *t* by them?"

<pre>
1. a   6. t
2. t   7. t
3. a   8. a
4. a   9. a
5. t
</pre>

17. Say: "Draw lines from a letter in one column to one like it in the second column."

<pre>
a   t
a   a
t   a
a   a
t   t
a   a
t   t
</pre>

18. Say: "Draw lines from a word in one column to the same word in the second column."

an	an
tin	tin
tin	an
tin	tin
an	an
an	tin

19. Say: "Draw a line from a letter in one column to the word that begins with the same letter in the second column."

t	an
a	an
t	tin
t	an
a	tin
t	tin
a	tin

Step 3: Learning to Write Manuscript Letters. The objective of this step is to reinforce children's rapid and easy recognition of letter names and to prepare them to use phonics in spelling. *As soon as children have learned to write a manuscript letter they can complete many of the activities in Steps 1, 2, and 3 by writing the letter, as well as by saying its letter name.* For this purpose it is useful to carry out the following activities. All activities refer to lower-case manuscript letters. Teach capital letters after the lower-case letters are mastered.

1. Teach children to write the letters that are being used in Steps 1, 2, and 3 as these are identified. Coordinate the teaching given in identifying letters, learning their names, and associating sounds with them with the teaching of the writing of these letters. There should be no question, then, as to what letter a teacher should teach children to write at any given time. It would be the one the child is learning about in the course of the activities in Steps 1 and 2. This also obviates the need for a handwriting "period." Handwriting is best taught as part of the ongoing phonics program.

2. Teach the writing of vowel letters *a, e, i, o, u* from the outset since no words can be written without vowel letters.

3. In the beginning allow children large spaces on unlined paper to write letters. As their skill increases, fold this paper to make "lines" and then introduce lined paper.

4. Place the model letter the child is expected to copy *on his or her desk.*
    Do not ask children to copy from the chalkboard. The response cards
    used in Steps 1, 2, and 3 can be utilized for this purpose.

5. Have children write often on the chalkboard so the teacher can
    supervise the way they make letter strokes.

6. Utilize a great deal of tracing. Have children run their fingers and
    their pencils over model letters given them. Stress the direction in
    which the writing strokes should be made: top to bottom, and left to
    right if letter has two parts. Some circles are made counterclockwise
    (*a, c, d, e, f, g, j, o, q*); some in a clockwise direction (*b, h, m, n, p, r,
    j*). To help children get the "feel" of the letters, paste sand on cards in
    the shape of letters. The roughness of the sand will make a greater
    impression as children trace the letters. Use cutouts of letters if these
    are available. Bend pipe cleaners into the shape of letters and glue
    these on cards. Using these special cards (sand, cutouts, pipe cleaners),
    have children close their eyes, feel the card, and tell its name.

7. Provide practice material that indicates the direction in which strokes
    should be made. For example:

    Do not have children write over dotted-line models, e.g., ⋮. This
    practice is generally too difficult for beginners. Besides making them
    write too slowly, it also is likely to inhibit the development of the
    rhythm needed for legible handwriting.

8. Have children work in pairs so that they can check each other's work
    in writing letters and make suggestions for improvement. A child will
    often be more critical of another's work than of his or her own.

9. Use a positive form of teaching psychology. Concentrate on the
    correctly formed letters children write rather than on their misshapen
    letters. Keep negative comments anonymous. If several children
    display a handwriting fault, work with them on it without mentioning
    individual faults by naming the children who made them.

10. Do not consider left-handed beginning readers to have less ability to
    learn to write letters than do right-handed pupils. There is no evidence
    to support this misconception.

11. Believe that children like to learn to write letters. The phonics teacher
    usually does not need an elaborate system of motivation to entice
    children to participate in letter-writing activity. Moreover, almost all

children find manuscript writing easy to master. This is doubtless due to the simplicity of manuscript forms. There are in essence only three strokes a child must learn to print letters: the straight line, the circle, the part of a circle (as in *c, s, r, e, h, m, n, u,* etc.). Some children, in fact, find that learning to write letters is easier than learning to read words. Nevertheless, one can find comments to the effect that a child must learn to read before being taught to write letters. Since there is no evidence to support this contention, and since knowing how to write letters is a great help to a child in quick recognition of letters, the unfounded notion that the writing of letters should be delayed can be disregarded. *Children should be taught to write letters as soon as they learn to identify letters.* They do not have to wait until they have learned to identify phonemes in words.

12. Use letter-writing abilities as evidence of readiness. While we are not completely sure as to precisely why, we do have much evidence that children's ability to discriminate, recognize, and name letters and numbers is the single best predictor of first-grade reading achievement [Durrell 1968]. We could infer from this evidence that children who learn to discriminate letters and learn letter names are those who attend to differences in shapes of things and of their names in general.

13. Use lower-case letters for the above activities since they will be seen by children learning phonics much more frequently than upper-case letters.

14. Follow a sequence in presenting letters. The teaching of the writing of letters should follow the sequence for letters used for Steps 1 and 2.

REFERENCES

Brown, Sandra S. "An Investigation of the Relationship Between a Knowledge of Letter Names and Sounds and the Mastery of an Initial Sight Vocabulary." *Dissertation Abstracts,* 27(1967):3358A.

Coleman, E. B. "Data Base for a Reading Technology." *Journal of Educational Psychology Monograph,* 61(1970): No. 4, Part 2.

Connell, Donna. "Auditory and Visual Discrimination in Kindergarten." *Elementary English,* 45(1968):51–54.

Dolby, J. L., and Resnikoff, H. L. *Prolegomena to a Study of Written English.* Palo Alto, Calif.: Lockheed Missiles and Space Company, 1963.

Dreyer, Harold B. "The Transfer of Learned Phoneme-Grapheme Relationships to Learning New Letters and Words Among Kindergarten Children." *Dissertation Abstracts International,* 30(1969):580A.

Dunn-Rankin, Peter. "The Similarity of Lower-Case Letters of the English Alphabet." *Journal of Verbal Learning and Verbal Behavior,* 7(1968):990–995.

Durrell, Donald. *Improving Reading Instruction.* New York: World Publishing Company, 1956.

Durrell, Donald. "Phonics Programs in Beginning Reading," *Forging Ahead in Reading,* ed. J. Allen Figurel. Newark, Del.: International Reading Association, 1968.

Gibson, Eleanor J. "An Analysis of Critical Features of Letters, Tested by a Confusion Matrix," *A Basic Research Program in Reading,* ed. Harry Levin. Cooperative Research Project No. 639. Ithaca: Cornell University Press, 1963.

Gibson, Eleanor J. "Perceptual Learning in Educational Situations," *Learning Research and School Subjects,* eds. Robert M. Gagné and William J. Gephart. Itaska, Ill.: F. E. Peacock, 1968.

Gibson, Eleanor J. *Principles of Perceptual Learning and Development.* New York: Appleton-Century-Crofts, 1969.

Gleitman, Lila, and Rozin, Paul. "Teaching Reading by Use of a Syllabary." *Reading Research Quarterly,* 8(1973):447–483.

Groff, Patrick. "A New Sequence for Teaching Lower-Case Letters." *Journal of Reading Behavior,* 5(1973):297–303.

Groff, Patrick. "A Phonemic Analysis of Monosyllabic Words." *Reading World,* 12(1972):94–103.

Groff, Patrick. "The Topsy-Turvy World of 'Sight' Words." *Reading Teacher,* 27(1974):572–578.

Hanna, Paul R., et al. *Phoneme-Grapheme Correspondences as Cues to Spelling Improvement.* Washington, D.C.: U.S. Office of Education, 1966.

Hanna, Paul R., Hodges, Richard E., and Hanna, Jean S. *Spelling: Structure and Strategies.* Boston: Houghton Mifflin, 1971.

Jenkins, Joseph R., Bausell, R. Barker, and Jenkins, Linda. "Comparison of Letter Name and Letter Sound Training as Transfer Variables." *American Educational Research Journal,* 9(1972):75–86.

Johnson, Roger E. "The Validity of the Clymer-Barrett Prereading Battery." *Reading Teacher,* 22(1969):609–614.

Johnson, Ronald J. "The Effect of Training in Letter Names on Success in Beginning Reading for Children of Differing Abilities." River Falls, Wis.: Wisconsin State University, mimeographed, undated.

Jones, Kenneth J. "Colour as an Aid to Visual Perception in Early Reading." *British Journal of Educational Psychology,* 35(1965):21–27.

King, Ethel M. "Effects of Different Kinds of Visual Discrimination Training on Learning to Read Words." *Journal of Educational Psychology,* 55(1964):325–333.

Lewis, Edward R., and Lewis, Hilda P. "Which Manuscript Letters Are Hard for First Graders?" *Elementary English,* 41(1964):855–858.

Lowell, Robert E. "An Evaluation of Selected Readiness Factors as Predictors of Success in First Grade Reading." *Dissertation Abstracts International,* 30(1970):2727A.

McKee, Paul. *Reading.* Boston: Houghton Mifflin, 1966.

Myers, Dorothy C. "The Effects of Letter Knowledge on Achievement in Reading in the First Grade." *Dissertation Abstracts,* 27(1967):2449A.

Nevins, Rosemary J. "The Effect of Training on Letter Names, Letter Sounds, and Letter Names and Sounds on the Acquisition of Word Recognition Ability." *Dissertation Abstracts International,* 34(1973):1490A.

Ohnmacht, Dorothy C. "Effects of Instruction in Letter Knowledge on Achievement in Reading in First Grade." Columbia: University of Missouri, mimeographed, undated.

Otto, Wayne. "Color Cues as an Aid to Good and Poor Readers' Paired-Associate Learning," *Perception and Reading,* ed. Helen K. Smith. Newark, Del.: International Reading Association, 1967.

Popp, Helen M. "Visual Discrimination of Alphabet Letters." *Reading Teacher,* 17(1964):221–226.

Rystrom, Richard. "Evaluating Letter Discrimination Problems in the Primary Grades." *Journal of Reading Behavior,* 1(1969):38–48.

Samuels, S. Jay. "Letter-Name Versus Letter-Sound Knowledge in Learning to Read." *Reading Teacher,* 24(1971): 604–608.

Samuels, S. Jay. "Modes of Word Recognition," *Theoretical Models and*

Processes of Reading, eds. Harry Singer and Robert B. Ruddell. Newark, Del.: International Reading Association, 1970.

Schoolcraft, Denzie R. "The Effectiveness of the Bender Gestalt Test for Children and the Knowledge of Letter Names in the Prediction of Reading Achievement with First Grade Children in a Rural Area." *Dissertation Abstracts International*, 33(1973):4988A.

Silvaroli, Nicholas J. "Factors in Predicting Children's Success in First Grade Reading," *Reading and Inquiry*, ed. J. A. Figurel. Newark, Del.: International Reading Association, 1965.

Smith, Frank. *Understanding Reading*. New York: Holt, Rinehart and Winston, 1971.

Smith, Nila B. *Reading Instruction for Today's Children*. Englewood Cliffs, N.J.: Prentice-Hall, 1963.

Smythe, P. C., et al. "Developmental Patterns in Elemental Skills: Knowledge of Upper-Case and Lower-Case Letter Names." *Journal of Reading Behavior*, 3(1971):24–33.

Speer, Olga B., and Lamb, George S. "First Grade Reading Ability and Fluency in Naming Verbal Symbols." *Reading Teacher*, 29(1976): 572–576.

Williams, Joanna P. "Reactions to Modes of Word Recognition," *Theoretical Models and Processes of Reading*, eds. Harry Singer and Robert B. Ruddell. Newark, Del.: International Reading Association, 1970.

9

TEACHING PHONICS:
LEVELS 2 AND 3

This chapter illustrates the way children can be taught to recognize (1) the correspondences between the spellings of *single consonant letters* and the sounds these spellings represent, and (2) the correspondences between the spellings of *consonant clusters* and the sounds these spellings represent.

At Level 2 in *Phonics: Why and How* children are taught to recognize single consonant phoneme-grapheme correspondences:

1.   At the beginnings of one-vowel words, as in *t*op.

2.   At the ends of one-vowel words, as in to*p*.

At Level 3 children are taught to recognize consonant cluster phoneme-grapheme correspondences:

1.   At the beginnings of one-vowel words, as in *st*op.

2.   At the ends of one-vowel words, as in ba*nd*, ba*ll*, and ba*th*.

3.   At the beginnings and the ends of one-vowel words, as in *stand*.

Levels 2 and 3 are combined in this chapter since the activities used to teach each of them are very similar. It is important to remember that the child's attention is directed *first* to single consonant letters, and *then* to consonant clusters. (Consonant clusters are often called "blends.") There is recent evidence that sound-spelling generalizations for initial consonant letter clusters such as *br, st,* and *th* are significantly more difficult for first-grade pupils to learn than single consonant sound-spelling correspondences [Hartley 1971]. Emmett Betts is right, therefore, in insisting that pupils need to be well grounded in the sound-spelling relationships of *s* and *t* before learning the consonant blend *st* [1962].

Sound-Spelling Relationships

1. Success in the activities at Level 2 depend on the child's having learned in Level 1 to perceive some of the letters used in words. Proceed to Level 2 and Level 3 only after the child has learned to discriminate some letters.

2. Do not teach children to listen to or make the sound of an individual letter. This is wrong on at least three counts: (a) letters do not "have" sounds; sounds are represented by letters; (b) sounding of individual phonemes is not a necessary activity; and (c) attempts to say isolated sounds in words results in a distortion of the sound of these phonemes. Phonemes can only be said in syllables.

3. Do not say, "This word (pointing to *tin*) begins like *tap*." Telling children that *tin* begins like *tap* is wrong because the teacher is doing the task the children should do. If children do not respond to questions such as, "Do *tin* and *tap* sound alike (look alike)? Where do *tin* and *tap* sound alike (look alike)?" they may have misunderstood the questions. If so, ask these questions another way. For example, "Listen to the first sound in *tin*. Listen to the first sound in *tap*. Are they the same? I will write *tin* and *tap* on the board. (Do so, one under the other.) Do they begin with the same letter? What is that letter?"

4. *Do not* get involved with vocabulary building with these phonics activities. We disagree with the advice that "the spelling program should, therefore, be to some extent a vocabulary program, providing the speller with more words which he may confidently use in real writing situations" [Personke & Yee 1971, p. 81]. We believe, to the contrary, that learning phonics is difficult enough for some children. To attempt to teach it with any but the most familiar words is a bad practice. We suggest that vocabulary building and phonics be divorced into two separate learning programs. Therefore, *do not* discuss in the phonics lesson the denotations, let alone the connotations, of a word being used. Instead, make sure that the words used in phonics are common to the children's speaking-listening vocabularies. Thus, in using a list of one-vowel words, the teacher should be careful to choose only those words that children already understand.

5. Do not waste children's time with exercises that have them pay

attention to how their lips are formed, how their tongue is placed, or how they expel breath as they articulate certain phonemes. This is not only a difficult matter to teach but contributes little to the objectives of phonics. These ill-advised attempts to teach children to associate sounds with the formations of the breath and vocal mechanisms take valuable time away from the teaching of the aspects of phonics that truly contribute to reading and spelling.

6.   Chapter 8 illustrated that the preferred order in which to teach children to recognize letters was as follows:

The other consonant letters should be taught in these pairs:

p-v   d-n   k-g   j-z   q-x   y-any letter

The activities with letters for Level 2 will follow this same sequence. Now, however, the child should go back through the sequence and learn the sounds these letters represent (in words).

7.   It is helpful first to teach children to perceive and name a letter; second, to write it; and third, to identify the sound that this letter represents. In this manner, the pupils' three senses of seeing, hearing, and touching (writing) are engaged in an integrated way as they learn phonics.

Notes on Level 3

As noted, Level 3 teaches children to recognize the sound-spellings of certain consonant-letter clusters. In the traditional writings on phonics certain clusters of consonant letters in words were called "blends." For example, William Gray noted that the child should "learn that two consonant sounds may be blended, and that such two-letter symbols as *st*, *sp*, or *bl* represent these blends" [1948, p. 151].

The term *blends* apparently stems from a notion that the two sounds one hears in *cr*, /k/-/r/ (as in *crash*), merge more with each other phonemically than they do with the following vowel sound /a/, or that /k/ and /r/ merge more than the vowel sound /a/ merges with the final phoneme, /sh/, in this word. Blends, according to Albert Harris, are parts of words "in which sounds partially merge but are distinguishable" [1962, p. 359]. One infers from this that blends merge more than do adjoining consonant-vowel sounds. Or, as Mildred Dawson and Henry Bamman claim, "*Consonant blends are the combinations of two or three consonants which, when pronounced, blend into sounds which still retain elements of the individual consonants:* bl-blue . . ." [1963, p. 168]. But, to them, *wh* is not a blend since it is part of a group of *"two-letter symbols which represent a single consonant unlike the sound of either of the separate consonants which compose the element"* [p. 169].

The term *blend* should not be used to refer to consonant-letter clusters in words, however. No part of the previous descriptions, or the supposed verifications of so-called "blends" can be shown to be accurate. There appears nothing in the literature on phonemics or phonetics that would lead one to conclude that any of the above *special* kind of blending that is assumed to take place with consonant-letter clusters actually does take place. Then, too, there is the misinformation connected with this notion. For example, /wh/ represents a sound unlike the sound of either of its separate phonemes. One must assume, therefore, that the notion of blends is mis-instructive as to the phonemic nature of these clusters. Instead of *blend,* the term *consonant-letter cluster* will be used in this book.

But of more importance in teaching consonant-letter clusters than this dispute over terminology is a determination of the order in which they should be taught. As Arthur Heilman rightly concludes, "There is a great deal of variance among teachers as well as among basal readers as to (a) when blends are dealt with, (b) which are taught first, and (c) how rapidly the blends are covered" [1961, p. 224]. Evidence presented by George Spache indicates that three well-known basal reading series do not agree on this matter [1964, p. 285–288].

Nor does there appear to be any agreement among the textbooks for teachers on teaching reading. For example, Donald Durrell would have teachers teach practically all the clusters in the first grade [1956, p. 232]. According to Gray none should be taught in the first grade, and only a few in the second grade [1948, p. 316]. Guy Bond and Eva Wagner [1960] avoid the issue. They make no suggestions at all as to the point in time the clusters should be taught.

Since we have no information as to how any of the arrangements or teaching sequences for consonant-letter clusters were arrived at, whether these arrangements have any merit, as such, is unknown. We do not know, for example, to what extent the *readability* of words using these clusters was taken into account in this determination. We do not know to what degree the relative *frequency of use* in printed matter of these words was considered, or whether the *total number* of words that use them was given any weight. Nor do we know whether the relative *spelling difficulty* of consonant-cluster words was seen as important. *Phonics: Why and How* considered all these aspects in determining the new sequence for teaching consonant clusters presented in the following pages.

TABLE 14. A RECOMMENDED SEQUENCE FOR INITIAL CLUSTERS

1. sh°	6. sp	11. th (*thing*)	16. fl	21. thr
2. st	7. pl	12. dr	17. pr	21. sw
3. gr	8. tr	12. wh (*when*)	17. cr	23. gl
4. cl	9. ch	14. bl	19. str	24. qu
5. th (*the*)	10. br	15. fr	20. sl	25. sk

° Not relevant for spelling since /sh/ is spelled *sh* at the beginning of syllables only 18 percent of the time [Hanna, Hodges, & Hanna 1971]. All others relevant for spelling *and* reading.

Source: Groff [1971–72], p. 63. By permission of the National Reading Conference.

To reach decisions on this sequence we asked these four questions:

1. Which initial consonant letter clusters are found in one-vowel words that are the easiest to spell?

2. What is the *average number of times* one-vowel words begin with each consonant letter cluster?

3. What is the *total number of different* one-vowel words that begin with each cluster?

4. Can children read more one-vowel words that begin with certain of these consonant letter clusters?

To find answers for these questions we consulted the *New Iowa Spelling Scale* [Greene 1955] for question 1, which gives the percent of children in grades two through eight who correctly spelled each of 5,507 high-frequency words;[1] for questions 2 and 3 we consulted the *Computational Analysis of Present-Day American English* [Kucera & Francis 1967]; and for question 4 the total number of high-frequency, one-vowel words beginning with the consonant clusters that fourth-grade children can *read silently* and *comprehend* [Dale & Chall 1948; Dale & Eichholz 1960].

We ranked each consonant letter cluster according to each of four criteria: ease of spelling; frequency of appearance in first 5,000 high-frequency words [Kucera & Francis 1967]; frequency of appearance in *different* high-frequency words; and readability.

Finally, we combined all the rankings. For example, *pl* ranked 3-7-8-17 in the four categories. Total rank score for *pl* is 35. The highest rank on the basis of this compilation is *sh:* total rank score, *15*. On the basis of this compiled rating the consonant-letter clusters appeared in the order shown in Table 14.

This same calculation was made for consonant-letter clusters that occur at the *ends of one-vowel words.* A combined ranking of the end

---

[1] For our purposes here we used the percent of fourth-grade children. By fourth grade all aspects of phonics should have been introduced.

clusters also results in a recommended sequence for teaching these clusters in one-vowel words. The combined rank of the consonant-letter cluster *ll* using this procedure is 8 (1-3-3-1 rank in the above four different categories, respectively). According to this, *ll* has the highest rank of all these clusters. For *ss*, as another example, the combined rank is 48 (15-13-10-10 in the four categories).

We recommend that the sequences in Tables 14–15 be used in the teaching of consonant-letter clusters [Groff 1971–72]. These sequences appear to be better for the following reasons:

1. They combine in their formulation several features of the difficulty and frequency of one-syllable words that use the clusters in initial and end positions in these words.

2. They deal only with one-syllable words, the kind of words with which the greatest success in phonics is possible.

3. They are clusters in the initial positions of these one-syllable words. It has been shown repeatedly that children are likely to have greater success attending to spelling-sound correspondences in the initial position of words than elsewhere. After this, the teaching of clusters in end positions of words has a greater chance of success.

Teaching Level 2

To teach children to perceive the correspondence between initial consonant phonemes and one-letter graphemes, it is best to use one-syllable words (*tip, tap*). The words used at Level 2 should have a one-vowel phoneme (to include diphthongs). As needed, these words will have one consonant phoneme (*to*), two (*time, top*), and three (*test*). The sounds in these words should always be in this order (C)C-V-C(C).

The vowel sounds in these words can be spelled in a variety of ways. At Level 2 the child's attention is not directed to the middle position of words since we are concerned only with associating single phonemes with one-letter graphemes.

TABLE 15. A RECOMMENDED SEQUENCE FOR END CLUSTERS

1. ll	6. nt	11. nk	16. sh	21. sk	26. ct
2. nd	6. ch	12. ss	17. rn	22. lt	27. pt
3. st	8. th	13. rm	18. mp	23. lk	28. mb
4. ng	9. ld	14. rk	19. ft	24. ff	29. rl
5. ck	10. rt	15. rd	19. gh	25. lf	30. lm

Source: Groff [1971–72], p. 64. By permission of the National Reading Conference.

1. Present pictures of a *toe, tire, tent,* etc. Have the class listen carefully as the teacher reads each word and shows the picture. Have the class say the words as the pictures are shown. Have the class think of other words that begin like *toe, tire, tent.* Ask the pupils to name all the objects in a picture that begin like *toe, tire, tent.*

2. Present pictures of a *toe, tire, saw, tent, six.* Have the class listen as the teacher reads each word while showing the picture. Then have the class pick out the two pictures whose beginning sounds are not the same as the other three.

3. Say: "Let's look at these pictures." Present pictures of a *tail,* a *tack,* something or someone *tall,* a *team, ten* things, *two* things, a *tire,* a piece of *toast,* a *toe,* a *tongue,* a *tooth,* something with a *torn top,* a *tub* or *tank,* etc. Say: "Let's say the names of these things. I'll write their names on the board. What letter do you see at the beginnings of these words?"

4. Say: "Let's listen to these words: *tag, toy, take.*" Ask a pupil to repeat each word after the teacher says it. Write the words on the board, directly under each other. Say: "What letter do they begin with?"

5. Say: "What are these?" *(teeth)* (Point to teeth. Child says, "teeth.")

> "How many fingers?" *(two) (ten)*
> "Your shoelaces are tied . . ." *(tight)*
> "Bread we eat for breakfast is . . ." *(toast)*
> "This is the bottom. This is the . . ." *(top)*
> "What is on the wheel of a car?" *(tire)*
> "What did I do to this paper?" *(tear-tore)*
> "What looks like a frog?" *(toad)*
> "What part of my finger is this?" *(tip)*
> "What did I do with my finger?" *(touch)*
> "If I pull on this, I . . . it." *(tug)*
> "A shovel is a . . ." *(tool)*
> "What is this?" *(toe)*
> "What does the clock tell?" *(time)*
> "What sound does the clock make?" *(tick tock)*
> "There are nine players on a baseball . . ." *(team)*
> "If a truck pulls a car, it . . . it." *(tows)*
> "If someone bothers you, they . . . you." *(tease)*
> "What am I doing?" *(tap)*

As children are able to give the *t-word* responses for these questions write the words on the board one directly under another. Ask: "What letter do these words begin with?"

6. Say: "Can you think of some other words that begin like these words?" (words gained in item 5). Write these words that begin with *t*.

7. Say: "Hold up your *t* card (previously given to each child) if you hear a word that begins with the *t* sound: *teeth, ten, sun, time*." Use a list of *t* words to make up lists of words to use for this activity. Choose some other words besides *t* words from the lists to include in this activity.

8. Say: "Hold up your *t* card if you hear a word that begins like *tag*." Use the lists of words made up for item 5.

9. Read a sentence that has several *t* words. Children hold up hands when they hear a *t* word.

10. Say: "Let's look around the classroom and name everything we can see that we think begins like *toe, tire,* or *tack*." As children name things, write them on the board. Have them check each time to be sure that the names begin with *t*. The teacher also can arrange to have several small objects such as a tool, a tack, a top, and so on available for this procedure.

11. Fold newsprint or a length of brown paper into two parts. On one part children paste pictures whose names begin with *t* and on the other half, names that begin with *s*.

12. Say: "How many words can we think of to put in this slot?"

    Susan will play with her t_____.

    Write the t_____ on the board. Write each word the class gives on the board. Check to make sure it begins with *t*.

13. Say: "Can you think of a word that would fit this slot? There is more than one word that will fit."

    Mike likes to play with his _____t. (cat, bat, jet, pet)
    Karen has a new t_____. (toy, top, doll)

14. Have children write either *s* or *t* if they hear the sound in a word. Give the children a page with the numbers 1, 2, 3, etc., written on it. The children write the letter, if they hear it, by the numbered word.

15. Say: "Hold up one finger if you hear the sound of *t* at the beginning of a word I say. Hold up two fingers if you hear the sound at the end. Listen: *top*. Is the *t* sound at the beginning or the end? Listen: *pot*. Is the *t* sound at the beginning or the end? Listen: *tot*. Beginning or end?" Continue with other one-vowel words that begin and end with the phoneme /t/.

16. Say: "Listen to this word: *top*. In which square does the *t* go?" Write on the board three squares.

☐   ☐   ☐

17. Say: "Listen to this word: *hat*. In which square does the *t* go?" Write on the board three squares.

☐   ☐   ☐

18. Play beginning or end phoneme-grapheme bingo. Give children cards on which words have been written in squares that begin or end with *t*. For example:

at	tap	take
it	Free	fit
sit	tell	tip

First, write _____ *t* or *t*_____ on the board. Children put a counter on the word with this form on their card. After this, write the entire word and have children play as before.

19. Say: "Let's write the letter that will make a word." Write on the board *at*. Say: "This is *at*. Let's say it. Can we add this (write *t* and *s*) to at to make a word?" Continue with other phonograms (see Chapter 8).

 Play letter-sound bingo. Give children cards on which letters have been written in squares. For example:

t	s	s
t	Free	t
s	t	s

Say: "Listen to this word. If it begins (or ends) with a *t* (or *s*) put a counter on a *t* (or *s*)."

20. Say: "Can you think of an animal whose name begins with the first sound you hear in *top* (or *sit*)?" Write the names they offer on the board. Ask: "Does this word have the same first letter as *top*?"

21. After children have learned five to ten consonant phoneme-grapheme correspondences, the teacher can present a picture-letter game. Here each child has a small pocket chart that holds five or six cards. These cards have a letter on one side and a picture on the other. One child holds up a card holder so that another child sees

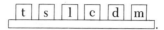

On the other side of each of these cards is drawn a picture whose name begins with the letter shown. If the child shown the card can guess the name of the picture, he or she scores a point.

22. Another useful game is "Portholes." Make holes through which a pencil will pass at regular spaces in a piece of heavy construction paper. Over each hole place a picture and its name. On the reverse side of this perforated sheet put a letter above each hole. The game is played as one child sticks a pencil through a hole on the picture side. The child on the other side notes the letter above this hole, and proceeds to guess the name of the picture. The pupil scores a point for each correct guess.

23. "Half-Moons" is another letter-sound game. Letters to be learned are printed on cards that have a jigsaw puzzle form:

Then, this beginning or end letter is fitted onto other cards:

24. "Brick Wall" is even more challenging. Here children are given a basic left-side "wall" on which they "build" words. For example, after they have learned a few consonant phoneme-grapheme correspondences, they can build a wall like this:

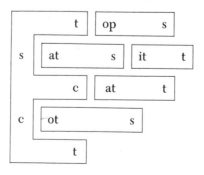

25. Say: "Can we trade the first letters in these words?" Write $\genfrac{}{}{0pt}{}{tip}{sip}$ on the board. "Can we trade these first letters?" Write:

take	top	tell
sack	sack	sail

26. Toward the end of this level, alternate spellings for the same sound should be taught in this way. The phoneme /k/, for example, is spelled *k* and *c.* Say: "Let's read these words: *king, kite, keep.* Now, let's say these words: *can, cup, cap.*" Write the words in this way:

k	ing
k	ite
k	eep
c	an
c	up
c	ap

    Say: "Do these words begin with the same sound? What two letters can you use to spell this sound?"

27. After several correspondences have been learned, this activity is useful. Say: "Jim had a dog. (Write *dog* on the board.) Jim had a large dog. (Write *large dog* on the board.) Who can think of some other thing about Jim's dog that begins like large?"

28. Say: "What word in the first sentence helps you know the word in the second sentence?" Write on the board:

The dog was fat.	The toy fell on the floor.
I lost my h____.	Can you t____ a story?

29. Say: "Where in these three words do you hear the same sound?" Write these words on the board and say them: *tip, tap, top.* Draw a square around the final letter in each word. Now say: "Where in these three words do you hear the same sound: *dog, tag, rag?*" Write, say, and mark as above. Now say: "Where do you hear the same sound in these three words: *cat, mat, fat?*"

To develop children's awareness of the single consonant phoneme-grapheme correspondences at the *ends* of one-syllable words, use the kinds of activities given here for the development of this awareness of *beginning* sounds and spellings. Now, offer children examples that direct them to the final consonant letter of these words.

Teaching Level 3

As previously noted, the purpose of Level 3 is to teach children to recognize consonant-letter cluster phoneme-grapheme correspondences at the beginnings and endings of words. The activities described for Level 2 are for the most part also usable for this purpose. Since the adaptation of these for use with Level 3 is rather obvious, no further examples seem needed.

It should be noted, however, that the teaching of consonant-letter clusters can follow two patterns. These clusters can be taught in the recommended sequence as entities. In this fashion children can be given cards on which the separate clusters *sh, st, gr,* etc., are printed. They then are engaged in activities much like those described for Level 2. For example, the children can hold up their *sh* card if they hear the sound at the beginning of a word. They can play bingo games involving this cluster. They can write *sh* as they hear it in words and can add it to given phonograms.

A second useful activity is to lead children to realize that they can build or recognize many new unfamiliar words by changing a single letter in a consonant-letter cluster. For this purpose a list of words (for example, *lack, lame, lank, last*) to which single letters can be added (in this case, *b*) to make words with clusters (*black, blame, blank, blast*) should be used. Here is an example of how such an activity can be conducted.

Tell the pupils that they are now going to create a different word by adding another sound before *top.* Ask them—

1.   to listen to the word *stop* as you pronounce it;

2.   to say *stop* and listen to the word as they say it;

3.   to tell what sound was added to *top* to make *stop.*

Write *s* before the word *top* on the chalkboard and ask the class to say *top* and *stop* and listen to the difference between the two words. Discuss this difference with the class. Remind the pupils that while the cluster seems to be almost one sound, it is really two separate sounds and must be written with two separate letters [Hanna, Hodges, & Hanna 1971, p. 138].

Other examples of this would be:

1.   Say: "Look at these words." (Write on the board in this fashion.)

> lack
> link
> rake
> tall
> ring

Read these words over and add *b* to each word. What is the one word you cannot add *b* to? Why can't we add *b* to *tall?*" Elicit the idea that *bt* never go together at the beginning of a word.

2.   Say: "Make a different word out of each of these words by adding s to it:

> led
> pot
> tub
> pin

3.   Say: "Listen to this word *stop*. Say it." Write on the board *top* and *stop*, one word under the other. Say: "What letter is added to *top* to make *stop?* Listen again to the differences in *top* and *stop*. Look at this word. (Write *pin*.) Let's say it. What happens when I add *s* to *pin?* Can you say the word?" Repeat this for several other words of this kind.

4.   Say: "Listen to the *th* sound at the beginning of these words." Say these words and write them on the board one under the other:

> thin
> thank
> third

"Hold up your hand if you hear the *th* sound at the beginning of these words. Hold up your fist if you hear it at the end." Say and write these words:

bath	teeth
cloth	thump
thick	thief
fifth	thorn
thing	truth

Say: "Hold up your hand when you hear a *th* in this story:
    The *third* boy in line had some*th*ing in his *mouth*. Was it a *tooth?* No, a *tooth* was too *thick*. A *thin cloth* would fit his *mouth*. Was it a *cloth?* No. It was something that came up his *throat*. It was his *breath*." (Write the words as the children recognize them.)

It can be seen that the activity in item 4 deals with a two-letter grapheme that represents one phoneme. It is necessary to alert children to these graphemes if the form of teaching as given in this lesson is used. There are only three of these at the beginning of words: *ch, sh,* and *th* (four, if we include *wh*). By putting words that begin with these graphemes into a special category, children should soon recognize that they must be seen to represent a single sound.

It is wise to teach the spellings of /th/ (*thing*) and /th̷/ (*then*) at separate times. It is not necessary to try to teach children to distinguish between these two sound-spelling correspondences.

REFERENCES

Betts, Emmett A. "Phonics: Consonants." *Education,* 82(1962):533–536.

Bond, Guy L., and Wagner, Eva Bond. *Teaching the Child to Read.* New York: Macmillan, 1960.

Dale, Edgar, and Chall, Jeanne. "A Formula for Predicting Readability." *Educational Research Bulletin,* 27(1948):11–20.

Dale, Edgar, and Eichholz, Gerhard. *Children's Knowledge of Words.* Columbus: Ohio State University Press, 1960.

Dawson, Mildred A., and Bamman, Henry A. *Fundamentals of Basic Reading Instruction.* New York: David McKay, 1963.

Durrell, Donald D. *Improving Reading Instruction.* New York: World, 1956.

Gray, William S. *On Their Own in Reading.* Chicago: Scott, Foresman, 1948.

Greene, Harry A. *New Iowa Spelling Scale.* Iowa City: The State University of Iowa Press, 1955.

Groff, Patrick. "Sequences for Teaching Consonant Clusters." *Journal of Reading Behavior,* 4(1971–1972):59–65.

Hanna, Paul R., Hodges, Richard E., and Hanna, Jean S. *Spelling: Structure and Strategies.* Boston: Houghton Mifflin, 1971.

Harris, Albert J. *Effective Teaching of Reading.* New York: David McKay, 1962.

Hartley, Ruth N. "A Method of Increasing the Ability of First Grade Pupils to Use Phonetic Generalizations." *California Journal of Educational Research,* 22(1971):9–16.

Heilman, Arthur W. *Teaching Reading.* Columbus: Charles E. Merrill, 1961.

Kucera, Henry, and Francis, W. Nelson. *Computational Analysis of Present-Day American English.* Providence, R.I.: Brown University Press, 1967.

Personke, Carl, and Yee, Albert H. *Comprehensive Spelling Instruction.* Scranton: Intext Educational Publishers, 1971.

Spache, George D. *Reading in the Elementary School.* Boston: Allyn & Bacon, 1964.

10

TEACHING PHONICS: LEVEL 4

In Level 4 children are taught to recognize the sound-spellings of closed syllables, or phonograms.[1] These are one-vowel phonograms that use single-letter vowel graphemes. They are found in words

1. Spelled with beginning single consonants, as in *c*at;

2. Spelled with beginning consonant clusters, as in *st*op;

3. Spelled with ending consonant clusters, as in da*sh*, ta*ll*, ha*nd*;

4. Spelled with beginning and ending consonant clusters, as in *crash*.

Phonograms whose vowels are represented by single-letter graphemes are taught at this early level principally because these phonograms represent certain predictable sound-spelling correspondences. We found in our analysis of high-frequency monosyllabic words [Groff 1972] that the graphemes *a, e, i, o, u* represented the sounds /a, e, i, o, u/ in 86 percent of the phonograms in these words.

Teaching Vowel Sound-Spellings Through Phonograms

We do not recommend that vowel letters be taught as such, or that the child be taught to make single vowel letter-sound associations. We agree with Paul

---

[1]The terms *closed syllable* and *phonogram* are used interchangeably for the sake of convenience. It is obvious that a closed syllable such as *met* is not necessarily a phonogram. The phonogram of *met* is *et*.

McKee that "at the present time the question of what to do about teaching letter-sound associations for vowels as part of instruction in beginning reading is unsettled and highly arguable" [1966, p. 103]. This is largely due to the fact that vowel graphemes can represent a numerous and varied set of vowel sounds. It is also due to the perplexity of many phonics writers as to what to do in phonics with the middle parts of words (where vowels more commonly occur), which are the parts with which children make the most errors in spelling and reading. One writer on phonics simply says that beginning instruction in single-vowel sound-spelling relationships "assumes that the pupil has learned what the vowels are and that they have at least two sounds" [Dechant 1969, p. 52]. This appears, however, much like saying that it is easy to teach phonics *after* children have already learned it.

There seems little doubt that phonics must help the child develop a system for determining which of the sixteen vowel phonemes to give to a vowel grapheme. Some writers on phonics agree with us that the graphemes that *follow the vowel grapheme in a word* generally act as signals to the pronunciation of that vowel grapheme. However, in spite of this knowledge of the effect of these *spelling patterns* of words on their pronunciation, many writers on phonics have persisted in the belief that, in reading, the vowel grapheme in a word first should be isolated and then an attempt should be made to say its phoneme in isolation; only then should this vowel phoneme be spoken as part of the spelling pattern. For example, for the word *paste* the child would be taught to see *a* and *e* as vowel letters, to remember that the *e* at the end of the word is not representative of a sound, that the *a* is given the sound /ā/ because the *e* is "silent," and that the grapheme cluster *aste* is pronounced /āst/. Or, following other advice, "The safe rule is: Always teach the initial consonant in conjunction with the vowel that follows if sounding is to function" [Hildreth 1958, p. 350]. The child would have to go through the first three steps of the routine outlined for *paste,* then give a sound for *p,* say /p/ and /ā/ together, and finally, say /pā/ and /st/ together. All of this appears to us to complicate the matter of word recognition unnecessarily. There is an effective yet simpler way, which we have adopted.

It is important to teach the child to proceed from the initial grapheme in a word to the final grapheme, and then to the phonogram. We have illustrated previously how the first two parts of this sequence can be accomplished. It appears that in the first stages of word recognition, a child's recognition of the initial and final graphemes of a word are adequate for this purpose. This is especially so if the child is taught to apply this recognition to one-vowel words with a C-V-C sequence of graphemes.

McKee studied the abilities of a group of first-grade children to recognize words without having been taught any of the letter-sound associations represented by vowels. He notes "that these first-grade pupils had no trouble reading an unfamiliar primer story in which all the words included were familiar to them in print and a blank was substituted for each vowel sound in each word" [1966, p. 104]. We believe that with the aid of beginning and final consonant graphemes such pupils will be able to read many words that are *not familiar* to them in print. It should be possible for them to read words with letters omitted from them even though they do not know some vowel letter-sound correspondences they represent.

No more pie, I am f___ll.
A f____l was called on the batter.
That trick doesn't f____l me.

(The advantage of knowing some function words—*at, on, the*—is also apparent.)

Levels 2 and 3 taught pupils to move from left to right, the order in which phonemes are pronounced in words. In learning to read phonograms, however, pupils will often have to read from right to left. That is, to determine the sound of the vowel letter in the phonogram, they will have to recognize the consonant letters that follow it. These consonants signal the sound the vowel letter represents. For example, we cannot read the *co* of *co*____ until we see the consonant letters that fit the slot (co-*b*, co-*ld*, co-*rd*, co-*me*).

Notes on Teaching Phonograms

At Level 4 we teach children other cues to word recognition, since the use of initial and final consonant graphemes often will not suffice. Mature readers pay less attention to the vowel letters than to the consonant letters because it is possible for them to "fill in" the missing vowel sounds from the context. We know what they "should be" or "must be." It seems reasonable to predict, as well, that children who are taught to use context cues, to read words so as to fit each successive one to previous ones, that is, to attempt to make sense, will also utilize this "vowel-letter cue reduction" process. They also will learn to get along with a greater dependence on consonant letters than on vowel letters if the context of what they read can be used to support certain intelligent guesses they make about vowel letters.

The information about the correspondences between a vowel letter and the sound or sounds it represents is a crucial matter for children to learn, nonetheless. There are several important aspects of teaching children this information that must be considered:

1. Instead of teaching children to attend to vowel graphemes as isolated parts of words, teach them to recognize the vowel grapheme in a phonogram: *the vowel grapheme plus the final consonant grapheme, at,* as in c*at*.

When children are taught to identify the isolated vowel sound, they are asked to notice if the vowel sounds in words (*sat, pan, bag*) are alike or different. They then are asked to write the vowel sound [Hanna, Hodges, & Hanna 1971, pp. 133–134]. We begin, instead, by asking children to recognize whether words *rhyme*. This is generally easier for children to do. That is, they can tell whether *pan* and *can* read aloud "make a rhyme" before they can identify isolated vowel sounds. One major reason, then, for beginning with rhymes (or phonograms, as we will call these VC clusters) is that this is the easiest way to teach vowel sound-spellings.

2. The reader of *Phonics: Why and How* doubtless realizes by this point that there can be many graphemes used to represent a single vowel phoneme. Nonetheless, one of the highly useful generalizations to demonstrate for children is that of the spelling of the *closed syllable* (VC). Pupils also will learn they can base recognition of the VC combination on the assumption that the vowel letter in this case will represent a *checked* vowel. Another reason for beginning with phonograms, then, is that from the beginning pupils are presented with phoneme-grapheme generalizations they will find that make word recognition predictable.

3. The problem of how to handle the optional spellings for final sounds in one-vowel words or syllables (a*dd*, bu*tt*er) is much simplified if the phonogram approach is used. It also simplifies the problem of reading certain spellings such as *dipping, bumping*. The syllabication rule to follow for these words is: "Divide the word after the second consonant letter" (*dipp-ing*).

4. By learning phonograms pupils do not have to wait until they can identify the separate sounds in two- and three-phoneme words, as such, to begin to write words. As soon as pupils can write the vowel letters and a few consonant letters, they can write phonograms. For example, when pupils can write the five vowel letters and two consonant letters (*t-n*), they can write the following ten phonograms: (t)*an*, (t)*en*, (t)*in*, *on*, (n)*un*, *at*, (n)*et*, *it*, (n)*ot*, (n)*ut*. When pupils have learned three more consonant letters, they can write the words *ben, bin, ban, bun; can; den, din, dan, don, dun; fin, fan, fun;* etc. Have them write the words here that are in their listening vocabularies. Most experienced teachers would agree that teaching children to write these few letters takes only a relatively short time. Moreover, with the exception of *ot* and *ut*, these phonograms occur in the top five percent of the most frequently seen phonograms in common words [Jones 1970].

5. The use of phonograms effectively reduces the chances that the

phonics teacher will be inclined to teach sounds in isolation. We have repeatedly stated that the isolation of sounds is both unnecessary for the teaching of phonics and contrary to what linguistics says about the true nature of these sounds. Therefore, we would be afraid that the chart of letters for sounds for children to follow, as suggested by Paul Hanna, Richard Hodges, and Joan Hanna [1971, p. 136], could lead to such isolated sounding:

Spelling of:

Picture	*First sound*	*Second sound*	*Last sound*
(a bed)	b	e	d

It is apparent that such a chart could misdirect the child to attempt a *buh-eh-duh* sounding of *bed*, which is quite the wrong thing to do, of course. The risk of encouraging such errors is greatly reduced by teaching *ed* as a phonogram to which a child adds the *first sound* of *big*.

6. The recognition of phonograms as the basic approach to recognizing vowel letters eliminates the question of whether instruction should begin with letters that represent free or checked vowels. Since a very high percent of closed syllables (VC clusters) use checked vowels, plus /o/, it is quite reasonable to begin with checked vowels and then move to free vowels.

7. If the phonics teachers use phonograms, they will not be required to have their pupils do aural-oral practice to distinguish between the sounds that certain clusters (*ch, sh, th, ng*) represent (*lunch, dish, with, sing*), versus the sounds that other consonant-letter clusters (*st, sk, lt, ft*) represent *at the endings of syllables or one-vowel words* (*best, desk, belt, raft*). It will remain for the teacher to demonstrate that some clusters can be added to *words* (as can single letter graphemes) for example, *th-read, b-read.*

8. It is relatively easy to show the pupil how a short phonogram can be extended. For example, *(c)ar* can be extended to *art, (c)art; arm* to *(h)arm; (f)or* to *(f)ort, (f)ord, (f)orm.* This is another application of the rule: Find the phonogram by going past the vowel letter until the consonant letters stop, unless you see a suffix.

9. The phonogram approach easily adapts itself to the linguistic controls on its identification. That is, as pupils later mature in their ability to search for phonograms, they will also notice that this search is conditioned by whether

    a. The word has a prefix. Thus, they note *mis-chance*, not *misch-ance.*

b. The word has a suffix. Thus, they note *ap-art-ment*, not *ap-artm-ent*.

c. A consonant-letter cluster should stand alone. This is usually the case. Thus, they note m*is*-ch*ance*, not m*isch-ance*.

d. There is an impermissible cluster of phonemes (affixes excepted). Thus, they note c*on-vent* since no word ends /onv/. There are few high-frequency words with such impermissible consonant-letter clusters (affix words excepted).

e. There is open juncture (this is closely related to *item d*). Thus, they note *ap-art-ment* since the impermissible cluster /rtm/ requires an open juncture after /rt/.

f. The word is a compound word, or has little words in it. Thus, they note d*oll-house*, and not d*ollh-ouse*.

g. A cluster in the word is made up of two same consonant letters. This cluster should stand alone and not be divided. Thus, they note d*oll-ar*, not d*ol-lar*.

Teaching Plural Forms

We believe that the recognition of *s* and *es* on one-syllable words will pose few problems for children for two reasons—one logical, one empirical. Logically, we would expect school children not to be confused by the idea of number because all of them in their everyday experiences have come to gain the concept of singular and plural long before they enter school. They recognize early in life the advantage of having more than one thing, for example, two pieces of candy, or another toy. Empirically, we know from experimental studies of children's language that they can *produce* the correct *s* or *es* plurals for pseudowords by the age of six. To determine this Jean Berko [1958] asked children to listen to a text read to them that said, for instance:

This is a wug (or gutch).   (Pictures of a "wug" or "gutch" shown.)
Now here is another one.
There are two of them.
There are two _____.

Then she asked them to fill in the blank. The percentage of correct answers by first graders was 89 percent where /z/ or /s/ had to be added (*wugs*). This dropped to 37 percent correct answers, however, when /əz/ was required (*gutches*). Thus, we would infer that children should have little trouble learning to recognize *s* as an inflection of a one-vowel root word, but that the recognition of *es*, which generally turns this inflected word into a polysyllabic word, would be more difficult.

Partial substantiation of this inference comes from Irene Hanson's study of first-grade children's ability to learn generalizations concerning variant word endings and the application of them in contextual material [Hanson 1966]. Among the endings taught was *s*, added to nouns and verbs. The children given instruction in these generalizations scored significantly better on an experimental test of the application of *s* to words than did a control group of children who "used the same periods of time for independent reading."

Note well that in all the levels to follow the plural forms of the particular words being taught should also be presented. Have pupils read both singular and plural forms.

Teaching Level 4

In suggesting the following activities for Level 4 we assume that the pupil has learned to identify some letters and how to match letters and their names; to recognize single sound-letter correspondences; and to recognize consonant-cluster, sound-letter correspondences. If this is not the case, children are not ready for Level 4. A quick survey by the teacher to determine whether this learning has taken place is appropriate before beginning Level 4.

At this point should the teacher directly teach that the term *vowel letter* equals *a-e-i-o-u*? We think this is unnecessary. Children who practice the following activities will learn that phonograms begin with *a-e-i-o-u*. It is of no great importance, then, whether they can say these are vowel letters. In sum, there is no specific value at this time for a child to know the term *vowel letter*.

Begin by having the child see and name the letters in phonograms.

1. Write two phonograms on the chalkboard, e.g., *an* and *in*. (See Chapter 5 for a list of high-frequency phonograms that can be used.) Children are given two cards, one with *an* and the other with *in*. Clip the upper corners of the cards to aid children in holding them up the right way.

2. Say: "This is *a-n, an*." (By saying the word as well as the name of the letters some incidental perception of the whole phonogram is encouraged.) "This is *i-n, in*. Say the letter names with me: *a-n, i-n*." Do not require the naming of the word at this step.

3. Say: "Look at your cards. Hold up *a-n*." Alternate a few times. Be sure that the children are holding up the correct card.

4. Say: "If I write what is on your card, hold it up." Alternate writing *an* or *in* with *ab, ad, ag, it, ib, ig,* or any other consonant phonogram the letters of which the children have previously learned to identify.

5. Say: "Can you find *a-n* in this word?" Write ⬚t⬚ |an|. "In these?" Write ⬚t⬚ |ab|-⬚r⬚ |an|-|m| ⬚f⬚ |an|.

6. Say: "If you see *a-n* in a word, hold up your *a-n* card. If you see *i-n* in a word, hold up your *i-n* card." Alternate writing *tan, tin, fan, fin,* etc.

7. Say: "What are the names of the two letters on this card?" Have children do this several times during the teaching of any two phonograms.

8. Say: "How many *a-n*'s can you find in this row? Count them. Show how many with your fingers." (Repeat for *i-n, in.*)

an	it	an	an
it	it	it	an
an	it	it	an
an	an	an	an

9. Present pairs of words that are alike except that one contains the first phonogram (*an*) and the other contains the second (*in*), for example, *tan-tin, fan-fin, dan-din.* Say: "What part of this word (write *tan*) is different from this word (write *tin*)?" Write the words one under the other.

10. Give children work to complete in this format, presenting several rows:

an—an	in	an	in
in—in	in	in	an

Say: "See *a-n*, circle all the words in the row that are just like it. Let's do the first row together."

11. Say: "Mark the one in each row that is different from the others."

it	it	it	an
an	it	an	an
it	it	an	it
an	an	it	an

12. Say: "Put a line under the two in each row if they are alike."

it	it
an	an
an	it
an	an
it	an

13. Say: "Look at these numbers (1 through 9). Some numbers have *a-n* by them. Some have *i-t* by them. What numbers have *a-n* by them? Which have *i-t* by them?"

1. it	6. an
2. an	7. an
3. it	8. it
4. it	9. it
5. an	

Begin now having the child hear the phonograms in words.

1. Write the word *sat* on the board. Say: "What is a word that rhymes with *sat?*" As the first word is mentioned, erase the *s* from *sat* and substitute the new consonant letter, *b*, for example. Have the class read the new word, *bat*. Now say, "What is a word that rhymes with *bat?*" Continue as with *sat*.

2. Say: "Listen to this. I have an old cat who is very fat. Who can tell me the two words that rhyme?" Write these on the board. Erase *c* and *f* to show *at*. Add *c* to *at* and ask, "What is this word?" Do the same with *f*.

3. Say: "Listen to this. The man hit the fly with a pan. What words rhyme? What do I need to do to change this (write *man* on board) to *pan*?" Elicit the idea. Erase *m*, add *p*.

4. Say: "Listen to this. The kitten was fat. Which of these words (write *rat* and *run*) rhymes with *fat?* Why is *run* not like *fat?* Does it look like *fat?*"

5. Say: "Fill in this blank." Write on the board: The cat was _____at.

6. Say: "Raise your hand if you hear two rhyming words." Read pairs of one-vowel words that either rhyme or do not.

7. Read sentences as these aloud. Write the rhyming words one under the other on the board.

   It's fun to eat a bun.

   Which do you want—a rake or a cake?

   My cat was lost today.

   He threw his cap into my lap.

8. Say: "Choose the word that rhymes and fits." Write on the board:

   He has my tack.

   Please give it _____. (Offer *pack, lack, rack, back*.)

9. Say: "Can you think of words that rhyme with *can?*" Children may think of *man, ran, fan, pan, tan, van.* Write these on the board, one under the other. "What two letters are the same in these words? We will call *an* a phonogram since it makes these words rhyme." (It is necessary at some point to introduce the term *phonogram* and give many examples of it. Later when this term is used, children will know to what it refers, saving much time in teaching.)

10. Say: "What is a color that rhymes with *sled?* What is a toy that rhymes with *tall?*" Write *sled* on the board and all the rhyming words given for it. Do the same with *tall.*

11. Say: "Listen to this phonogram: *un.* Let's see how many words we can make with the letters we know." Write some consonant letters on the board. Point to each letter and say, "Put it on the front of *un.* Now say the word."

12. Say: "If these words have the same phonograms, put a line under them. Put a mark only if they have the same phonogram."

mark-bark	tall-bell	tell-tan
tell-bell	tin-tan	bell-bark

13. Set up phonogram charts such as the following:

First Sound	Phonogram
b	ed
	ig
	an
	op
	ib
	us

First have the class put the sound /b/ with these phonograms. Then try other beginning sounds. Always write the words.

14. Say: "Listen to this phonogram: *an.* Do you hear *an* at the beginning or end of this word: *ant?* (Write on the board to verify.) Do you hear *an* at the beginning or end of this word: *plan?*" Verify by writing on the board.

15. Say: "Listen to this phonogram: *ed.* Find *ed* in these words and underline it." (Write *sled, bed, fed,* etc.)

16. Say: "What is this phonogram?" Say "*ed*" and write it on the board. "Let's add *b* to it. What word do we have? Now let's add *f.* Now *r,*" etc.

17. Say: "Find the phonograms in these words: *pan, pin, pun, pen.*" Write the words on the board as the pupils say them. Write the phonograms one under the other:

> *an*
> *in*
> *un*
> *en*

Then say: "What letter makes these phonograms different?"

18. Say: "Hold up your phonogram card when you hear your phonogram in a word I say aloud." Give each child two cards on which are written *og* and *ag*. Read aloud a list such as *dog, log, sag, bag, bog, lag, rag, fog.* Make sure that the response of each child is correct after each word. (The teacher can type or ditto copies of each story in the basal reader, stories dictated by pupils, or other reading materials that are being used with the class. Have the children underline all the phonograms indicated by the teacher. After almost all the common phonograms are learned, have the class mark any phonogram in the duplicated story that they think they see.)

19. Write *t* and *s* on the board. Say: "Put these letters in front of these phonograms to make new words":

> __an   __en   __in   __on   __un

20. Write these words on the right side of the board:

> hat
> tin
> fin
> bat
> bin
> cat

Give children *at* and *in* phonogram cards. Have them match the phonogram with the word.

21. Play phonogram bingo. Say: "Listen to these words as I read them." Write the words on the board at first. Then, play the game without writing them on the board. "Put a counter on the square that has a phonogram you hear."

at	an	at
in	free	an
it	it	in

22. Say: "Each of these phonograms has a number." Write:

> 1. at
> 2. in

"Put the number of the phonogram by these words."

> _____bat
> _____din
> _____sit
> _____fat, etc.

23. Generate a list of one-vowel words using a selected phonogram as a base. Ask children to attach letters to the phonograms to make words:

> un   and
> run   land
> fun, etc.   sand, etc.

24. Give the class two phonogram cards, one with *in* and one with *at*. Say: "This is *in*. This is *at*. Hold up your *in* card if you see it in a word I write on the board. Do the same for *at*."

25. Say: "I will write a letter on the board. Bring up your *in* card or your *at* card to see if we can make a new word." Write:

> c   at
> r   in
> t   (on one side of the board and)   in   (on the other).
> b   at
> f   at

26. Say: "Draw a line from one to the other to make a word." (See item 25.)

27. Say: "What are these letters?" (Write *f* and *p*.) "If this is *pit*" (write it), "this must be _____" (write *fit*). Follow these steps with several other combinations with other phonograms.

28. Use some context-cue activities involving the phonogram words taught in the above activities (see Chapter 19). Try to include a context-cue activity within as many of the above activities as is possible.

REFERENCES

Berko, Jean. "The Child's Learning of English Morphology." *Word*, 14(1958):150–177.

Dechant, Emerald. *Linguistics, Phonics, and the Teaching of Reading.* Springfield, Ill.: Charles C. Thomas, 1969.

Groff, Patrick. "A Phonemic Analysis of Monosyllabic Words." *Reading World,* 12(1972):94–103.

Hanna, Paul R., Hodges, Richard E., and Hanna, Jean S. *Spelling: Structure and Strategies.* Boston: Houghton Mifflin, 1971.

Hanson, Irene H. "An Investigation of the Effects of Teaching Variant Word Endings to First Grade Children." *Dissertation Abstracts,* 26(1966):6552.

Hildreth, Gertrude. *Teaching Reading.* New York: Henry Holt, 1958.

Jones, Virginia W. *Decoding and Learning to Read.* Portland, Oreg.: Northwest Regional Educational Laboratory, 1970.

McKee, Paul. *Reading.* Boston: Houghton Mifflin, 1966.

11

TEACHING PHONICS: LEVEL 5

Children are taught to recognize another kind of closed syllable, or phonogram, in Level 5. These are one-vowel letter phonograms that end with the marker letter *e*. This diacritic *e* serves as a sign for the immediately previous vowel letter to help indicate which sound the first vowel letter represents. For our purposes diphthongs are regarded as single vowels.

In *cake*, for example, the marker *e* signals that the previous *a* represents /ā/. At Level 5 children are taught to recognize phonograms that end in the marker *e* (often wrongly called "silent e") (1) as spelled with single letters, as in *cake, home, nice, cute*, and (2) as spelled with single vowel letters (in words with beginning and/or ending consonant clusters) as in *tribe, paste*. The single vowel letters for the above spellings in (1) and (2) represent the vowel sounds /ā, ē, ī, ō, yōō/.

The Usefulness of the "Marker e"

There are three studies that we know of on the usefulness of marker *e*. These studies [Bailey 1967; Clymer 1963; Emans 1967] determined what percent of high-frequency words spelled with one vowel letter plus the marker *e* (e.g., *bone*) follow this rule: the first vowel is "long" and the *e* is "silent." These are the spellings of words given above (*cake, tribe*). It will be remembered that traditional phonics writers consider "long" vowels to be the sounds /ā/, /ē/, /ī/, /ō/, /yōō/. These three studies reported, respectively, that words at elementary-school level conform to the rule to these percents: 63, 57, and 63. Examples of spellings that these researchers say would not conform to the rule are *leave, house, groove, cause, voice, prince, nurse, carve, serve.* One of these researchers, Robert Emans, also indicated that if one goes to the extent of excluding words ending in *ive* and *le* that the "utility" percent of marker *e* for preceding *a* and *i* could be raised to 71. The percentages found in the three studies dropped significantly, however, when these three researchers asked whether "in many two and three syllable words, the final *e* lengthens the vowel in the last syllable."[1] In this case the percents were 46, 46, 42.

New Analyses Needed

It appears to us, however, that an additional analysis of the general corpus of words these investigators consulted is needed for two reasons. First of all, the above studies analyzed both monosyllabic and polysyllabic words. But they did not give separate reports for one-syllable and multisyllable words. We believe nonetheless that data on the phonemic properties of one-syllable words are needed for phonics. It can be argued that phonics is best taught with monosyllabic words. This is basically so because these shorter words are more predictable than polysyllabic words in their sound-spelling relationships. It was calculated from the data of our study of high-frequency monosyllabic words that 73 percent of vowel sounds in the 1,274 closed-syllables studied represent either "long" or "short" vowel sounds: /ā, ē, ī, ō, yōō/ or /a, e, i, o, u/ [Groff 1972]. An analysis of the words in the *New Iowa Spelling Scale* used for this study also reveals that polysyllabic words are approximately twice as hard for children to spell as monosyllabic words [Greene 1955]. This is another important consideration in beginning phonics.

Then, too, monosyllabic words have only stressed vowel sounds. This is an important advantage in learning phonics since the vowel sounds given to syllables often become relatively unstressed when the syllable is said in a polysyllabic word, for example, *ant* /ant/ versus import*ant* /ənt/. It is also held by linguists that polysyllabic words consist of a series of syllabic pulses whose timing and stress are not predictable to any great degree [Groff 1971, pp. 23–24]. We believe, therefore, that the variant nature of vowel sounds in polysyllabic words dictates against the early use of these long words in phonics. They should be reserved for the later stages of phonics instruction.

---

[1] No spelling of words has such a causative effect, of course. What these researchers were trying to ask was this: With what frequency does the "long" vowel sound occur in the final syllable of one- or two-syllable words that end in *e*?

A second reason that further analysis exclusively of monosyllabic words is needed lies in the quality of the analyses in the above studies, which has come under sharp negative criticism, especially from linguists. Ronald Wardhaugh, for example, observed that the above studies on phonic generalizations "would have benefited from a much closer attention to linguistic data than any of the authors chose to give . . ." [1968, p. 433]. He sees them as "a good example of the type of investigation of which [John] Carroll [another linguist] speaks in which adequate methodology is dissipated on material which is often linguistically indefensible" [1968, p. 433]. On a later occasion Wardhaugh notes that in these studies,

> no attempt was made to examine the generalizations themselves for their linguistic sense or to order them in any way. The only criterion was their usefulness, not their soundness. . . . The generalizations seem to be a haphazard set in which rules about accent, word-splitting, silent letters, and special combinations are presented randomly. Burmeister's conclusion that not many of them are very useful is hardly surprising, because it is hard to imagine that a child could ever learn to read by applying a set of rules of this kind [1969, pp. 10–11].

Any analyses of the phonemic nature of words to be used as a basis for phonics teaching should keep these criticisms prominently in mind.

Our analysis of high-frequency monosyllabic words [1972] revealed these data about single-vowel letter marker *e* words:

1. Fifty-eight percent had the spelling CVC*e*, as in *bake*. The vowel sounds /ā, ē, ī, ō, yōō/ occurred in these words 91 percent of the time.

2. Thirty-one percent had the spelling CCVC*e*, as in *blame*. The vowel sounds /ā, ē, ī, ō, yōō/ occurred in these words 97 percent of the time.

3. Four percent had the spellings CVCC*e* or CCVCC*e*, as in *waste*, *change*. The vowel sounds /ā, ē, ī, ō, yōō/ occurred in them 100 percent of the time.

4. Seven percent had the spellings CVCC*e* or CCVCC*e*, as in *judge*, *bridge*. The vowel sounds /a, e, i, o, u/ occurred in them 88 percent of the time.

The goal of Level 5, accordingly, is to lead children to realize that a very high percent of single vowel letter marker *e* phonograms have the vowel sounds /ā, ē, ī, ō, yōō/. To accomplish this goal children must learn to read a different vowel sound for a vowel letter than they have at previous levels. Before, they have learned to read one-vowel letter phonograms with the sounds /a, e, i, o, u/. At Level 5 they are moved to phonograms that use free vowel sounds (beyond /o/), and that end in the marker *e*.

Teaching "Marker e"

There are several different ways that traditional writers on phonics have suggested that the marker *e*, or "silent e" as they call it, should be taught. Emerald Dechant suggests that to teach this phenomenon, the child must first be directed to identify or discriminate the "short" and the "long" vowel sounds. He contends it is proper to ask the child: "What sound occurs in the word *mule*? In the word *go*? Are these short sounds or long sounds? Why?" Then, after having the child look at *came*, *flame*, and *dame*, the teacher should say, "How many vowels are pronounced? Which vowel is silent? What happens to the first vowel when the *e* is silent and is preceded by a single consonant?" [1969, p. 92]. We believe all this to be unnecessary and therefore a wasteful use of the time available for teaching phonics. As we have described it, teaching children to recognize vowel sounds *as they occur in phonograms* makes the procedure described by Dechant superfluous. We insist that vowel sounds should not be learned outside their natural speech environment, the syllable. A child attempting to answer the question, "What sound occurs in the word *mule*?" would be forced to try to isolate the vowel sound, and thus to violate the principle that speech sounds are only genuine when heard in syllables. Moreover, the answers that Dechant apparently leads children to give to his question—"Are these vowel sounds in *mule* and *go* short sounds or long sounds? Why?"—would be inaccurate descriptions. He obviously wants the child to respond to the question "Why?" by saying, "The vowel sound in *mule* is long because there is an *e* at the end of the word." It is inappropriate to lead children to this conclusion. The /yo͞o/ sound in *mule* is heard simply because that is the way the word is pronounced. The spelling of the word does not *cause* this pronunciation.

That the child must state the generalization for marker *e* words also is heavily emphasized in other traditional writing on phonics. For example, Ruth Gallant believes that to learn to respond to marker *e*, a "visual clue to the long sound," as she calls it, the teacher should present a list of words illustrating "long" vowel "clues." Then, the "pupil marks the long vowel (and silent letter if silent *e* or double vowel clue is used). Lead pupils to discover and state the clue common to each group" [1970, p. 85]. Arthur Heilman also requires children to put diacritical marks on words with marker *e* (*hate*), but *after* they have stated the generalization, "the final *e* is silent and the first vowel is long" [1964, p. 63].

Again, we emphasize that taking the time that is necessary to bring children to the stage where they can *name* the generalization involved in any sound-spelling correspondence is not needed for children to comprehend and use such generalizations. The writers on phonics who insist that children must state the generalization that is involved in such correspondences, or put diacritical marks on words, never explain how these activities *add* to children's ability to read words. It is obvious, of course, that in the activities of this sort children *must be able to read the words involved before they can successfully complete the activity.* There is no evidence, however, that such activities are needed or useful.

We feel that the "labeling" activities required by Carl Wallen [1969] are equally objectionable. He claims that if a child labels *made*, for example, as $\frac{made}{CVCE}$ this will overcome confusions later in perceiving *made* as different from *mad*. In other words, he believes that it is easier for the child to discriminate $\frac{CVC}{CVCE}$ than $\frac{mad}{made}$. For example, "Look closely at the word you just gave me, *late*. Does it have the same labeling as the other words?" [p. 60]. It appears to us this activity is superfluous and unessential. Moreover, it puts excessive emphasis on the terms *vowel* and *consonant*. There is no evidence, either, that marking letters as vowels or consonants ever helps children to learn to read.

Instead of these complicated, extraneous procedures, we believe that the best way to teach a child to perceive and to be sensitive to the marker *e* in the words selected for Level 5 is to follow the procedures described for Level 4.

Accordingly, the teacher is encouraged to adapt the activities given for Level 4 for use with the marker *e* words of Level 5:

1. Since marker *e* words should be taught as phonograms (*ake* for *bake*), it is appropriate to have many exercises using phonograms as parts of words that rhyme. Rhyming activities are relatively easy for children to understand and participate in.

2. Activities involving the addition of single consonant letters and consonant clusters to marker *e* phonograms can be used.

3. Phonograms can be chosen from a list or recalled from memory to complete exercises where an initial consonant or consonant cluster is given, as in s_____ (*side*), sp_____ (*spoke*).

4. Marker *e* phonogram cards can be used for many activities. These cards are used by children to signal which phonogram they hear, or see written.

5. Children can identify words that have indicated marker *e* phonograms and put these into categories or lists. Children find it intriguing to be allowed to select their own special marker *e* phonogram, and then go on a search to find words in which it is found.

6.   As children practice with marker *e* phonograms, the teacher can evaluate their abilities to detect marker *e* phonograms in two ways. One is to have children read words or sentences to the teacher in which certain selected marker *e* phonograms are involved. This is a time-consuming activity, so it is often necessary, two, to have children underline all the marker *e* phonograms of a certain kind in copy prepared for this purpose. The latter practice has the possible danger, of course, that the child will be able to mark a phonogram correctly without being able to actually read the word in which it is embedded. This emphasizes the need to have someone listen to the child read words involving these phonograms and to give immediate feedback as to the child's accuracy with them. Older children, teacher aides, or helping parents can be utilized for this.

7.   Playing games with marker *e* phonograms is conducive to heightened interest for pupils, and probably a corresponding higher degree of learning than nongame activities. (See the appendix for descriptions of several of these games.)

8.   The plural forms of the marker *e* phonograms should be demonstrated for pupils. The general ways to do this are given in Chapter 10, Level 4. This activity should be the one with which the teacher concludes, at any particular time, the work to be done with marker *e* phonograms.

9.   Finally, we want to emphasize the special value of teaching marker *e* words as "contrastive spelling patterns," as Fries calls them [1963, p. 201]. One of the best ways for the child to learn to respond habitually to *hat* as /hat/ and *hate* as /hāt/ is to see these spelling patterns repeatedly in frames such as

hat,   ___at
hate, ___ate,

I hate my hat,   I _____ him,   or,   hat   rate
                                        mat   gate   (connect
I lost my _____.   rat   mate   the
                                        gat   hate   words).

REFERENCES

Bailey, Mildred H. "Utility of Phonic Generalizations in Grades One through Six." *Reading Teacher*, 20(1967):413–418.

Clymer, Theodore. "Utility of Phonic Generalizations in the Primary Grades." *Reading Teacher*, 16(1963):252–258.

Dechant, Emerald. *Linguistics, Phonics, and the Teaching of Reading.* Springfield, Ill.: Charles C Thomas, 1969.

Emans, Robert. "Usefulness of Phonic Generalizations Above the Primary Level." *Reading Teacher,* 20(1967):419–425.

Fries, Charles C. *Linguistics and Reading.* New York: Holt, Rinehart and Winston, 1963.

Gallant, Ruth. *Handbook in Corrective Reading: Basic Tasks.* Columbus: Charles E. Merrill, 1970.

Greene, Harry A. *New Iowa Spelling Scale.* Iowa City: The State University of Iowa Press, 1955.

Groff, Patrick. "A Phonemic Analysis of Monosyllabic Words." *Reading World,* 12(1972):94–103.

Groff, Patrick. *The Syllable: Its Nature and Pedagogical Usefulness.* Portland, Oreg.: Northwest Regional Educational Laboratory, 1971.

Heilman, Arthur W. *Phonics in Proper Perspective.* Columbus: Charles E. Merrill, 1964.

Wallen, Carl J. *Word Attack Skills in Reading.* Columbus: Charles E. Merrill, 1969.

Wardhaugh, Ronald. "Linguistics—Reading Dialogue." *Reading Teacher,* 21(1968):432–441.

Wardhaugh, Ronald. *Reading: A Linguistic Perspective.* New York: Harcourt Brace Jovanovich, 1969.

12

TEACHING PHONICS: LEVEL 6

At Level 6 the child is introduced to what we call *vowel-cluster* graphemes—often called vowel digraphs—as in f*oo*t, s*ee*n, p*ea*ch. At this level children are taught to recognize these in closed syllables (phonograms) in the following kinds of words:

1. Those spelled with vowel-letter clusters and single consonant letters (*seat, boat, fail/raise, seen*)

2. Those spelled with other vowel-letter clusters and single consonant letters (*boil/voice, foot, boot, loud/down*)

3. Those spelled with vowel-letter clusters plus beginning and/or ending consonant-letter clusters (*steal, peach, beast*)

4. Those spelled with other vowel-letter clusters and consonant-letter clusters (*spoil, shook, cloud/house, clown, round, ground, smooth/groove*)

In each of these kinds of spellings, the grapheme is made up of two letters (exceptions: *voice, house, groove*), and represents a single vowel sound. (As has been mentioned earlier, diphthongs are not taught as such in *Phonics: Why and How.*)

Phonograms and the Diphthong

The major objective of Level 6 is to teach children to recognize phonograms that are spelled with two-letter vowel graphemes and the marker *e*. We have said that in each of these kinds of spellings the vowel grapheme is made up of two letters, and represents a single vowel sound.

It is readily apparent this is not altogether true, since Levels 5 and 6 both involve words with diphthongs, for example, *foot*. As has been explained, a diphthong is a gliding complex of sounds that involves a change of resonance, and that begins with a recognizably single vowel sound but ends with another vowel sound. While each diphthong "is separable phonetically into two units, the diphthongs are single units phonemically" [Wise 1957, p. 63].

The reader at this point should remember that phonetics refers to the science of speech sounds, the forms of all speech in all languages. Phonemics, on the other hand, is the study of the individual sounds or linguistic units of a particular language, as these units act to determine meaning in that language. From phonemics we learn that a diphthong (which is spoken within the confines of a single syllable, and is a gliding together of two vowel sounds) *functions as does a single vowel, for purposes of distinguishing meaning.*

Because a diphthong in its phonemic function often is not easily distinguishable from a single vowel sound, we consider it appropriate in teaching phonics to view it as a single vowel. Thus, when we refer to one-vowel words, we mean one-syllable words with single vowel sounds and/or diphthongs. The avoidance of the term *diphthong* when teaching children is another example of how to abstain from the use of complex linguistic information, when it is not necessary for children in order for them to apply phonics in reading and spelling. The complexity of this matter is noted by linguists who say that a large number of diphthongs could be listed since "nearly all the vowels are diphthongized to some extent, and these resonance changes are necessary for accurate pronunciation" [Carrell & Tiffany 1960, p. 121]. *The idea of diphthong is best avoided when teaching phonics.*

The Utility of Vowel-Letter Cluster Markers

In Level 6 we move to word spellings that could be said to have "silent" letters. Under the rule: one sound-one letter, this would be so. The second vowel letter in *seat*, for example, could be said to represent no sound, and therefore to have no usefulness. One can argue that the *a* in *seat* is not a so-called "silent" letter, however, if by silent letter it is meant that *a* serves no function. The *a* in *seat* does have utility. It acts as a visual marker for the sound that one should give the letter *e* in *seat*. It signals that this letter is given the /ē/ sound. You know full well by now that the twenty-six letters of English orthography are not enough to make possible the optimum rule of one letter-one sound. The *a* in *seat* serves, then, to signal the reader not to read the word *seat* as /set/, but as /sēt/.

TABLE 16. PREDICTABILITY OF SIGNAL FUNCTION OF
CERTAIN VOWEL CLUSTERS°

Vowel Clusters	Clymer	Emans	Bailey	Burmeister
oa as /ō/	97%	86%	95%	94% of time
ee as /ē/	98%	100%	87%	86%
ea as /ē/	66%	62%	55%	51%
ai as /ā/	64%	83%	60%	74%

° As indicated earlier, some of these studies have weaknesses of design, and therefore their findings must be used selectively. The data we use from them here appear to be authentic.

Moreover, the predictability with which it performs this service is impressive. This is apparent from five studies of how well words conform to phonics generalizations. Theodore Clymer [1963], Robert Emans [1967], Mildred Bailey [1967], Lou Burmeister [1968], and Paul Hanna and his associates [1966] studied this matter respectively in primary grade books, in words used beyond the primary grade levels, in basal readers for grades one through six, and with a 17,000–word "common core" vocabulary.

The studies of Clymer, Emans, Bailey, and Burmeister show that the signal marker, or diacritic function of certain vowel-letter clusters can also have predictability. The percent of utility, or the percent of times the following clusters or digraphs occur when they represent the indicated sounds, is shown in Table 16.

Our analysis of these and other such correspondences in high-frequency monosyllabic words exclusively [Groff 1972] resulted in findings similar to those of Clymer, Emans, and Bailey, as seen in Table 17.

One must be careful *not* to infer that these data mean, for example, that when /ō/ is heard in words, it is spelled *oa* 97, 86, 95, or 94 percent of the time. The foregoing data were not gathered by this kind of analysis. Instead, they are the results of finding words that had, for example, the spelling *oa,* and *then* determining what sound this *oa* spelling represented. This turned out to be /ō/ the high percentage of times indicated. On the other hand, a study other than ours shows the percent of times in which /ō/ in words is spelled as *oa* is low, only 5 percent. Then, /ā/ is spelled as *ai* only

TABLE 17. PREDICTABILITY OF SELECTED
VOWEL-LETTER CLUSTERS IN MONOSYLLABIC WORDS

Vowel Clusters			Percent	Example
oa	as	/ō/	94%	*coat*
ee, ee-e	as	/ē/	98%	*beef, cheese*
ea	as	/ē/	77%	*bead*
ai, ai-e	as	/ā/	97%	*fail, raise*
ei	as	/ā/	78%	*vein*
ie, ie-e	as	/ē/	89%	*brief, niece*

9 percent of the time, /ē/ as *ee* 10 percent, and /ē/ as *ea* 10 percent [Hanna et al. 1966]. This illustrates, again, the different problems the child has in learning to read versus learning to spell.

In Level 6 /o͞o/ and /o͝o/ are taught as parts of phonograms. We thus avoid a problem that traditional phonics brought on itself, which was trying to "explain" these sounds. "Explaining the sounds of *oo* is much more complicated than actually learning to pronounce the frequently used words which contain this letter combination" [Heilman 1964, p. 69].

Instead of trying to "explain" to pupils the phonemic differences between these sounds, the child should be led to realize that the phonogram in which the spelling *oo* is a part will be a dependable signal for the pronunciation of *oo*, whether this be read /o͞o/ or /o͝o/. Notice how the final consonant letter of the phonograms in these words signal to the reader which of the two sounds the *oo* spelling represents:

Column 1	Column 2
/o͞o/	/o͝o/
poo*l*	
roo*m*	woo*d*
foo*d*	boo*k*
moo*n*	
hoo*p*	
boo*t*	
too*th*	
proo*f*	

With the exception of the single consonant letter *d* (*food-wood*), this system works quite well. Therefore, within a short time, the child should come to realize the value of these spelling signals. The teacher should first teach the phonograms in the first column above, of course. Then, the exceptions *ood* and *ook* can be given.

The vowel-letter clusters given in Table 18 are less predictable in their representation of the sounds indicated for them (with the exception of /oi/—*oi*). Two of the previously mentioned studies of phonic utility indicate

| | | | TABLE 18. PREDICTABILITY IN SELECTIVE VOWEL CLUSTERS | | |

Vowel Clusters			Burmeister	Emans	Groff
oi	as	/oi/	98% of time	—	100% of time
oo	as	/o͞o/	59%	74% of time	65%
oo	as	/o͝o/	36%	26%	30%
ou	as	/ou/	35%	—	59%
ow	as	/ou/	48%	—	59%

the percent of times these spellings occur where they represent the indicated phoneme. These and our data on monosyllabic words are shown in
Table 18.

Again, we should note these percentages do not refer, for example, to
the number of times /oi/ is spelled as *oi* in words. The 98 percent represents
the number of times where *oi* was seen in words and represented the
sound /oi/.

As an aid to this learning in Level 6, a control is placed on the number
of different vowel-letter clusters that are taught. These are limited to those
that show the highest degrees of predictability. These are clusters we have
shown that consistently demonstrate their utility as markers for the vowel
sound. In a large percentage of cases the second letter of the clusters *oa, ee,
ea, ai* signals that the first letter of the pair is given the free vowel sound.

Traditionally, phonics teachers have told children to remember,
"When two vowels go walking, the first one does the talking." Or, that "the
first vowel in a pair says its name, and the second is silent, or is a ghost
letter." These are inaccurate statements, of course. Moreover, we doubt if
such mnemonics are necessary if the phonogram approach to vowel sounds
is used. The teacher should be careful not to give pupils wrong information
as a memory aid. For example, the teacher *should not* "explain how the
second vowel, which is quiet, makes the first vowel say its own name" [Scott
& Thompson 1962, p. 261].

Teaching Level 6

Since the major goal of Level 6 is to further children's ability to perceive
phonograms, the activities are substantially the same as those given previously. The only new perceptual task demanded of children at Level 6 is to
see the vowel-letter cluster, plus a single consonant or consonant-letter
cluster, as in s*eat*, b*oil*, st*eal*, cl*own*, p*each*, gr*ound*. This activity requires
children to recognize single consonant letters, consonant-letter clusters, and
phonograms. Since they have done all this before, the only additional or new
task should be attending to a phonogram with *two* vowel letters.

Accordingly, the teacher is directed to the activities described in
earlier levels, especially 4 and 5, and is encouraged to adapt them for use
with these new phonograms. These activities involve the following:

1.   Using phonograms as rhyming words

2.   Adding single letters to phonograms

3.   Adding consonant clusters to phonograms

4.   Filling in phonograms when the initial consonant or consonant cluster
     is given: s_____ (*seat*), sp_____ (*spoil*)

5. Using phonogram cards, cards on which the phonograms of Level 6 are written, for children to signal which phonogram is heard in words read or written by the teacher

6. Identifying words that have an indicated phonogram and putting these into lists

7. Marking phonograms in prepared copy that has many words spelled with vowel-cluster phonograms

8. Playing phonogram bingo

(Also see the appendix for descriptions of games that can be played with phonogram cards.) The plural forms and the possessive forms of the phonograms of Level 6 should also be demonstrated with pupils.

REFERENCES

Bailey, Mildred H. "Utility of Phonic Generalizations in Grades One through Six." *Reading Teacher,* 20(1967):413–418.

Burmeister, Lou E. "Usefulness of Phonic Generalizations." *Reading Teacher,* 21(1968):349–356.

Carrell, James, and Tiffany, William R. *Phonetics.* New York: McGraw-Hill, 1960.

Clymer, Theodore. "Utility of Phonic Generalizations in the Primary Grades." *Reading Teacher,* 16(1963):252–258.

Emans, Robert. "Usefulness of Phonic Generalizations Above the Primary Level." *Reading Teacher,* 20(1967):419–425.

Groff, Patrick. "A Phonemic Analysis of Monosyllabic Words." *Reading World,* 12(1972):94–103.

Hanna, Paul R., et al. *Phoneme-Grapheme Correspondences as Cues to Spelling Improvement.* Washington, D.C.: U.S. Office of Education, 1966.

Heilman, Arthur W. *Phonics in Proper Perspective.* Columbus: Charles E. Merrill, 1964.

Scott, Louise B., and Thompson, J. J. *Phonics.* St. Louis: Webster, 1962.

Wise, Claude M. *Applied Phonetics.* Englewood Cliffs, N.J.: Prentice-Hall, 1957.

13

TEACHING PHONICS: LEVEL 7

In Level 7 children are taught to recognize phonograms in which the vowel grapheme precedes *r*. These are phonograms where the letter *r* follows:

1. The free vowel /o/ as in *arm, part, park, carve;*

2. The checked vowel /e/ as in *care, scarce, hair, there, bear, their;*

3. The free vowel /ô/ as in *cord, door, score, four, war;*

4. The free vowel /ī/ as in *fire;*

5. /ûr/ as in *her, burn, nurse, fir, bird, worm, were, nerve, worse.*

Level 7 is concerned with "*r*-colored" vowel sound spellings. These are words with vowel sounds followed by *r* sounds. The *r* sound is affected by the vowel sound, although it may appear to be the other way around. As Claude Kantner and Robert West conclude, "We would not be far wrong if we think of *r* as being dragged all over the mouth cavity by the various sounds with which it happens to be associated. This means that different sounds that we recognize as *r* are sometimes produced by fundamentally different movements" [1960 p. 169]. This helps explain why linguists call *r* sounds *glides*. A glide sound is one in which the speech mechanism moves without interruption from the position of one sound to that of another. For example, the tongue moves all the time a vowel-*r* sound is being made.

Should the teacher of phonics demonstrate for children, for example, that the vowel sound in *arm* is the same as the vowel sound in *odd*? We think that this is neither appropriate nor necessary since it is not entirely accurate

information. For the purposes of describing a complete set of vowel phonemes for "Western" dialect we say these sounds are the same. It is obvious
that this is not entirely true. Most linguists would say that there is some
distinctive phonetic difference between these vowel sounds in *arm* and *odd*.
These are not phonemic differences, however. The substitution of one of
these two vowel sounds for the other in *arm* and *odd* would not give the
other word a new meaning. We are confident, therefore, that for the
purposes of *Phonics: Why and How* we can somewhat reduce the number of
sounds needed for this program (as given in the tables in Chapter 3.)

Letter *r* Phonograms

Letter *r* phonograms are singled out for special treatment because of the
variant nature of the grapheme-phoneme correspondences that they exemplify. Note above the number of different spellings for /e/ +r and /ûr/.

It can be seen, too, that no distinction is made in "Western" dialect
between the vowel sounds in

there	/er/	and	*end*	/end/
arm	/orm/	and	*odd*	/od/
ear	/ir/	and	*in*	/in/

Sound-Spellings of Letter *r* Phonograms

Some attempts have been made to study the relationship of vowel-*r* sounds
and spellings. Theodore Clymer [1963], Mildred Bailey [1967], and Robert
Emans [1967] say, respectively, that 78, 86, and 82 percent of the elemen-
tary-grade words they studied were spelled to follow this rule: "The *r* gives
the preceding vowel a sound that is neither long nor short." Remember,
phoneticians disagree that this is a "rule" of pronunciation (cf p. 37). This
would imply that the way to teach these sound-spelling correspondences
would be first to have taught children the so-called "long" and "short"
vowel sounds and then to teach them to realize that the vowel sounds before
r are neither "long" nor "short."

It is not possible for us to use these rules for our program of phonics,
however, since phoneticians object, and because the terms *long* and *short*
"are nothing more nor less than conventional misnomers" [Lefevre 1970, p.
102]. Not using accepted linguistic designations for these sounds leads
Emans, for example, to say that the first vowel sound in *certainly* is not
"short" or "long," but the last vowel sound in *insecure* is. Linguists would
say that the former vowel sound is an *r*-colored vowel or a stressed syllabic

TABLE 19. PREDICTABILITY OF VOWEL-*r* SPELLINGS

Sound	Spelling	Percent	Sound	Spelling	Percent
/ûr/	er	40	/er/	ar	29
	ur	26		are	23
	ir	13		air	21
	Total	79		ere	15
				Total	88
/or/	ar	89	/ir/	er	32
	are	5		ear	25
	Total	94		eer	18
				ere	14
				Total	89

Source: Hanna et al. [1966].

/r/ (ûr). The latter sound they call a diphthong. Should we gather that what is meant by "long" and "short" is this distinction: *r*-colored vowel vs. diphthong? Apparently not, for Clymer says the vowel sound in *horn* follows the above rule, while the vowel sound in *wire* does not. Both of these vowel sounds are diphthongs. The confusing nature of the information from Clymer, Bailey, and Emans is readily apparent.

We must turn, instead, to data that indicate the percent of spellings in words given to the sounds /ûr/, /er/, /or/, and /ir/. These are as shown in Table 19.

If the child is taught to recognize the vowel-*r* phonograms that involve these different spellings, the teacher can be confident that almost all the spellings of the indicated sounds will be covered. And this can be done without teaching a child the wrongly applied names, "long" and "short" vowel sound.

We examined the peculiarities of the sound-spelling correspondences of the vowel sound followed by an /r/ sound and, sometimes, a marker *e* in high-frequency monosyllabic words [Groff 1972]. We found 9 different vowel-*r* sounds, but 5 of them accounted for 95 percent of these words. These were the sounds /ôr/, /ûr/, /or/, /er/, and /ir/. Table 20 shows the percent of times each of these sounds is represented in the total group of

TABLE 20. NINE VOWEL-*r* SOUNDS AND THEIR SPELLINGS

Sound	Percent	Examples of Spellings
/ôr/	28	*roar, coarse, more, born, four, source, door, war*
/ûr/	25	*her, bird, burn, nurse, worse, word, were, heard*
/or/	21	*barn, large, heart*
/er/	11	*hair, heir, care, bear, there*
/ir/	10	*deer, pier, fierce, here, dear*
Others	5	*fire, choir, cure, poor*

TABLE 21. PREDICTABILITY OF SOUND-SPELLING
CORRESPONDENCES OF VOWEL-*r* WORDS

Spelling	Sound	As in	Percent Occurrence	Exceptions
ar	/or/	barn	89	quart, war, warm, warn
or	/ôr/	born	82	word, world, worm, worth
ir	/ûr/	bird	100	
ar-e	/er/	care	71	charge, large, starve
ear	/ir/	dear	50	heard, learn, bear, heart
or-e	/ôr/	more	91	worse

vowel-*r* spellings and gives examples of the different spellings used to represent each sound.

The most frequently occurring spellings and the degree to which they predictably represent the indicated sounds in monosyllabic words (Percent Occurrence) is shown in Table 21.

Other correspondences which have relatively low frequencies of occurrence in high-frequency monosyllabic words, but which have 100 percent predictability, are shown in Table 22.

The tables indicate which of the "*r*-colored" vowel sound-spellings should be taught. As with other sound-spelling relationships, we would suggest that the order in which these be taught correspond with how frequently these sounds occur in high-frequency words and the predictability of their spellings. As the tables imply, this is difficult to do for the "*r*-colored" vowel sound-spellings.

This order is the best that can be determined:

1. /ûr/ as in *her, bird*

2. /ôr/ as in *born*

3. /or/ as in *barn*

4. /ôr/ as in *more*

5. /er/ as in *care, hair*

6. /ir/ as in *dear, here*

TABLE 22. VOWEL-*r* SOUND-SPELLING
CORRESPONDENCES WITH 100 PERCENT PREDICTABILITY

Spelling	Sound	As in	Spelling	Sound	As in
air	/er/	hair	ier, ier-e	/ir/	pier/fierce
er	/ûr/	her	oar, oar-e	/ōr/	roar/coarse
eer	/ir/	deer	oir	/ïr/	choir
eir	/er/	heir	ur	/ûr/	burn
ir-e	/ïr/	fire			

Teaching Level 7

The activities for developing this perception of vowel-*r* phonograms can precede much as was described for other phonograms in Level 4. These activities can be seen to involve the following:

1. Using phonograms as rhyming words

2. Adding single letters to phonograms

3. Adding consonant clusters to phonograms

4. Filling in phonograms when the initial consonant or consonant cluster is given: f_____ (*farm*), sp_____ (*spark, spare*)

5. Using phonogram cards on which the phonograms of Level 7 are written, for children to signal which phonogram is heard in words read or written by the teacher

6. Identifying words that have the indicated phonogram, and putting these into lists

7. Marking phonograms in prepared copy that has many words spelled with the vowel-*r* combination

8. Playing phonogram games (see appendix)

REFERENCES

Bailey, Mildred H. "Utility of Phonic Generalizations in Grades One through Six." *Reading Teacher*, 20(1967):413–418.

Clymer, Theodore. "Utility of Phonic Generalizations in the Primary Grades." *Reading Teacher*, 16(1963):252–258.

Emans, Robert. "Usefulness of Phonic Generalizations Above the Primary Level." *Reading Teacher*, 20(1967):419–425.

Groff, Patrick. "A Phonemic Analysis of Monosyllabic Words." *Reading World*, 12(1972):94–103.

Hanna, Paul R., et al. *Phoneme-Grapheme Correspondences as Cues to Spelling Improvement*. Washington, D.C.: U.S. Office of Education, 1966.

Kantner, Claude E., and West, Robert. *Phonetics*. New York: Harper & Row, 1960.

Lefevre, Carl A. *Linguistics, English, and the Language Arts*. Boston: Allyn & Bacon, 1970.

14

TEACHING PHONICS: LEVEL 8

In Level 8 children are taught to recognize monosyllabic words as *open syllables*. Open syllables are one-vowel words that end in free-vowel phonemes. Table 23 gives (1) spellings of vowels found in such open-syllable words, (2) the sounds they represent, (3) a typical word in which the spelling is found, (4) the number of open-syllable, high-frequency monosyllabic words in which this spelling is found [Greene 1955], and (5) the percent of occurrence the given spelling-sound relationship represents. In other words, when children see *a* in an open-syllable, high-frequency monosyllabic word, they will always read this as /o/. As can be seen in Table 23, the only spellings for which there are more than one pronunciation each are *ew, ow,* and *ey*.

In the first stage of Level 8, six open syllables are taught. Given below are the spellings for the open syllables that occur most frequently in monosyllabic words. These represent, with 100 percent predictability, single vowel sounds (except *ow,* which represents /ou/ 72 percent of the time). These spelling-sound correspondences are as follows:

1. *aw* for /o/, as in s*aw*

2. *ay* for /ā/, as in pl*ay*

3. *e-ee* for /ē/, as in b*e* and b*ee*

4. *ew-ue* for /o͞o/, as in bl*ew* and bl*ue*

5. *ow-o* for /ō/, as in l*ow* and g*o*

6. *y* for /ī/, as in m*y*.

TABLE 23. PREDICTABILITY OF SPELLINGS OF OPEN-SYLLABLE VOWELS

Spelling	Sound	As in	Number	Percent Occurrence	Exceptions
a	/o/	ha	3	100	
aw	/o/	paw	7	100	
ay	/ā/	bay	17	100	
e/ee	/ē/	be/bee	13	100	
ea	/ē/	sea	3	100	
i	/ē/	ski	1	100	
ie	/ī/	die	4	100	
igh	/ī/	high	1	100	
o	/ō/	go	3	100	
oo	/o͞o/	too	2	100	
oe	/ō/	toe	2	100	
oh	/ō/	oh	1	100	
ou	/o͞o/	you	1	100	
owe	/ō/	owe	1	100	
oy	/oi/	boy	3	100	
u	/o͞o/	flu	1	100	
ue	/o͞o/	true	3	100	
uy	/ī/	buy	2	100	
wo	/o͞o/	two	1	100	
y	/ī/	my	10	100	
ew	/o͞o/	blew	10	83	(sew, few)
ow	/ō/	low	13	72	(cow, how, now, plow, vow)
ey	/ā/	grey	2	67	(key)

At the second stage of Level 8, open-syllable spelling-sound correspondences that occur with high predictability but with relatively infrequent occurrence are taught. The following spelling-sound correspondences occur with 100 percent predictability in high-frequency, open-syllable monosyllabic words. For example, all words like *ma* and *pa* have the *a*-/o/ correspondence; all ending in *ie* are given the /ī/ sound.

1. *a* pronounced as /o/, as in h*a*

2. *ea* and *i* pronounced as /ē/, as in s*ea* and sk*i*

3. *ie, igh,* and *uy* pronounced as /ī/, as in d*ie*, h*igh*, and b*uy*

4. *oe, oh,* and *owe* pronounced as /ō/, as in t*oe, oh,* and *owe*

5. *oo, ou, u,* and *wo* pronounced as /o͞o/, as in t*oo*, y*ou*, fl*u*, and t*wo*

Open-Syllable Sound-Spelling Relationships

Open syllables are those that begin with a consonant sound and end with a vowel sound. It is important to know, too, that open syllables, "those with the vowel (open) arrest are by far the least common in isolated syllables" [Carrell & Tiffany 1960, p. 248]. They probably constitute less than 10 percent of this group. (For a discussion of how syllables begin and end see Chapter 5.) We [Groff 1972] found 8 percent of the high-frequency monosyllabic words [Greene 1955] were open syllables.

We are concerned in Level 8, as in all preceding levels, that words with predictable correspondences of sound and spelling be used to teach phonics. It has been determined that the previous lists of sounds and spellings represent predictable correspondences. For example, in the 17,000 most frequently used words where the spelling *ay* is seen in the final position in a syllable, it represents the sound /ā/ 98 percent of the time [Hanna et al. 1966].

Table 24 presents such data. The left side represents the sound-spelling correspondences that are taught at Level 8. Those on the right side will be taught later as children learn to analyze the structure of polysyllabic words in Level 10. Numbers in parentheses represent the rank order of occurrence of the spelling in the final position of syllables. For example, the spelling *a* occurs the most for the sound /ā/ in open syllables. All percents represent the degree to which the spelling represents the given sound in open syllables.

TABLE 24. PREDICTABILITY OF SOUNDS
GIVEN OPEN-SYLLABLE VOWEL SPELLINGS

Sound	Spelling	Percent of Occurrence	Sound	Spelling	Percent of Occurrence
/ā/	(2) *ay*	98	/ā/	(1) *a*	86
/ē/	(1) *e*	99			
	(2) *ee*	33			
/ī/	(2) *y*	99	/ī/	(1) *i*	71
/ō/	(1) *o*	87			
	(2) *ow*	83			
/o͞o/	(4) *ew*	90	/o͞o/	(1) *u*	88
	(6) *ue*	100		(2) *oo*	14
				(3) *o*	57
				(4) *ou*	69
/o/	(2) *aw*	68	/o/	(1) *au*	55
/ou/	(1) *ow*	61			
/oi/	(1) *oy*	100			

Teaching Open-Syllable Words

Teaching open-syllable words raises some new issues for the phonics teacher. Up to this point, pupils have been accustomed to working with words that ended in consonant letters or consonant-letter clusters (pa*t* or pa*th*), or consonant letter plus marker *e* (ca*ke*). They have been taught to see the vowel letters (*a, e, i, o, u*) as the first parts of phonograms, and then marker *e* as a signal letter.

Now pupils are presented with five new tasks:

1. To hear and see that vowel sounds and letters can be at the ends of words (*go, he*)

2. To realize that *y* and *w* at the ends of words do not represent the consonant sounds they have learned that they represent at the beginnings of words (*day, saw*)

3. To note that vowel letters can represent different vowel sounds than they have previously learned they represent (*pot-go*)

4. To understand that vowel-letter clusters can occur at the ends of words (*see*)

5. To sense the difference between marker *e* (at*e*) and the final letter *e* (h*e*) that represents a sound

In short, Level 8 reminds pupils that they must be versatile in application of vowel sound-spelling correspondences. From this point to the conclusion of their phonics program, pupils will increasingly become aware that the spelling system is not as simple as the preceding levels taught to them have indicated it to be. Children probably are aware of this, to some extent, since by this time they doubtless have learned to recognize some words that are not spelled according to the patterns given in the previous levels.

This point also may be an appropriate time for the phonics teacher again to determine how well children have mastered previous levels. And, if the teacher has not lately rearranged classroom groups for the teaching of phonics, this may be an especially timely point in the program to do it. If children have not mastered Levels 5 to 7, the probability for their success in Levels 8 to 10 especially is endangered. Rearranging groups of children for phonics lessons will give the teacher an opportunity to help the slower learners in the class to review and reinforce their understanding of the predictable spellings of words given at previous levels.

Because open syllables end only in free vowels, never in checked vowels, one's first impulse might be to teach the letters that represent these vowel sounds in isolation. It is suggested often that this be done (but wrongly, as we shall demonstrate). Children often are told that the vowel letter or letters, *ay*, for example, "say" the name of the letter *a*—/ā/. Following this, it is suggested children mark the long vowel sound in *ay* by crossing out the "silent" letter. They are asked how many vowel letters they see and how many vowel sounds they hear. Then, children are told to "blend" *pl* with *ay*, and say the word. The immature reader, who inevitably does this "blending" slowly, says a disyllabic word something like /po͞ohl+āē/, thus illustrating the impossibility of saying the sounds of phonemes unless they are said within a syllable.

Despite this linguistic truism there are authors of books on reading instruction who consistently violate this fundamental rule. A notable offender is Siegfried Engelmann [1969]. He suggests, for example, children be taught to read *rot* by saying /ûr/-/ûr/-/ûr/-/oh/-/oh/-/oh/-/to͞oh/. This pronunciation, let alone /ûrohto͞oh/, is far from the true pronunciation of the word *rot*, of course.

We have insisted so far in *Phonics: Why and How*, contrary to opinions such as Engelmann's, that all the teaching of sounds must be done within syllables so that the child learns to recognize these sounds in their true linguistic environment. Therefore, we must be opposed to any notion that letters representing vowel phonemes in open syllables be taught in isolation. Neither do we believe that the complicated process of isolating sounds, marking "silent" letters, "blending" sounds, and giving the "rule" is necessary to teach children to recognize open syllables. An effective, yet simpler, approach is as follows.

In Levels 1 to 7 free vowel phonemes have been heard and their graphemes seen in phonograms or closed syllables. The task of Level 8 is to give the child experiences in hearing free vowel phonemes, and seeing their graphemes, at the ends of words. The following examples illustrate how this is done for the vowel sounds in *he, play,* and *go*. Use these examples as models for teaching the remaining open-syllable vowel sound-spelling correspondences:

1. Say: "Listen to this word and tell me the last letter in it. *Seed.*" Children should readily come up with *d*, since they have had such activities for some time. Write *seed* on the board to prove they are right.

2. Say: "Do you think there is a *d* at the end of this word? *See.*" Children should say, "No." Write the word *see*. Under it write *seed* to show again that *d* was added to *seed*.

3. Say: "Let's look at these two words":

> *seen*
> *see*

"What are the words? What is added to *seen* that is not in *see?*"

4. "What are some words that rhyme with *see?*" Children should say *me, he, three, free, tree.* Write these. "What letter or letters do we see at the end of these words?"

5. Say: "Listen to these words. Hold up a finger if they end like *see.* Hold up a fist if they end like *seed.*"

    seen, me, free, seep, seem, he

6. Say: "Fill in the blank."

    I can s_____ him.
    Have you s_____ him?

    The remainder of the types of closed syllables can be taught the following ways:

7. Say: "Listen to this word. *My.* Does it rhyme with *sky?*" Write *my* and *sky* on the board.

8. Say: "What letter do these two words end with?" Write *dry* and *fry.*

9. Say: "Can you think of a word that rhymes with *my* and *sky?*" As children give the words, write them on the board so that *y* is lined up for each word.

10. Say: "Look at this word." Write *drop.* "Now let's take this off." Erase *op.* "Now let's add *y.* What word do we have?"

11. "Which consonant cluster can you add *y* to?" Write:

    sh_____ br_____ cr_____ fr_____ dr_____ bl_____

12. Say: "Listen to these three words. How many rhyme with *my?*" Write the words *dry-fry-free* on the board.

13. Say: "Listen to these words." Write the words *me-free-key-sea-row-ski* on the board. "Which one does not rhyme?"

14. Say: "Now look at these words." Write *we, key, tea, ski, low.* "Which one does not rhyme with the others?"

    Continue items 13 and 14 with combinations like these until the children readily hear and see the endings:

    day, they, jaw   by, toe, guy, die, high
    slow, go, oh, two, toe   grew, too, true, boy, who

15. Say: "Which are the two words that rhyme?"

    by-bay-be-blow-now-die

16. Give children cards on which the words *bay, he, snow, plow, drew,*

boy, draw are written. They say a few open syllables. Children hold up
a card if they think it rhymes with a word being said, e.g., Teacher: *lie.*
Child holds up *by* card.

REFERENCES

Carrell, James, and Tiffany, William. *Phonetics.* New York: McGraw-Hill,
1960.

Engelmann, Siegfried. *Preventing Failure in the Primary Grades.* New York:
Simon & Schuster, 1969.

Greene, Harry A. *New Iowa Spelling Scale.* Iowa City: The State University
of Iowa Press, 1955.

Groff, Patrick. "A Phonemic Analysis of Monosyllabic Words." *Reading
World,* 12(1972):94–103.

Hanna, Paul R., et al. *Phoneme-Grapheme Correspondences as Cues to
Spelling Improvement.* Washington, D.C.: U.S. Office of Education,
1966.

15

TEACHING PHONICS: LEVEL 9

In Level 9 children are taught to recognize certain closed syllables (phonograms) that occur infrequently. These phonograms are read as follows:

1. /ō/ before *l* as in *cold, colt.*

2. /ī/ before *gh* as in *night.*

3. /ī/ before *nd* as in *find.*

4. /o/ before *ll* and *l* as in *all, salt.*

Also taught at this level are words in which the marker *e* does *not* signal free vowels as in *edge, prince, chance, fence, budge* (exception: *solve*); and words in which /o͞o/ is represented by *u̇* as in *pull, put.*

The teaching of these words is delayed until Level 9 for two reasons: (1) words with these sound-spelling correspondences occur relatively infrequently, and (2) we want to introduce the single-vowel letter grapheme with these sounds at a time distant enough from the same graphemes with /a, e, i, o, u/ sounds so that children at Level 4 will not be presented with the contradictory material the Level 9 sound-spelling correspondences offer. That is, we hope children will have the correspondences of other levels firmly fixed in their minds before being given those of the present level. We contend that success in phonics depends on such a movement, that is, from the main body of correspondences to the correspondences that occur less frequently and are in conflict with rules taught previously.

At Level 9 children will learn that phonograms with VCC*e* spellings

TABLE 25. SOUND-SPELLING CORRESPONDENCES
IN HIGH-FREQUENCY MONOSYLLABIC WORDS

Correspondence	As in	Percent Occurrence
/ī/ before *ght*	*tight*	100
/ī/ before *ld-nd*	*child, bind*	100
/ō/ before *ld-lt-ll*	*cold, bolt, roll*	100
/ō/ before *st*	*host*	100
/o/ before *ll-lt*	*ball, salt*	100

also may be given the sounds /a, e, i, o, u/. Some of the features of these phonograms signal which vowel sounds they take. For the clusters *nc* (*chance*), *lv* (*twelve*), and *dg* (*hedge*), children will learn to give the above checked vowel sounds and /o/. The marker *e* here also can be said to indicate the /s/ sound for *c*, and the /j/ sound for *g*. Other postvowel consonant-letter clusters will signal the use of such free vowel sounds as *st* (*waste*), *th* (*bathe*). The cluster *ng* gives no such useful signal. Note the vowel sounds in *plunge, range,* and *cringe.*

It can be seen that the postvowel consonant-letter clusters in the words in Table 25 signal the free vowel sounds /ō, o, and ī/. They indicate where the *o* is read as /ō/, *a* as /o/, and *i* as /ī/. The instances in which this occurs are shown in Table 26.

Teaching Level 9

At this level the main task for the pupil is to recognize these additional phonograms. The general task, then, is the same as it was for previous levels when phonograms were taught. Accordingly, the activities for developing the perception of the phonograms at Level 9 can proceed in much the same way as described for Levels 4, 5, 6, and 7.

TABLE 26. POSTVOWEL CONSONANT
CLUSTERS AS SIGNALS FOR FREE VOWEL SOUNDS°

ght	ld	nd	lt	ll	st
__aght°°	*bald*	band	*halt*	*fall*	mast
__eght°°	held	bend	belt	fell	nest
tight	*mild*	*bind*	tilt	fill	mist
__oght°°	cold	bond	*bolt*	*roll*	*most*
__ught°°	__uld°°	fund	cult	gull	must

° Italicized words are taught at Level 9; the others at Level 4.

°° No such spelling.

In Level 9 the major emphasis should be placed upon impressing pupils with the need to be versatile in the reading of phonograms. In teaching Level 9 phonograms, therefore, it is desirable to have many activities in which pupils see a series of words that end with the same consonant-letter cluster, for example, *ll*, and that have the same spelling pattern, *CVCC*, but where certain selected numbers of words represent the vowel sounds /a, e, i, o, u/ and others the vowel sounds /ō, o, ī/. This can be seen for the following:

mast	nest	mist	most	must	bank
fall	fell	fill	roll	gull	tax

Typical activities of this nature would be done by saying: "Let's read this list of words." (Use Level 9 words.) "Now, let's mark the phonograms in them. Can you think of a rhyming word for each of the words?"

Say: "Put *a, e, i, o, u* in the blank and read the word." Write m___st. Continue this with all the post-vowel consonant-letter clusters (except *ght*) in Level 9: *ld, nd, lt, ll, nk, x, xt.*

Finally, present the plural forms of all the words taught at Level 9.

III

The "How" of Phonics: Teaching Polysyllabic Words

16

THE SPECIAL PROBLEMS OF POLYSYLLABIC WORDS

In Levels 1 through 9 we have dealt exclusively with the use of one-syllable words. For the reasons given earlier, for a period of time a child's learnings of phonics are better accomplished with monosyllabic words than if both monosyllabic and polysyllabic words are used.

We now turn to the manner in which children should be taught to recognize the syllables in polysyllabic words. Before the specifics are given, however, it is necessary to discuss further the peculiar nature of these longer words. Especially, we need to describe here the particular problems the pupil faces in learning to recognize words of more than one syllable and, in general, how the teacher of phonics can deal effectively with these difficulties.

The Relative Difficulty of Monosyllabic Versus Polysyllabic Words

We separate polysyllabic words from monosyllabic words and advise they be taught in this last level of phonics teaching for a very fundamental reason. Polysyllabic words are harder to read and to spell. A survey of the pertinent evidence and comment on this matter [Groff 1975] convinces us, as it did Arthur Gates and Eloise Boeker [1923] more than fifty years ago, that "the length of a word" is a factor that "demonstrably influences the difficulty of learning" a beginning reader faces.

Other evidence of the relative difficulty of polysyllabic words comes from a study by Betty Berdiansky, Bruce Cronnell, and John Koehler [1969]. They calculated the total number of spelling-to-sound correspondence "rules" necessary to read one- and two-syllable high-frequency words, that is, words children comprehend. They found there were many additional single-letter "rules" (what sound a letter is given) needed to read two-syllable words that were not needed to read one-syllable words.

Table 27 shows that thirty-five rules can be said to be necessary to read all the single-vowel letters in one-syllable words. To read these same single-vowel letters in two-syllable words, an additional thirty-eight rules are required. (We have combined or eliminated some of the rules cited in this study. The number of rules we name, here and below, are the result of this recalculation.) Table 27 also shows that it is said, for example, the *a* is found in seven different patterns of spellings (single-syllable words), each of which influences how the *a* is pronounced:

1. *name*: *a* plus one consonant (C) and marker *e*

2. *sat*: *a* plus C

3. *cart*: *a* plus *r* and C

4. *ball*: *a* plus l(l)

TABLE 27. RULES NEEDED TO READ VOWEL
LETTERS IN ONE- AND TWO-SYLLABLE WORDS

Spelling-to-Sound Correspondence	Number of Rules Necessary in One-Syllable Words (One Per Word)	Number of Other Rules Necessary in Two-Syllable Words (One Per Word)
a-as sounded in	7 (name, sat, cart, ball, wad, war, paste)	8 (acre, baby, April, saddle, above, vary, separate, axle)
e-as sounded in	7 (here, set, edge, name, wives, herd, we)	6 (hero, zebra, hidden, create, different, clever)
i-as sounded in	5 (fine, sit, bird, find, high)	9 (title, pilot, migrate, hidden, office, onion, liar, aspirin, river)
o-as sounded in	9 (home, gorge, lot, horn, word, roll, off, go, won)	7 (notice, only, hockey, sailor, poem, licorice, novel)
u-as sounded in	4 (use, gum, guest, bull)	7 (burgler, unit, bugle, sudden, lettuce, ruin, nature)
y-as sounded in	3 (rhyme, myth, try)	1 (baby)
Total	35	38

5. w*a*d: *a* (said to represent a different vowel sound than heard in *ball*;
            not heard in the "Western" dialect of this book)

6. w*a*r: *a* plus *r*

7. p*a*ste: *a* plus CC and marker *e*

Then, it is said there are eight additional patterns of spelling, in one of
the syllables in two-syllable words, which also affect the pronunciation of *a*.
Similar "rules" as these, which are too lengthy to demonstrate here, have
been worked out for these additional eight spellings.

The number of other rules necessary to read the two-syllable words

TABLE 28. RULES NEEDED TO READ VOWEL CLUSTERS

Spelling-to-Sound Correspondences	Number of Rules Necessary in One-Syllable Words (One Per Word)	Number of Rules Necessary in Two-Syllable Words (One Per Word)
ai	1 (rain)	1 (captain)
ay	1 (day)	0
au	1 (cause)	0
aw	1 (cause)	0
ea	3 (each, deaf, earn)	0
ee	1 (feel)	0
ei	1 (rein)	1 (ceiling)
ew	1 (new)	0
ey	1 (they)	1 (money)
ie	2 (die, field)	1 (movie)
oa	1 (boat)	0
oe	1 (toe)	0
oi	1 (join)	0
oo	2 (boot, book)	0
ou	5 (count, young, group, fought, soul)	0
ow	2 (glow, now)	0
oy	1 (toy)	0
ue	1 (blue)	0
ui	2 (fruit, build)	0
Total	29	4

Adapted from Berdiansky, Cronnell, & Koehler [1969].

given here is, of course, different from that offered for the child to learn in *Phonics: Why and How*. The present text, for example, does not attempt to teach the child the schwa /ə/ sound. Nonetheless, Table 27 is a graphic example of the fact that the longer series of letters found in polysyllabic words create spelling contexts for vowel letters that are different in appearance from those for vowel letters in monosyllabic words. Doubtless these different contexts in polysyllabic words require that the child be taught some additional spelling-to-sound correspondences. It is doubtful, however, whether the number of these is as great as the list given by Berdiansky, Cronnell, and Koehler. *Phonics: Why and How* takes a more conservative view of the number needed. Table 28 shows that very few additional rules are needed to read vowel clusters in two-syllable words than are needed to read these in monosyllabic words.

As one would suspect from our previous discussions of consonants, only a very small number of additional rules are needed to read single-consonant letters and consonant clusters in two-syllable words than in one-syllable words (see Table 29).

TABLE 29. RULES NEEDED TO READ CONSONANT LETTERS

Spelling-to-Sound Correspondences	Number of Rules Necessary in One-Syllable Words (One Per Word)	Number of Other Rules Necessary in Two-Syllable Words (One Per Word)
b-as sounded in	2 (boy, climb)	0
c-as sounded in	2 (city, cat)	0
d-as sounded in	1 (dad)	0
f-as sounded in	1 (fat)	0
g-as sounded in	3 (gem, gave, get)	0
h-as sounded in	2 (home, hour)	0
j-as sounded in	1 (job)	0
k-as sounded in	2 (kill, know)	0
l-as sounded in	2 (like, yolk)	0
m-as sounded in	1 (man)	0
n-as sounded in	2 (no, sink)	0
p-as sounded in	1 (pot)	0
r-as sounded in	1 (run)	0
s-as sounded in	4 (sun, nose, house, wives)	0
t-as sounded in	1 (let)	1 (often)
v-as sounded in	1 (vase)	0
w-as sounded in	2 (wet, wrong)	0
x-as sounded in	1 (box)	0
y-as sounded in	1 (yet)	0
z-as sounded in	1 (zoo)	0
Total	32	1

Adapted from Berdiansky, Cronnell, & Koehler [1969].

Pronunciation rules for consonant-letter clusters divide themselves into two categories. In group 1 are rules for pronouncing these clusters in one-syllable words. There are no additional rules needed for pronouncing group 1 clusters in two-syllable words. Group 2 rules are needed for pronouncing these clusters in two-syllable words since the clusters do not appear in one-syllable words. The spelling-to-sound rules for these clusters only apply to two-syllable words. Table 30 shows consonant clusters and the number of rules (one per word) needed to pronounce them.

Richard Hodges' data [1968] also help confirm our reasoning that monosyllabic words are easier for young children to learn than polysyllabic ones. Hodges found that these shorter words are more predictable in their phoneme-grapheme correspondences than are the total 17,000 most-used words. For monosyllabic words he found simple phoneme-grapheme correspondences (the use of one grapheme to represent one phoneme) to occur 81 percent of the time. For the 17,000 words in general this fell to 73 percent. This seems to us one probable reason why, with beginning readers, as the length of words increases the number of those recognized decreases [Richard 1935; Gates & Boeker 1923]. Garrett Richard says that practical experience shows that shorter words are easier to recognize.

Richard Bloomer's study arrived at substantially the same conclusion for spelling. He found that the best predictor of spelling difficulty among the variables tested appears to be length of the word [1956]. We found the spelling difficulty of the polysyllabic words in the *New Iowa Spelling Scale*

TABLE 30. RULES NEEDED TO PRONOUNCE
CONSONANT CLUSTERS

Group 1	Group 2
ch 2 (chip, ache)	*bb* 1 (bubble)
ck 1 (kick)	*cc* 1 (accuse)
ff 1 (off)	*dd* 1 (hidden)
gg 1 (egg)	*le* 1 (little)
gh 1 (high)	*mm* 1 (summer)
ll 1 (fill)	*nn* 1 (funny)
ng 1 (song)	*pp* 1 (apple)
ph 1 (phone)	*rr* 1 (hurry)
qu 1 (quick)	
ss 1 (mess)	
sh 1 (show)	
tt 1 (mitt)	
tch 1 (match)	
th 3 (thin, they, bathe)°	
wh 1 (when)	
zz 1 (buzz)	

Adapted from Berdiansky, Cronnell, & Koehler [1969].
° Need not be taught as different rule.

[Greene 1955] to be approximately twice that of monosyllabic words listed.

George Spache's conclusion that "the length of a word [in reading] is immaterial in your ability to learn it and retain it" [1970, p. 96] must be interpreted with this previous evidence in mind. It appears that Spache bases his opinion in part on findings, such as those reported by Melvin Howards [1964], that monosyllabic words have many meanings attached to them, while this is not the case for polysyllabic words. On the basis of this probability Howards contends that "it may be more efficacious to teach [the meaning of] longer words and words from the sciences than it is to teach little 'easy' words" [p. 381].

While it is indisputable that polysyllabic words generally have fewer denotations than do monosyllabic words,[1] it does not follow, necessarily, that they should be used in beginning phonics to replace shorter words. We have indicated our belief in the importance of utilizing children's spoken language in phonics (as nearly as possible) so as to neutralize problems of word meanings. Thus, for instance, the phonics teacher would use the term *bank* only in a context that is familiar to the pupils. If this is done, then Howards' argument for using polysyllabic words evaporates. Furthermore, his idea that word-structure analysis skills are easier to apply than simple phoneme-grapheme rules, or phonogram rules, is dubious, especially since it is based on the notion that "the meanings of the root and prefix [of a polysyllabic word] can be taught quickly with good transfer to many derivative words" [1964, p. 381]. Actually, there is no evidence that this is the case [Groff 1972].

The /ə/ in Polysyllabic Words

It is apparent from Tables 29 and 30 that one major cause of the additional rules needed to read two-syllable words, versus one-syllable words, is the schwa sound /ə/. It has been shown that the schwa sound /ə/ can be spelled twenty-two different ways [Hanna et al. 1966]. Our objection to teaching about the /ə/ is based on more than this information alone, however, since nine other vowel phonemes are spelled in an above average (average: 12 ways) number of ways [Hanna]. Our argument against teaching the /ə/ is based, instead, on the conclusion that knowledge about the /ə/, which is applied when reading certain syllables in polysyllabic words, can be inferred by the pupils—*if they are well-rooted in all the other aspects of phonics used to read one-syllable words.*

---

[1] Only about one third of the 500 most frequently used words are polysyllabic. Yet, these 500 words are said to have over 14,000 dictionary definitions. See William V. Haney, *Communication: Patterns and Incidents* (Homewood, Ill.: Irwin, 1960), p. 48.

In learning to read one-syllable words, children have learned all the vowel sound-spelling relationships (except those of the /ə/). At this point (or all along the way), rather than to teach them that they will no longer be able to depend on their hard-earned knowledge of vowel sound-spelling relationships, another stratagem is employed.

This is to encourage children to use their single-syllable vowel phonics knowledge to infer (to make intelligent, linguistic guesses) about unknown words. For example, suppose pupils face the unknown word *juvenile*. Their knowledge of predictable single-syllable phonics rules would tell them this is probably pronounced /juvenīl/. This pronunciation obviously would not result in a recognizable word. Now, their phonics knowledge directs children to try /jyo͞ovenīl/.

As will generally be the case with such words, we maintain, the pronunciation /jyo͞ovenīl/ is close enough to the American pronunciation of this word, /jyo͞ovənəl/, that children can at this point correctly match their reading pronunciation with the correct pronunciation of the word, and thereby understand the meaning of the string of letters, *juvenile*.

Frederick Brengelman [1970] has provided further insight into the spelling of polysyllabic words where the rules of stress reduction (the rules for spelling /ə/) must apply:

> It is clear that our spelling of polysyllables is not based on their "surface" or actual pronunciation. In terms of generative grammar, our spelling is a representation of a higher level than what we actually hear. . . . Our spelling of words other than stressed monosyllables thus seems to be designed to keep morphemes as recognizable as possible. This, of course, explains the use of g for both /g/ and /j/ in *analog* and *analogy*. It also explains why a syllable such as /šən/ in words such as *distortion, Grecian, coercion, mission,* and *shun* is spelled in these various ways . . . [pp. 131–132].

Syllabication

The previous illustrations demonstrate that the /ə/ sound (the free, less-accented vowel) occurs in polysyllabic words. Monosyllabic words use accented vowel sounds. The problem shown here, of children trying to read *juvenile* as an unknown polysyllabic word, cannot be solved merely by having them give all vowel letters a certain vowel sound. Children can learn to read polysyllabic words well, though, if they are shown how to break up these words, syllabicate them, into units they can pronounce and then recombine into recognizable words.

The advice teachers have been given over the years as to the syllabication of words has been faulty, unfortunately. For example, most phonics writers have endorsed William Gray's notions that the teacher should "lead pupils to formulate the generalization that when the first vowel letter in a [polysyllabic] word is followed by one consonant letter, the first syllable usually ends with the vowel letter" [Gray 1948, p. 214]. This would require the vowel in this first syllable to be "long"—/ā, ē, ī, ō, ū/—according to Gray. Gray's rule is misleading, however. We found 247 polysyllabic words among the 1,000 most frequently used words [Kuchera & Francis 1967] in which the first vowel letter of a word was followed by one consonant letter. But only 55, or 23 percent, of these 247 words were pronounced according to Gray's rule, e.g., *ba-sis, re-cent, wri-ting, mo-ment, fu-ture*. Moreover, it would be doubtful for several reasons that one would identify the first syllable of some of these 55 words in the way the Gray rule would require, e.g., *e-ven, u-nited, o-pen, sto-ry, li-kely, sta-tement*.

Gray's second syllabication rule says, "Call attention to the double consonant following the first vowel in words like *rabbit*. Then divide the words into syllables; that is *rab-bit*. Lead pupils to note that in each case the first of the double consonants is at the end of the first syllable" [p. 213]. This is also wrong. We have previously noted, in Chapter 5, the erroneous basis on which Gray rests his second notion, that the proper way to syllabicate *rabbit* is *rab-bit*. This is dictionary syllabication, which we have shown has little relationship to true syllabication. Such a dictionary division represents nothing more than some anonymous typesetter's decision as to how to break this word at the end of a line of print.

The phonogram syllabication of this word would be *rabb-it*. This phonogram syllabication is better for several reasons. One, the child has had experience with monosyllabic phonograms that end with double consonants (*will*). So, *rabb* of *rabbit* would be seen as another of these. Two, the frequency of the pronunciation of the first vowel grapheme of double-consonant disyllabic words (*batter, better, bitter, dollar, butter*) as /a, e, i, o, u/ is comparable for closed syllables in general. We calculated from a list of high-frequency words of this nature [Greene 1955][2] that the single-vowel graphemes represented these sounds the indicated percent of the time:

a as /a/—66 percent, *e* as /e/—96,

$$i \text{ as } /i/—100, o \text{ as } /o/—67, u \text{ as } /u/—83.$$

The 66 percent for the *a* as /a/ includes only words with this spelling: C(C)aC(C). If we include words like *accord* or *affair,* the percentage drops to 44. Three, the syllabication *rabb-it* is preferable since it is in accord with the kind of knowledge about graphemes that the phonics teacher should pass along to pupils. Children should be taught that sometimes two letters constitute a single grapheme. Thus, the five graphemes in rabbit are

---

[2]Excluding plurals, past tense inflections, and compound words.

r-a-bb-i-t. If one taught children to divide the word as *rab-bit* and split the grapheme *bb*, children would be wrongly led to add a phoneme (and a grapheme) to the word. They would be led to say /*rab-bit*/ and to count six graphemes. All of this unnecessarily complicates, confuses, and misteaches the basic idea of phonics, that is, that certain graphemes represent certain sounds, and one should learn to recognize them as such.

In short, we advise the phonics teacher *not* to teach children to syllabicate words with the mistaken rules that previous writers of phonics have offered for this purpose. While we would agree with Arthur Heilman that "the ability to break words into syllables is a very important word-analysis skill" [1964, p. 78], the phonics teacher would be in error to accept Heilman's (that is, Gray's) rules for doing this with disyllablic words. These are (1) to divide syllables between double consonants, or between two consonants (*hap-pen, bas-ket*), and (2) to divide syllables so that a single consonant between vowels usually goes with the second vowel (*fa-mous, ci-vic*).

We have seen how this advice is wrong for words like *happen*. It is also erroneous for words like *basket*. In the identification of phonograms, children are taught from the first to read the vowel letter of the phonogram and as many consonant letters as there are to follow. They read VC(*at*); VCC(*ask, ell*); VCCC(*atch*); and phonograms that include the marker *e*. The division of *bask-et* for *basket* is a logical continuation of this practice. In short, in a polysyllabic word pupils read for a phonogram a vowel grapheme plus all the consonant letters up to the next vowel grapheme, which begins a new phonogram. This is conditioned, of course, by affixes and impermissible combinations of consonants (*ex*pert, earne*stly*, ca*nv*as, gover*nm*ent). By trying to pronounce the impermissible combinations in phonograms, children discover where these affect the application of the basic phonogram rule given in *Phonics: Why and How*. This basic phonogram rule obviates the need for another rule that some phonics writers think should be taught, that is, do not divide consonant digraphs (*ch, th*, etc.).

It appears to us that the data on the frequency with which the /a, e, i, o, u/ sounds occur for single-vowel graphemes in stressed syllables also discredit the second rule that is generally given: "When a consonant occurs between two vowels, syllabication usually occurs before the consonant." We have shown that it is preferable to teach children to read such words (*direct, marine, water*) according to our phonogram rules so that they will be more successful in reaching a reasonable approximation of the sound of the word. Then, if children are taught to shift to /ā, ē, ī, ō, yo͞o/ if one of the previous groups of sounds does not work, they should be able to read practically all polysyllabic words. Again, no special or extra teaching is necessary to do this. Children merely continue to practice the phonogram recognition rules learned for monosyllabic words.

In addition, the notion that words should be syllabicated in the V-CV pattern obviously is not based on linguistic evidence. To be a rule, the syllabication V-CV would have to be based on a high incidence of the free vowel sound for the first vowel in words spelled V-CVC. However, our analysis of the high-frequency disyllabic words [from Greene 1955] did not prove this to be the case. Only 78 (28 percent) of the 279 such words that we studied[3] had this correspondence. Examples of this correspondence would be:

VCVC   VCVC

bacon   grateful

Examples of the exceptions to this correspondence would be:

VCVC   VCVC   VCVC

above   before   canal

Thus the syllabication V-CVC cannot be supported by the evidence of the kinds of vowel sounds found for the first vowel letter in these spellings.

The remaining rule generally given by previous writers of phonics reads: "Whenever *le* ends a word and is preceded by a consonant, the last syllable consists of the consonant and the *le* (*ta-ble, mid-dle, peo-ple*)" [Dechant 1969, p. 123]. We have indicated so far our dissatisfaction with the dictionary syllabication in the examples that are given here. Emerald Dechant is right, nonetheless, in stressing the need for the child to be observant of the *le* spelling.

As we have previously noted, /l/ (and /m, n, r/) may be said to assume the function of a vowel in the unstressed syllable of certain words, for example, *chasm, button, father, beetle.* The sound /l/ can serve as a separate syllable in such words as *kettle* and *handle,* hence the name given to it: syllabic /l/. In *beetle* it is usual to produce the /l/ without any other speech sound made between it and the /t/ sound. To make this syllabic /l/, the position of the tongue is such that when the preceding sound is made, all the speaker has to do is drop the sides of the tongue so that the breath for /l/ escapes at the sides of the tongue. Since the breath used for /l/ escapes sideways over the tongue, this phoneme is called the *lateral* sound.

The *le* spelling survives from the period of Old English (about A.D. 450–1100) when the use of a final *e* in spelling was more common than today. For example, in Old English (OE), adverbs were regularly made by adding a final "weak" *-e* to the corresponding adjective. A remnant of this can be seen in our modern expression *Stand fast!* (not *fastly*). In OE this was *Stand faste!* So those who resist modern social admonitions against saying *Go slow,* or *Come quick,* actually have the history of the language on their side.

---

[3] We did not include disyllabic words with plural inflections, those in the past tense, nor those with *ing* or *ly* endings.

The phonics teacher should also realize that the *le* spelling does not occur frequently. In his analysis of over 40,000 syllables in the 17,000 most frequently used words, Paul Hanna [1966] found only 651 syllables with this spelling. The *le* spelling was found at the end of the syllable in all cases except one. In a list of the 5,500 most commonly used words [Greene 1955] we found only 37 disyllabic words ending in *le* (no monosyllabic words had this spelling).

This evidence about the *le* spelling leads to the conclusion that teaching about the *le* spelling that involves the establishment of some rule of syllabication is wrong. A more sensible way to deal with the *le* spelling is simply to teach it the same way that certain affixes are taught. That is, children should be conditioned through activities designed for this purpose to visualize the *le* as standing alone, and *not as part of a syllable involving any letters that precede it*. In brief, the advice to syllabicate words like *bundle* as *bun-dle* is not helpful in recognizing this word. A better syllabication to teach is *bund-le*. Here children apply the basic phonogram rules learned earlier, while remembering that *le* stands separately at the end of words.

Should the Meaning of Affixes Be Taught?

It is readily apparent to mature readers that affixes (prefixes and suffixes) occur often in polysyllabic words. Because of this pupils doubtless should be taught to identify the affixes, as such, in words. This knowledge will enable pupils to speed up and improve the accuracy of their syllabication of polysyllabic words.

A pertinent question regarding the teaching of affixes as a means of breaking polysyllabic words into their separate syllables, however, is whether it is worthwhile to teach children the "meaning" of affixes. For example, should the phonics teacher instruct children in the fact that these affixes have the indicated meanings?

Prefixes		Suffixes	
a-:	against, without, of, to	*-er:*	one who
ab-:	from, away	*-or:*	doer
com-:	together	*-ent:*	state of
pre-:	before	*-tion:*	state of
pro-:	forward	*-able:*	able, like
re-:	backward, again	*-less:*	without

We surveyed the writings of over forty leading experts in reading and spelling as to their opinions on this matter [Groff 1972]. The majority of these authorities endorsed the notion of teaching the meanings of affixes.

They believe that such knowledge helps elementary school children (at least from the third grade upwards) to recognize words, to spell better, to develop larger vocabularies, or to be more critical readers. Moreover, some of these experts said the study of these meanings was intriguing fun for children.

The opponents of the idea either had no comment on the matter (damning it by no praise), or objected to it on logical or empirical grounds. The logical objection is typified by the remarks of Leo Schell:

> The obvious problem is that these prefixes have meaning to an elementary school child only when there is a known base word. Even though in Latin these prefixes were attached to base words, over the years these bases have lost their independent standing and the prefixes have become known as "absorbed prefixes." In such words, knowledge of the meaning of the prefix is virtually worthless.
>
> Suffixes present difficulties in two ways. Many suffixes have multiple meanings; e.g., -*ment* may mean act, condition, or concrete instance. To use the suffix to help derive the word's meaning, the reader must (1) recall these three meanings, (2) choose the appropriate one, and (3) apply this meaning to the base form—a prodigious task for most elementary school pupils. Surely, there must be a *more efficient* procedure [1967, pp. 133–134].

While there continues to be favorable opinion as to the value of teaching the meanings of affixes, and elaborate programs even have been designed for this purpose [Dale, O'Rourke, & Bamman 1971], there is no relevant empirical data to support the notion. Lois Otterman's study [1955] on this problem showed that even with extra time given to such teaching to seventh graders, learning the meanings of prefixes did not significantly affect the reading skills of these children. One must ask, too, what if her control group had been given, for example, equal extra instruction (which they did not get) in a nonaffix reading vocabulary building program? In short, Otterman missed a good opportunity to compare these two approaches. And, by not giving her control group equal instructional time, Otterman committed an unpardonable research sin, according to modern standards. This "card-stacking" in favor of her experimental group renders her findings dubious, indeed. Thus, we can question the fact that her program even is a good way to develop spelling gains. In fact, Otterman's evidence (all we could find) suggests that lessons designed to build up children's reading vocabularies or spelling skills should not take up time with the learning of the meanings of affixes.

This information that the teaching of the meanings of affixes does not result in significantly larger gains in reading adds support to our advice *not* to teach the common open syllable prefixes *be-, de-, pre-, pro-,* and *re-*. If there were evidence that knowledge of the meanings of these prefixes was of use in reading, one would be tempted to teach the prefixes, even though the pronunciation of the vowel letter in these prefixes (in disyllabic words) is the free vowel sound /ē or ō/ only 4 percent of the time. The fact that such knowledge brings no such special gains confirms our decision that to teach these prefixes as prefixes is time-wasting and superfluous.

Some Limitations of Phonics
for Polysyllabic Words

Carol Chomsky [1970] broaches the seldom considered question as to whether there is an order or sequence in which polysyllabic words should be taught. In a partial answer she notes that for the skilled reader *nation* and *nationality* are not different words in the sense that *nation* and *notion* are. She rightly observes that the reader recognizes at some point (not yet determined by research) that the second of the above pair of words, *nationality,* is a variant form of *nation.* Accordingly, the reader may not have to read all the parts of *nationality* in, for example, a sentence like *What is that man's nationality? What is that man's nation?* gives almost the same degree of meaning. There are many such examples that one could work out—for example, *The parents were anxious about the sick child* versus *The parents had anxiety about the sick child.*

Thus, in addition to teaching words in groups such as *notion, motion, nation, ration, cushion, pension* to teach the suffix (*ion, tion*), the phonics teacher should also teach such groupings as *apply, applies, applied, applying, applicant, application, applicable, applicator, applique, appliance, applicative, applicatory.*

We believe this to be one thing Noam Chomsky calls for when he says, "It may very well be that one of the best ways to teach reading is to enrich the child's vocabulary, so that he constructs for himself the deeper representations of sound that correspond so closely to the orthographic forms" [1970, p. 18]. The point here is that although children may not be able to attach a single peculiar meaning to each of these above derivations of *apply* as they see them in print, being able to recognize *apply* teaches them that all the other eleven forms are connected to the meaning of *apply.* Having such information, children can "read" several of the variant forms of *apply* without having to totally process their affixes. It should be apparent that this is quite the opposite tack from trying to teach children the meaning of all the affixes involved in *apply* and its eleven variant forms. The dubious rationale for this latter procedure is that children can presumably deduce the meanings of the variant forms by employing knowledge of the meanings of affixes. There is no evidence [Groff 1972] this can be done effectively, however, nor even that one could take the time to do it in reading. Instead, to learn to read *application,* for example, it is likely that children should be taught to note the "apply" part of *application*, and react to the slot in the sentence it fits (for the sake of meaning). Notice how this works:

1. He will   *apply*   for a job.
2. He will *make an application* for a job.

If children read the second sentence as *He will make an apply for a job*, they essentially have gained the meaning of the sentence.

More on the nature of this kind of useful linguistic guessing will be described in the chapter on context cues. For now, it can be seen that the silent reading of sentence 2 would be different from the oral reading of this sentence. That is, children may be able to read sentence 2 silently, but not orally, if by "read" we mean to understand the essential meaning of the sentence. The phonics teacher, who is fundamentally concerned with children's abilities to process written material phonologically, must concede that rapid silent reading involves the above kind of successful estimations of polysyllabic words, a way of reading that may not appear to be successful if a child is asked to read aloud, however.

It was also observed by Carol Chomsky that "good spellers, children and adults alike, recognize that related words are spelled alike even though they are pronounced differently. They seem to rely on an underlying picture of the word that is independent of its varying pronunciations" [1970, p. 303]. She confirms the idea that in learning to spell polysyllabic words, which are variant forms of another word, it is wise for children to think first of certain of these forms. Children should be first taught to spell the form that has the potentially confusable vowel sound in a stressed syllable, she says. For example, children should be taught to spell *preside* before *president*, since the second vowel sound in these words is more stressed in *preside* and less stressed in *president*. Therefore, to spell *president* children should think: *preside*. They can thus visualize that the second vowel sound in *president* will be spelled with *i*. This makes good sense. Accordingly, children should be taught to spell the words in the first column here before learning to spell those in the second column. The affected part is shown below in italics.

1.	2.
pres*i*de -----------	presid*e*nt
dem*o*cracy	dem*o*cratic
hist*o*rical	hist*o*ry
maj*o*rity	maj*o*r
criti*c*al	criti*c*ize
na*t*ive	na*t*ion
si*g*nature	si*g*n
sof*t*	sof*t*en

REFERENCES

Berdiansky, Betty, Cronnell, Bruce, and Koehler, John. *Spelling-Sound Relations and Primary Form-Class Descriptions for Speech-Comprehension Vocabularies of 6–9 Year-Olds.* Inglewood, Calif.: Southwest Regional Laboratory for Educational Research and Development, 1969.

Bloomer, Richard H. "Word Length and Complexity Variables in Spelling Difficulty." *Journal of Educational Research,* 49(1956):531–536.

Brengelman, Frederick H. "Dialect and the Teaching of Spelling." *Research in the Teaching of English,* 4(1970):129–138.

Chomsky, Carol. "Reading, Writing and Phonology." *Harvard Educational Review,* 40(1970):287–309.

Chomsky, Noam. "Phonology and Reading," *Basic Studies on Reading,* eds. Harry Levin and Joanna P. Williams. New York: Basic Books, 1970.

Dale, Edgar, O'Rourke, Joseph, and Bamman, Henry A. *Techniques of Teaching Vocabulary.* Palo Alto: Field Educational Publications, 1971.

Dechant, Emerald. *Linguistics, Phonics, and the Teaching of Reading.* Springfield, Ill.: Charles C Thomas, 1969.

Gates, Arthur I., and Boeker, Eloise. "Study of Initial Stages in Reading by Pre-School Children." *Teachers College Record,* 24(1923):469–477.

Gray, William S. *On Their Own in Reading.* Chicago: Scott, Foresman, 1948.

Greene, Harry A. *New Iowa Spelling Scale.* Iowa City: The State University of Iowa Press, 1955.

Groff, Patrick. "Long Versus Short Words in Beginning Reading." *Reading World,* 14(1975):277–289.

Groff, Patrick. "Teaching Affixes for Reading Improvement." *Reading Improvement,* 9(1972):28–30.

Hanna, Paul R., et al. *Phoneme-Grapheme Correspondences as Cues to Spelling Improvement.* Washington, D.C.: U.S. Office of Education, 1966.

Heilman, Arthur W. *Phonics in Proper Perspective.* Columbus: Charles E. Merrill, 1964.

Hodges, Richard W. "Phoneme-Grapheme Correspondences in Monosyllabic Words," *Forging Ahead in Reading,* ed J. Allen Figurel. Newark, Del.: International Reading Association, 1968.

Howards, Melvin. "How Easy Are 'Easy' Words?" *Journal of Experimental Education,* 32(1964):377–382.

Kuchera, Henry, and Francis, W. Nelson. *Computational Analysis of Present-Day American English.* Providence: Brown University Press, 1967.

Otterman, Lois M. "The Value of Teaching Prefixes and Root Words." *Journal of Educational Research,* 48(1955):611–616.

Richard, Garrett E. "The Recognition Vocabulary of Primary Pupils." *Journal of Educational Research,* 29(1935):281–291.

Schell, Leo M. "Teaching Structural Analysis." *Reading Teacher,* 21(1967):133–137.

Spache, George. "Reaction to Models of Perceptual Processes in Reading," *Theoretical Models and Processes of Reading,* eds. Harry Singer and Robert B. Ruddell. Newark, Del.: International Reading Association, 1970.

17

TEACHING POLYSYLLABIC WORDS

At this level children are taught to recognize the syllables in polysyllabic words, including those that

1. Are compound words, as *into, watchdog, playground, cowboy;*

2. Are inflected words, as *walking, dipped, running, ladies, judges, greatest, higher;*

3. Have common closed-syllable prefixes, as in *ab*sent, *ad*vise, *com*pel, *dis*patch, *en*tire, *ex*cite, *in*cline, *sub*mit, *un*like;

4. Have common closed-syllable suffixes, as in bank*er*, arm*or*, differ*ent*, descrip*tion*, discus*sion*, form*al*, enjoy*able*, develop*ment*, tight*ness*, light*en*, care*less*, care*ful*, desir*ous*, differ*ence*, ignor*ance*, fortun*ate*, defec*tive;*

5. Have common open-syllable suffixes, as in deep*ly*, deliver*y*, hones*ty;*

6. Do not have any of the above characteristics, but which follow the sound-spelling correspondences taught at previous levels.

Breaking Words into Parts

The identification of polysyllabic words requires children to break these longer words into manageable wholes or parts. There are several ways to do this.

1. With compound words like *cowboy* children should be taught to look for two words within the larger word. Paying attention to familiar words within words is much like the phonogram approach to word recognition previously learned.

2. The practice of finding "little words in big words" other than compound words has been equally praised and condemned. We analyzed high-frequency words to find the extent to which monosyllabic words (e.g., *it*) could be spoken as accented syllables in any bigger words without appreciably distorting the sound of the bigger word (e.g. *pen-penny*). We concluded this is possible 65 percent of the time [Groff 1973]. Accordingly, the practice of finding little words in bigger ones, with this stipulation in mind, does have some limited usefulness for phonics.

3. When monosyllabic words such as *walk* are inflected[1] to *walking* and *walked*, they become polysyllabic in the first case, but not in the second. To read such words as *walking* the beginning reader must recognize the familiar word *walk*, the familiar phonogram *ing*, and say the two as one. The same holds true, for example, for the inflected forms *faster* and *fastest*. For words that take a past-tense inflection, for example, *walked*, the application of the rules for phonogram recognition would lead children to give these inflected verbs an /ed/ pronunciation as in *walked* /wok-ed/. In short, they would say these verbs as disyllabic words, words of two syllables.

    Unfortunately, this generalization for pronouncing these past-tense words as disyllables does not hold for the majority of high-frequency verbs. Instead, one finds, when given the past-tense inflection, about 70 percent of these verbs do not become disyllabic words. For example, changing *bake* into the past tense form (*baked*) does not add a syllable to the word, /bāk/ as versus /bākt/. This merely adds a consonant sound /t/ to *bake*.

    This seems to complicate the matter of teaching children to recognize the majority of tense-inflected verbs. However, if children are taught to recognize one element of this inflectional system, this problem can be resolved. Thus, if a monosyllabic word ends in either of the sounds /t/ or /d/, it will become a disyllabic word when the inflection *ed* is added. If the word ends in other sounds, it will not become a disyllabic word. This rule is strengthened by the fact that 96 percent and 93 percent of the syllables which end in the sounds /d/

---

[1] By *inflected* we mean the addition of a suffix to a verb that does not change it from a verb to another part of speech. Notice, on the other hand, how the addition of *derivational* suffixes, *ness*, *en*, *ly*, changes the grammatical function of *light* (adjective): light*ness* (noun), light*en* (verb), light*ly* (adverb).

and /t/ are spelled *d* and *t* (*had, pat*) [Hanna et al. 1966]. Our analysis of high-frequency monosyllabic verbs reveals that 100 percent of these verbs have these correspondences: /d/-d and /t/-d.

4.   Some writers on phonics insist that to teach pupils to perceive the *s* and *es* inflections, they must be given exercises to develop the ability to "decide whether the *s* is pronounced as *s* or as *z*" [Dechant 1969, p. 107]. Dechant suggests the use of activities such as these in which the child indicates either *s* or *z*:

as   *his*

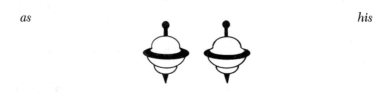

s or *z*   *s* or *z*   *s* or *z*

We contend such exercises should *not* be given. They are difficult and unnecessary. Normal children can adequately pronounce the /s/ and /z/ in the above words. They already have learned to discriminate well between these two sounds as they learned to listen to and speak words with these sounds. It is a waste of time, therefore, to take pupils through such activities. What pupils learning to read need is not activities to distinguish the /s/ and /z/ sounds, but rather activities that lead them to visually discriminate the *s* and *es* at the ends of words. The activities we have given for plurals of one-vowel words can be readily applied to polysyllabic words that end in *s* or *es*.

5.   Another problem regarding the past-tense inflection of monosyllabic verbs comes when the final consonant letter is doubled, as in *patted*. We have seen that the sound at the end of a verb will determine whether one pronounces it as a disyllable when the verb is given the past-tense inflection. This rule does not extend to the verbs whose final consonant letters are doubled when their inflected forms are spelled with *ed*. For example, in *pitted* and *pinned* we note that the first inflected word is pronounced /pit-əd/ and the second word /pind/. These pronunciations are signalled by the final consonant sound in *pit* and *pin*.

Notice, however, that in spelling the inflected forms the final *t* and *n* in verbs are doubled before *ed* is added. The doubling of the final consonant letters in verbs works, in certain cases, to aid the reader in the recognition of these words. We can see that different spellings for different words can help for this purpose:

bared—barred	moped—mopped	taped—tapped
bated—batted	pined—pinned	tubed—tubbed
hoped—hopped	raped—rapped	waded—wadded
mated—matted	robed—robbed	waged—wagged

The value of this contrastive spelling (C—CC) is largely lost, however, since about 80 percent of past-tense verb forms with doubled final consonant spellings would not present any reading problem if their final consonant were not doubled. For example, there appears to be no reason to double the final consonant letter of *wet* to write *wetted*, since there is no word, *wete*. That is, *weted* would not be confused with any other word. Then, for some inexplicable reason, the past-tense form of *bus* can be spelled either *bused* or *bussed*.

Nonetheless, the spelling rule for doubling a consonant letter at the end of a word is quite apparent: If a monosyllabic word ends in a single consonant letter that is directly preceded by a single vowel letter, the consonant letter is doubled when *ed*, or *ing*, is added. If children can remember this rule it will be very helpful for them in spelling these forms, of course.

6.   For the purposes of spelling, children should be given practice in seeing how the *y* at the end of certain polysyllabic words is changed to *i* before these words are given a plural inflection, a past-tense inflection, or other changes.

To spell these verbs children must be taught to recognize that the *y* is changed to *i*, for example, when the following are added:

es—abilit*ies*	*ment*—merri*ment*	*ful*—piti*ful*
ance—compli*ance*	*ness*—readi*ness*	*less*—penni*less*
ous—injuri*ous*	*er*—empti*er*	*est*—hungri*est*
ed—buri*ed*		

They must also realize that with some additions the change is *y* to *a*, as in occup*a*tion, memor*a*ble. Sometimes the addition is longer: *cation*—appli*cation; zation*—coloni*zation*.

7.   For words like *absent* children may see a familiar part, *sent*, and then apply their phonogram knowledge to read *ab*, a closed-syllable prefix. For words such as *excite*, children may have to depend more heavily on their skills of phonogram recognition since neither *ex* nor *cite* can be recognized as words. From the rules learned for these two phonograms, they will give the sounds /eks/ and /sīt/. This will function to give children a pronunciation for *excite* that should be close enough to the normal intonational pattern of this word to make it recognizable.

It is helpful here to recall the fact that a relatively few prefixes make up the great majority of those used. Russell Stauffer found that 15 prefixes account for 82 percent of all the prefixes to be found in a list of the most frequently used 20,000 words [1942]. These prefixes, in the order of their frequency, are as follows:

1. com-	4. un-	7. dis-	10. en-	13. sub-
2. re-	5. in-(into)	8. ex-	11. pro-	14. be-
3. ad-	6. in-(not)	9. de-	12. pre-	15. ab-

Of the 20,000 words studied by Stauffer, 24 percent had prefixes.

8. The common "open" syllable prefixes *be-, de-, pre-, pro-, re-* need not be taught. It is better to teach children to read these within phonograms. Accordingly, a child would read *before* as /bef-ôr/. The advantage is that no added or special instruction in these "open" prefixes need be given. Pupils merely apply the phonogram rules they have learned for monosyllabic words. Moreover, the pronunciation of *before* as a result of phonogram decoding is as close to its normal sound as if the free vowel sound were given, /bē-fôr/.

The opinions of linguists give us little help in deciding this. It is said that checked vowels (e.g., as heard in *recite*) *cannot* occur at the ends of morphemes [Kurath 1964]. Yet in our study of 138 high-frequency disyllabic words [Greene 1955] beginning with *be-, de-, pre-, pro-, re-*, we found only six (4 percent) of these words (*decent, prepaid, previous, program, recent, retail*) in which the vowel letter of the prefixes (*o, e*) represented the free vowel sound /ō, ē/. In all the other such words the prefix vowel letter is given some other sound. We estimate that this low percentage would obtain for the less-frequently used disyllabic words involving these prefixes.

We cannot totally accept the above opinion, since how could *re-* in *recall* (pronounced with a checked vowel /i/) not be a morpheme? It (*re-*) fits the standard definition of morpheme, that is, the "smallest meaningful units in the structure of the language . . . which cannot be divided without destroying or drastically altering the meaning . . ." [Gleason 1961, p. 53].

Another opinion that is of no help states that for two forms to be the same morpheme "they must have the same phonemic structure and the same lexical meaning" [Liebert 1971, p. 101]. Using this logic, the *re-* in *reread* /rē/ and *relive* /ri/ would be different morphemes. Obviously, this is not the case.

Accordingly, we come to our own conclusion as to how to teach the prefixes *be-, de-, pre-, pro-, re-*. Liebert describes the ofttimes conflicting and confusing aspects or sources for the analyses of morphemes. "Because of these sources of possible confusion, all 'conclusions' in morphemic analysis are considered tentative. Further analysis of the language may at any time upset some well-established hypothesis" [1971, p. 102]. We believe our decision for the teaching of the aforementioned prefixes to be the result of such an analysis.

9. The child accustomed to finding phonograms may read *before* as /bef-ôr/. It can be heard that this is not as close to *before* as is /eks-sīt/ to *excite*. Complicating the matter here is the fact that the first vowel sound in *before*, as in many other open-syllable prefixes, is given the /ə/ sound. We have purposely not dealt with the /ə/ sound before this time because it occurs almost exclusively in polysyllabic words. In reading the syllables of polysyllabic words, the child is often baffled by the variant sound-spelling correspondences found in these syllables since about one half of them have the /ə/ sound [Affleck 1967]. The solution to this is to teach the child to give all syllables in polysyllabic words an accented, that is, a non-/ə/, sound. This reading will come close enough to the true sound of the word to make it recognizable.

10. The child should experience very few of the previously mentioned problems in recognizing common closed-syllable suffixes. According to Edward Thorndike [1941], the twenty most common closed-syllable suffixes are

-able	-ate	-ic	-less
-age	-ance, -ence	-ical	-ment
-al	-ent	-tion, -sion	-ness
-an, -ian	-er	-ish	-or
-ant	-ful	-ive	-ous

Most of these by now should be familiar as phonograms: *er, or, ent, ment, ful, ence, ance, ate, ness, less, en*. It will be necessary for the phonics teacher to make special efforts for the child to identify *-tion* and *-sion*, though, since these are unpredictably spelled suffixes. Although *-tion* and *-sion* are commonly said to be suffixes, sometimes they are not. At times, *-ion* is the suffix. This occurs when the final consonant sound of some words is changed to /sh/ before the suffix *-ion* is added. Note how this is done in *act-action, success-succession*. To the contrary, note how the last sound in *posit* is maintained for *positive*. Compare this with *position* where the final sound in *posit* is changed to /sh/. While in some words, as in *subscribe-subscription*, *-tion* is the suffix, more commonly when the final consonant sound of the word is not changed the suffix will be *-ation* or *-ition*. Note, for example, *admire-admiration, compose-composition*.

11. Common open-syllable suffixes will be easy for the child to learn to read: they all end in *y*. The single task for the child here is to remember that this *y* (as in happy) represents the /ē/ sound.

Teaching How to Syllabicate Words

The phonogram approach to syllabication (Chapter 5), in essence, teaches the child to identify this cluster of letters: a vowel grapheme, plus a consonant grapheme(s), V-C(C) (as in *pat* or *lack*). This approach first conditions the child to give the /a, e, i, o, u/ phonemes to vowel grapheme(s), and the appropriate predictable consonant speech sound(s) to the consonant grapheme(s) that follow the vowel grapheme. From this point the child learns to read phonograms with other vowel sounds.

Fundamentally, this works the way that Virginia Jones [1970] has described it. Assume, for example, that pupils have learned to recognize the phonograms *in* and *ish* in the words, *pin* and *fish*. They now can apply these to read *finish:*

Known: pin fish

Unknown: fin ish

Essentially the same process is used with scores of other polysyllabic words:

Known:	fun	her	rock	pet	gun	her	hand
Unknown:	un der		rock et		un der		stand

The same sort of analysis is called for with words in which the final *y* is changed to *i* before a suffix is added:

Known: penn y   less

Unknown: penn 'i less

Here, of course, the child has learned the recognition of the open syllable *y*. Other words involve somewhat more complicated analyses:

Known:	tack	lid	bent	rat	if	lick	a	tion	tub	bill	pant
Unknown:	ac	cid	ent	grat	if	ic	a'	tion	jub	il	ant

We can see that with *accident, gratification,* and *jubilant* that correspondences between the phonograms in the shorter words and those in the longer words are not exactly the same. Nonetheless, *ac* is not too distant in spelling from *ack*, nor *ick* from *ic*. We note that *tion*, which is unpredictably spelled, is recognized as such without the customary extension from a monosyllabic word. *Jubilant* presents the most difficult task of transposition of known phonograms of the three words. According to phonogram teaching, this word would be pronounced /jub-il-ant/. It is at this point that a test is made of whether instruction in phonogram recognition has developed in pupils the notion of a versatile use of vowel sounds. If it has, they will automatically shift the sound given to the first syllable to /o͞o/ or /yo͞o/, and give the word the pronunciation /jyo͞ob-il-ant/, which should be close enough to

/jȳoob-əl-ənt/ for them to recognize the word if they have it in their memories. We agree in principle with Paul McKee, who has observed that "when the pupil encounters the strange word *about, call, care,* or *asked,* for example, and thinks first for the *a* the short sound or the long sound, he has little if any trouble in shifting quickly to the sound that letter has in the familiar spoken word called for by the context and the consonants" [1966, p. 108]. We believe *Phonics: Why and How* explains how this is possible.

Teaching Level 10

In summary, only the following skills are needed by the child to analyze polysyllabic words. These are the skills taught at this level.

1. Ability to recognize familiar monosyllabic words as they are combined to make polysyllabic words (compound words)

2. Ability to recognize that certain affixes and the spelling *le* "stand alone," and therefore are peculiar pronunciation units

3. Ability to syllabicate words based on the use of the rules for recognizing phonograms taught at earlier levels in this text

4. Ability to combine the recognition of affixes, *le*, and familiar phonograms as an integrated approach to recognizing polysyllabic words

On the other hand, instruction at this level does not include the following:

1. Teaching the meaning of affixes

2. Teaching dictionary syllabication rules

Compound Words

1. Say: "Look at these words." Write: *playground, horseshoe, birthday, dollhouse, cowboy.* "How many words are in each long word? How many syllables do you hear?" (Introduce the term *syllable* this way.)

2. Say: "Look at these pictures":

"What is the word for each of them?" Write it on the board.

3. Say: "Match the words in one column with those in the other to make compound words." (Introduce the term *compound word* in this way.)

for	hop
sun	get
bell	top
big	dog
bull	hop

4. Say: "Listen for two words in these sentences that will make a new word."

"This is my side" (point to the word).	"Let's take a walk."	(sidewalk)
"There is the cow."	"You are a boy."	(cowboy)
"Sue had a doll."	"Come over to my house."	(dollhouse)

Inflections In all activities involving the inflections *ed, ing, er, est,* the phonics teacher should keep in mind the distinction between the reading and spelling of inflected morphemes. That is, pupils can more readily recognize *dipping* from *dip* than they can remember to spell *pp* for /p/ in the word. Nonetheless, in exercises in which pupils are being taught to read the word *dipping*, it is necessary to call attention to the two *p*'s in *dipping*. The teacher need not ask pupils to pronounce *dipping* and to tell how many /p/ sounds they hear. A much better test of this understanding is to simply practice in the ways that we have illustrated with words in which the consonant letter is doubled. For a test of whether pupils have grasped the concept of inflections and are not simply memorizing words, have them read pseudowords with inflections: *vapped, lutting, leated, deaking, freams, dunches, hifter, gintest.*

For spelling this is quite another matter, of course. To spell words correctly, as we have pointed out, the child must remember which kind of words *generally* require a doubled consonant with certain inflections. It is appropriate when teaching the spelling of a word to lead children to a conscious awareness of these rules.

1. Say: "Let's add *ed* to these words: *skip, slap, bat.*" (Write them on the board.) "What letter besides *ed* did I add to *skip* to make it *skipped?*" Do this with the other words.

2. Say: "Let's add *ing* to these words: *skip, slap, bat.*" (Write them on the board.) "What letter besides *ing* was added to *skip* to make it *skipping?*" Do this with the other words.

3. Say: "Let's add *ed* to these words: *bake, move, ride.*" (Write them on the board.) "What letter in *bake* is dropped before I add *ed* to it?" Do this with the other words.

4. Say: "Let's add *ing* to these words: *bake, move, ride.*" (Write them on the board.) "What letter in *bake* is dropped before I add *ing* to it?" Do this with the other words.

5. Say: "What is different about these words: *bump-bake?*" Elicit from the pupils that one has an *e* on the end, and that one has the phonogram *ump* and the other the phonogram *ake.* "If we add *ing* to *bump* we have *bumping.*" (Write it on the board). "If we add *ing* to *bake* we get *baking.* Let's call *bump* and *bake* root words. What are the root words of these words?"

telling	riding	kicking	wading
making	living	barking	standing

"What are the phonograms of these words?"

6. Say: "Look at this sentence. Bill can _____. Give me a word to put in the blank. Now look at this sentence. Bill _____ on the way to school. Let's take our first word (e.g., *talk*) and see if we can fit it into the second sentence." Children might say "Bill talk . . . ," but will realize this is ungrammatical. They will eventually say, "Bill talked. . . ." When this happens, write *talked* in the blank. Then start over with a new word for Bill can _____.

7. Say: "Look at this sentence. Bill was _____. Give me a word that will fit this blank. (Write in the word, e.g., *walking.*) Now look at this sentence. Will the word you gave fit this sentence? Bill can _____. How can we change this second sentence so that *walking* will fit the blank?"

8. Say: "Think of an *ing* word to fit this sentence. _____ is fun." As the children give a word for the sentence, write it in the blank, erasing the previous word. Each time circle *ing.*

9. Say: "Let's try adding *ed* to words. Here is a list of words. Can we add *ed* to them?"

help	bump
pick	sail
ran	eat

10. Say: "Which is the correct pronunciation of *wanted?*" (Write on board):

$$
\text{wanted} \quad
\begin{matrix}
d \\
ed \\
t
\end{matrix}
$$

11. Say: "Let's try adding *ing* to words. Here is a list. Can we add *ing* to them?"

sing	go
fill	fly
feed	blow

The following three items should not be practiced until children can readily do the previous two exercises. (It should be noted that when *ed* or *ing* is added to a VC phonogram, the final C is doubled: clip*ped*, clip*ping*; but not if the phonogram has either a vowel digraph: ch*ea*ted, ch*ea*ting; or a consonant cluster: de*nt*ed, de*nt*ing.) When the phonogram ends in a final "silent" *e*, the *e* is dropped before *ed* or *ing* is added: *baked, baking.*

12. Say: "Here is a word we know. (Write *walk.*) Let's add these endings. (Write *s, ed, ing.*) Now what words do we have?"

13. Say: "What is added to *walk* and *play*?" (Write *walk, play.*) Write:

walked	played
walking	playing

14. Say: "What is added to *skip*?" Write on the board:

She can skip.	skip
The girls skipped.	skipped
They were skipping.	skipping

"Can you finish this?"

> The water will drip.
> The water_____.
> The water is _____.

15. Say: "What is added to *call*?" Write on the board:

Can you call him?	call
Who called him?	called
Who is calling him?	calling

"Can you finish this?"

> Who will pick it up?
> Who _____ it up?
> Who is _____ it up?

16. Say: "What are two ways words can end that mean more than one?" Children should respond: *s, es.* "Now look at these words. How are they changed to make them mean more than one?" Write:

child	mouse	foot	goose	shelf
children	mice	feet	geese	shelves

"Can you think of others like this?" If children can, write them on the board.

17. Say: "What is added to *farm*?" Write on the board:

He is a farmer.	farm
	farmer

"Can you finish this?"

   He works in a bank.
   He is a _____.

18. Say: "What is added to *bright*?" Write:

This color is bright.	bright
This one is brighter.	brighter
This one is brightest.	brightest

"Can you finish this?"

   Tie the knot tight.
   Tie the knot _____.
   This knot is _____.

19. Say: "Look at these lines. Match the words to the lines."

_____	shorter
_____	short
_____	shortest

20. Say: "All these months are warm. Match the month with the word."

April	warmest
June	warmer
August	warm

21. Say: "Imagine there are three boys. One is 4, one is 8, and one is 16. Match their age with the word."

4	tall
16	tallest
8	taller

Affixes For the teaching of other affixes besides inflections, many of the formats for the previous exercises can be used. The following are the general activities to use for developing children's perception of affixes:

1. Have children count the number of syllables in polysyllabic words. Say: "Listen to this: *cow-boy*. How many syllables? *Chim-ney*. How many syllables?" Read the words with a slight pause between the two

syllables. (Begin with disyllabic words and move on to those with three or more syllables.) Then, write the words on the board:

cow boy, chim ney

This gives an opportunity to illustrate how impermissible clusters of sounds indicate the boundaries of syllables. Say: *"chim-ney."* Write it on the board: *chim-ney.* Now say: *"chimn-ey."* Write it: *chimn-ey.* Ask whether the first or second pronunciation sounds right. Children will say the former, since to say *chimn-ey* one must add a syllable: 1-*chim*, 2-*n*, 3-*ey*. Say: "Notice how we can't make a phonogram out of *chimn.*" Continue to illustrate this point with other words with impermissible clusters.

2. Have children match root words within one column with affixes in another.

3. Have children add affixes to root words. Give children cards on which affixes are written. Write a root word on the board. Have children put their affix card at the beginning or end of the word and try to pronounce it.

4. Have children fill in blanks with the proper "affixed" words:

The boy was _____. (happy)
_____ is eating ice cream. (happiness)

5. Syllabicate words according to the phonogram approach illustrated on page 222.

6. Say: "Listen to *act*. (Say it.) Do you hear the last sound in *act* in *action*?" Say *action*. Write *act* and *action* on the board. "Do you see the same letter *t* in both *act* and *action*? Now listen to these two words: *locate-location*. Let's spell *locate*. (Write on board.) Now let's spell *location* right under *locate*."

locate
location

Continue with other such words.

7. Find root words in given "affixed" words.

8. To teach children to give the /yo͞o/ sounds to certain phonograms, present a list of words such as the following, with the vowel grapheme and phonogram underlined as indicated:

ab<u>use</u>	<u>u</u>nion	m<u>u</u>sic	pop<u>u</u>lar
circ<u>u</u>late	reg<u>u</u>lar	m<u>u</u>tual	p<u>u</u>pil
c<u>ute</u>	man<u>u</u>facture	occ<u>u</u>py	ref<u>use</u>
f<u>u</u>ture	m<u>ule</u>،	perf<u>ume</u>	sched<u>ule</u>

Say: "Instead of the regular way we would say the phonograms in these words, let's say the word *you* (write on the board) for the vowel letter in each phonogram." Have children find other words in which they think they hear the /yo͞o/ sound.

9. To teach children to give the /yûr/ sound to certain phonograms, read aloud the words that have such sounds as /yûr/ and /ûr/. For example, say: "Listen to these pronunciations. Tell me which is the better one." Read aloud:

/kûr-i-us/—/kyûr-i-us/   (curious)
/prōk-ûr/—/prōk-yûr/   (procure)
/sēk-ûr/—/sēk-yûr/   (secure)

Write the words on the board. Then, say: "Listen to these words. Which answer my questions? If someone is very angry, he is in a terrible /fûr-ē/—/fyûr-ē/. An animal that carries a pack in the mountains is a /bûr-ō/—/byûr-ō/. The sound a cat makes is /pûr/—/pyûr/." Write the words on the board.

10. Play games using affix cards (see Appendix).

REFERENCES

Affleck, Muriel A. *The Utility of Selected Phonic Generalizations When Applied to a Vocabulary for the Intermediate Grades.* Ed.D. Dissertation, Colorado State College, 1967.

Dechant, Emerald. *Linguistics, Phonics, and the Teaching of Reading.* Springfield, Ill.: Charles C Thomas, 1969.

Gleason, Henry A. *An Introduction to Descriptive Linguistics.* New York: Holt, Rinehart and Winston, 1961.

Greene, Harry A. *New Iowa Spelling Scale.* Iowa City: The State University of Iowa Press, 1955.

Groff, Patrick. "Should Youngsters Find Little Words in Bigger Words?" *Reading Improvement,* 10(1973):12–16.

Hanna, Paul R., et al. *Phoneme-Grapheme Correspondences as Cues to Spelling Improvement.* Washington, D.C.: U.S. Office of Education, 1966.

Jones, Virginia W. *Decoding and Learning to Read.* Portland, Oreg.: Northwest Regional Educational Laboratory, 1970.

Kurath, Hans. *A Phonology and Prosody of Modern English.* Ann Arbor: University of Michigan Press, 1964.

Liebert, Burt. *Linguistics and the New English Teacher*. New York: Macmillan, 1971.

McKee, Paul. *Reading*. Boston: Houghton Mifflin, 1966.

Stauffer, Russell G. "A Study of Prefixes in the Thorndike List to Establish a List of Prefixes That Should Be Taught in the Elementary School." *Journal of Educational Research*, 35(1942):453–458.

Thorndike, Edward L. *The Teaching of English Suffixes*. New York: Columbia University Press, 1941.

18

TEACHING
EXCEPTIONAL WORDS

Children will learn to recognize some *exceptional* words at each level of *Phonics: Why and How*. Exceptional words are those children see at any level that are not spelled in conformity with the spelling patterns that they have learned so far. As children learn sound-spelling correspondences at the different levels, they will quite normally observe that there are words to which these generalizations do not apply. This is especially the case for *vowel* sound-spelling correspondences.

Thus, this text cannot intentionally reserve all exceptional, unpredictably spelled words for a late stage of its phonics instructional program. It is obvious that all exceptional words cannot be ignored at previous levels. Primarily, children have to be given the names of some unpredictably spelled words early in their reading program because there are several of these in the most frequently used words in writing. It is generally agreed among researchers of the frequency of written word usage that 100 different words constitute about 50 to 60 percent of all the words one sees in print [Anderson & Groff 1968, pp. 10–11].

The words listed in Table 31 occur so frequently in writing that the phonics teacher cannot wait to present them at the later time they occur in the *Phonics: Why and How* program. Pupils will encounter them so often and soon in their reading that they must be told what they are. By this we mean pupils are simply given their names when they encounter these words. No attempt is made at this point to teach their peculiar sound-spelling correspondence, unless the child is at the instructional level at which this correspondence is presented.

It is clear that everything needed by children in phonics *cannot* be taught at once. Of necessity, we must delay the teaching of certain phonics items since our systematic ordering of the phonics items to be taught is based on a judgment of their priority. That is, phonics items for which children have a more fundamental or pressing need—those that are involved in the greatest number of words they encounter—are taught first. Those who claim to teach children *all* the phonics they need, *when* they need it (the incidental approach), are claiming to accomplish an impossible task. Moreover, there is no evidence that the incidental approach is as successful as systematic phonics. We must emphasize that our systematic phonics does insist that all children in the program move as quickly as possible through its levels. In the long run their peculiar needs are more carefully attended to in this way than is likely in some incidental approach that purports to teach children phonics only in the *order* in which they supposedly indicate a need for it.

Using Exceptional Words in Phonics

The general manner in which exceptional words become part of the phonics program, so as to allow for the use of syntax and context cues for word recognition, can be illustrated in the following way. For example, when the *ill* phonogram is being taught, garner sentences from children's language such as: Will you help me? I want to fill my glass. My name is Jill (or Bill). Danny is ill today. Did you spill your milk? To this group of sentences add ones like: This is the bill of this cap. When you are sick you get a pill. Be still! If you get cold you get a chill. (A dictionary of such rhyming words is found in Anderson and Groff [1968].)

Now write on the chalkboard: *Will you help me?* Read this sentence aloud to the group of pupils. Then, erase *will* from the sentence and write it in a column to one side of the board. Do the same with the other sentences given previously. Remaining on the board when this is done is a column of monosyllabic words exemplifying the *ill* phonogram, and sentences into which these *ill* words will fit. Again read the sentences leaving out the deleted *ill* words. Have the pupils identify which of the *ill* words fits into each of the sentences. Have the pupils tell what there is about the spelling of the *ill* words that is alike. Invite them to think about other words that are spelled with *ill*.

Two purposes are fulfilled in this lesson: (1) it teaches pupils to use *ill* as a cue to word recognition, and (2) it teaches pupils that words fit into sentences and thereby create meaning. From this the child makes the generalization that the remainder of a sentence often can act as a partial cue to the identification of an unknown word in the sentence.

Which Are the Unpredictably Spelled Words?

How many unpredictably spelled words are there among the most frequently used monosyllabic words, the ones highly useful for reading? According to Henry Kucera and W. Nelson Francis [1967] the one hundred most frequently used monosyllabic words are listed in Table 31.

What to Do with Function Words

Many of the hundred highest-frequency words are used so often because they are *marker,* or *function,* words (words other than nouns, verbs, adjectives, or adverbs). If one subtracts the function words from these one hundred most frequently used monosyllabic words (Table 31), the remainder is small, indeed. We are left with only a few nouns or noun-words: *I, time, years, way, world, he, they, each, we, she, you, me, them, him, her, it, one, man.* The only verbs are *made, said, like, make, state* (a noun?).

If we add adjectives to our group of nonfunction words, that is, the words that fit both slots in these sentences: The boy/book is _____; the _____ boy/book, we get *new, good, well. There* can be called an adverbial of place, rather than a function word. In sum, of the one hundred most used

---

TABLE 31. THE 100 MOST
FREQUENTLY USED MONOSYLLABIC WORDS

1. the	21. this	41. we	61. some	81. must
2. of	22. had	42. him	62. could	82. through
3. and	23. not	43. been	63. time	83. back
4. to	24. are	44. has	64. these	84. years
5. a	25. but	45. when	65. two	85. where
6. in	26. from	46. who	66. may	86. much
7. that	27. or	47. will	67. then	87. your
8. is	28. have	48. more	68. do	88. way
9. was	29. an	49. no	69. first	89. well
10. he	30. they	50. if	70. any	90. down
11. for	31. which	51. out	71. my	91. should
12. it	32. one	52. so	72. now	92. each
13. with	33. you	53. said	73. such	93. just
14. as	34. were	54. what	74. like	94. those
15. his	35. her	55. up	75. our	95. how
16. on	36. all	56. its	76. man	96. too
17. be	37. she	57. than	77. me	97. state
18. at	38. there	58. them	78. most	98. good
19. by	39. would	59. can	79. made	99. make
20. I	40. their	60. new	80. did	100. world

words, we can identify only twenty-seven that are not function words.

Function words are syntactical "keys" that the child can use to "unlock" the meanings of sentences. And since reading, as nearly as possible, should be to gain for the reader the intent of the writer of the material, it follows that the use of structure words for this purpose must be emphasized at all levels of the phonics program.

These "empty" words of the sentence, as Carl Lefevre calls them, [1964, p. 119], signal or mark the kinds of syntax, the parts of speech, to follow. To this extent they signal what a sentence is *likely* to mean. For example, in the blank that follows, a *noun marker, the* (the _____), tells us we will likely get a different message than the blank that follows these other markers:

verb marker:	am _____ (*going*)	has _____ (*gone*)
phrase marker:	up _____ (*the hill*)	down _____ (*the tree*)
clause marker:	when _____ (*he left*)	because _____ (*he left*)
question marker:	Who _____ (*was here?*)	What _____ (*is that?*)

Accordingly, it is important to determine whether function words should be taught with other words of the sound-spelling classification they exemplify, or whether they should be "always learned in relation to the words and functions they signal," as Lefevre insists. To him, "structure words, above all, are words that should never be taught in isolation, but always as they function in the language, in typical structural order and patterns" [1964, pp. 119–120].

We see no need to create this false dichotomy. No good phonics activity teaches function words only in isolation. The phonics teacher, however, should make the most of opportunities to teach these words both in the patterns in which they function, and as phonograms. For example, at Level 4 the function word *will* should be taught in conjunction with verbs it marks, e.g., *will bend, will cost, will dart, will fan, will get, will help, will jog.* It also can be taught with isolated words that fit its sound-spelling patterns as *bill, chill, drill, fill,* etc. The study by Chester [1972] supports this. He found that pre-reading first graders learned to read function words equally as well as content words whether these were taught in isolation or in sentence context. We know of no evidence that indicates that

> Such "word" teaching will keep the child from carrying his acquired speech tunes over to his oral reading; subsequently, in visual or silent reading, the mnemonic echoes from the printed page will not repeat the native intonation patterns for him. Thus intrinsic linguistic signals for important structural elements may be corrupted, or lost completely, through faulty reading methodology [Lefevre 1964, p. 120].

To the contrary, we suggest that all techniques that can contribute to helping the child to attain fluent word recognition should be endorsed.

Teaching the child to develop high-speed recognition responses to phonograms is one of the most important of these techniques. This activity, combined with the simultaneous reading of structure words with the other parts of speech they signal, is better than either of these techniques alone. When used together, the dire consequences of "word teaching" predicted by Lefevre is not likely to come to pass.

Exceptional Words and Children's Reading Materials

All reading systems are faced with the problems of what to do with exceptional words. Thus, the alleged control over such words by the writers of basal readers is by and large a fictional claim. According to the Spaches [1969], a survey found only 600 out of 12,000 words to be common to the vocabularies of twelve different basal readers. This study, and others [Groff 1961], indicate the lack of vocabulary overlap in these different readers. As the Spaches rightly observe, "Apparently each basal reader series has its own essential or core vocabulary that appears in no other series. How fundamental is a basal vocabulary which isn't even required to read common supplementary basals?" [1969, p. 101].

It has been suggested by critics of phonics that a high percent of the words a child will need to recognize when reading constitutes a relatively small number of words (one thousand different words constitute about 90 percent of all the words a child is likely to see). They say phonics is not justifiable in the terms of the time it takes since the child learning to read will recognize these words by "sight." As we have demonstrated, however, the notion that the beginning reader learns "sight words" is not supported by the research in word recognition [Groff 1974].

Moreover, no author of any merit for children can stay within any such thousand-word limit for very long. Authors' abilities to choose precisely the right word for a given situation in literature is essentially what makes for good writing. To make it possible for children to be able to read good literature soon, all through the levels of phonics instruction the phonics teacher must be willing to supply, on demand, the names of exceptional words children do not recognize. As well, outside the phonics lesson children should not be interrupted in their reading with instructions as to how to "figure out" unknown words that puzzle them. Neither should they be referred to the dictionary for this purpose. Such interruptions not only disrupt the pace of the reading, they dishearten pupils. They also act to reduce the amount of comprehension of what is read. Accordingly, the teacher must assume that good phonics teaching will transfer into pupils' regular reading practices. And that which does not transfer needs further teaching.

How to Teach Exceptional Words

The ways to alert children to the fact they will not be able to rely on their phonics generalizations or skills for the recognition of exceptional words require, *first,* that the teacher remind children of the great possibility that such words will occur in their reading. In a word, the phonics teacher must develop versatility in children's application of their sound-spelling knowledges. Most commonly, and this is what the teacher should tell children, children will learn they must be ready to give more than one vowel sound to a vowel grapheme in order to reduce an exceptional word to a pronunciation near enough to its pronunciation so that they can successfully interpret it. As we have shown, the exceptional, unpredictably spelled words are not necessarily unfamiliar words. In visual terms they may genuinely appear strange to the child, of course, since they do not lend themselves to the pronunciations that their spellings would suggest to be the likely ones.

Second, the teacher must give the child supervised practice in dealing with exceptional words. These techniques are varied in nature.

1. If the exceptional word is a function word, the teacher can present this (as was suggested above) in the typical patterns, phrases, clauses, or sentences in which they normally appear. This is especially useful for totally unpredictable words like *of.* And long before children are taught the /ou/-ou sound-spelling correspondence (/out/-*out*), they can be taught, for example, to read sentences like *John fell out of bed* by guessing from the context the word *out.*

2. The unpredictably spelled word can be presented with a picture that depicts the word and a sentence in which it fits. For example:

The _____ drinks the milk.

3. The use of context cues for determining the pronunciation of excep-

tional words can be used on many occasions. See Chapter 19 for details.

4. Configuration cues, the length and particular shape of a word, are of very limited usefulness to beginning readers for unlocking exceptional words, or any other words. Beginning readers seldom use configuration cues to recognize words [Groff 1974].

5. If pupils are blocked on an exceptional word, they can be encouraged to pay particular attention to the beginning and ending consonant letters of the word. Then, by inferring what word might be likely to appear in the slot of the unidentified word, they can mentally check to see if the word they infer has the same beginning and ending sounds as the letters of the unidentified exceptional word would suggest it should have.

Third, anyone who can recognize exceptional words should be recruited for this purpose to come to the class to supply exceptional words to children as they read. These prompters can be older children, parents, or children's relatives, other school patrons, and school aides. This practice is fast gaining acceptance by modern phonics teachers.

REFERENCES

Anderson, Paul S., and Groff, Patrick. *Resource Materials for Teachers of Spelling.* Minneapolis: Burgess, 1968.

Chester, Robert D. "Differences in Learnability of Content and Function Words Presented in Isolation and Oral Context When Taught to High and Low Socioeconomic Level Students." *Dissertation Abstracts International,* 32(1972):3833A.

Groff, Patrick. "The Problem of Vocabulary Load in Individualized Reading." *Reading Teacher,* 14(1961):188–190.

Groff, Patrick. "The Topsy-Turvy World of 'Sight' Words." *Reading Teacher,* 27(1974):572–578.

Hanna, Paul, Hodges, Richard E., and Hanna, Jean S. *Spelling: Structure and Strategies.* Boston: Houghton Mifflin, 1971.

Kucera, Henry, and Francis, W. Nelson. *Computational Analysis of Present-Day American English.* Providence: Brown University Press, 1967.

Lefevre, Carl A. *Linguistics and the Teaching of Reading.* New York: McGraw-Hill, 1964.

Spache, George D., and Spache, Evelyn B. *Reading in the Elementary School.* Boston: Allyn & Bacon, 1969.

19

TEACHING THE USE
OF CONTEXT CUES

We have indicated in previous chapters that words, as such, can give cues to their recognition. Recognition of *isolated* words depends on two things: (1) children's abilities to recall the sound correspondences of the graphemes they see in a word, and (2) their memory of the various combinations of letters that are used to spell English words, "sequential redundancy," as Frank Smith [1971] calls it. Most mature readers would agree, however, that words take (or are given) their meanings as a consequence of their occurrence in sentences. As the "natural" environment of the phoneme is the syllable, so in like manner the word depends for its explicit meaning on the sentence. As phonemes cannot be articulated accurately outside the syllable, so the word depends for the authenticity of its meaning on the sentence.

Phonics and Context Cues

We insert the matter of context cues into our discussion of phonics to define more accurately the place of phonics in word recognition and to illustrate better how phonics works in conjunction with context cues in the process of recognizing words.

Context cues to reading refer to the signals to the identity of a word found in the sentence in which the word rests. That is, what effect does the sentence have on the reader's ability to recognize any given word within it? We know the sentence must exert a considerable influence on word recognition since any mature reader will attest that it is possible to read for comprehension without actually identifying all the individual words or all the parts of all the words in the sentences. In other words, the more skilled the reader is the less visual information is required from the printed page. Readers who recognize words fluently have the ability to recognize the structures or patterns of sentences. And they are able to predict what the remainder of any "unread" passage will be.

Accordingly, the first teaching principle in Chapter 6 was that from the beginning of phonics instruction pupils should be taught to use the three cue systems to word recognition: (1) phonics, (2) their knowledge of word meanings, and (3) the sentence in which a word is found. So far, we have demonstrated only the first of these, phonics.

We have previously recommended that if a phonics teacher uses the actual language of the pupils as the material for phonics instruction that the second cue to word recognition, the semantics or meanings of words, can quickly come into play. Taking pupils' language as the material with which they will be taught to read is known as the "language experience" approach [Hall 1970].

We come now to the third aspect of word recognition, context cues. We have described in the various levels of this book why and how children are taught to recognize the various sound-spelling correspondences within words. It is obvious this is not enough. The child also can use context cues to recognize words. It is critical, therefore, for the phonics teacher to use sentences as well as isolated words in teaching. The teacher should consistently demonstrate for pupils how context cues are available to them as a means of recognizing words.

The numerous context cue activities found in this chapter should be seen as examples of exercises the phonics teacher should include in lessons that stress sound-spelling relationships. All such lessons can contain some of these context cue activities.

Research on Context Cues

Rose-Marie Weber [1970] found that even poor readers in the first grade use the grammar of the sentence as a context cue. She found that the difference in the grammatical acceptability of reading miscues (e.g., *penny* for *money; that* for *what* in *Puff did not say what she wanted*) is very small between good readers and poor readers in the first grade. Of the errors of good readers, 91 percent were grammatically acceptable. This compares with 89 percent for poor readers. It is equally important to note what the pupils in Weber's study did with their miscues that upset the grammaticality of the sentence as they read it. Good readers ignored only 15 percent of these miscues. (Weber does not tell whether these miscues were corrected so that the correct sound of the reidentified word was given or whether the correction simply made the miscue grammatically acceptable.) Poor readers passed over 58 percent of this kind of miscues.

The difference in attention to these miscues might be calculated to account for some of the difference in the reading abilities of the two groups of pupils on the standardized reading test Weber used, as one half of this test is made up of sentence reading.

Another important question to ask at this point is, Would not Weber's good readers have behaved much as poor readers if she could have tested them on their use of context cues for reading when they were *at the same stage of decoding ability* as the poor readers in this study? Would not they too have passed over 58 percent of their "grammar" errors at this point in the development of their reading skills?

Julian Hochberg's evidence indicating that the beginner is a word-by-word reader tends to substantiate this. As Hochberg correctly notes, ". . . the main task in skilled, literate reading is to extract information about some subject from an array of redundant and often irrelevant graphic symbols . . . [and] this ability is very different in goal, in methods, and in mechanism from the task of translating graphemes into speech" [1970, p. 88]. That beginning readers do process a sentence word by word was demonstrated by Hochberg. He found that the reading speed of immature readers was little affected as to whether they read the first or second sentence:

1.   ʀsomeʀthinkʀthatʀwildʀanimalsʀlikeʀtoʀliveʀinʀtheʀforestʀ
2.   some think that wild animals like to live in the forest

More advanced readers who were deprived of the blank spaces as cues (sentence 1) read the first sentence at a significantly slower rate than the second sentence. The immature readers here read both sentences word by word. The lack of spaces did not hamper them. The better readers, who apparently read in units larger than words, found sentence 1 more difficult to read since they were prevented from their customary use of larger units of reading.

Another of the context cues of the sentence is the boundary of each of the phrases in the sentence being read. It has been discovered that the boundaries of the phrases exercise a distinct effect on the reader. As Harry Levin and Eleanor Kaplan have commented, this discovery "suggests that readers have an elastic [eye-voice] span, which stretches or shrinks to phrase boundaries" [1970, p. 124]. The length of phrases does not affect the need of the reader to process reading matter phrase by phrase.

Before context cues become of much value in word recognition, "shopping-list" reading is to be expected for a time. Evidence of this "shopping-list" manner of reading by young children is reported by Marie Clay and Robert Imlach [1971]. In their study of the oral reading of second graders, they found the number of pauses these children made was closely related to their reading ability. The best readers in this group read an average of 4.7 words per pause. The poorest readers made 1.1 stresses or pauses per word as if they were reading a list of words [1971].

The extent to which context, in general, helps children in grades one, two, and three to recognize words has been reported by Kenneth Goodman. When reading words in a story rather than reading words in a list, "average first graders could read almost two out of three words in the story which they missed on the list. The average second grader missed only one-fourth of the words in the story which he failed to recognize on the list. Third graders were able to get, in the stories, all but 18 percent of the words which they did not know in the list" [1965, p. 641]. The accuracy of Goodman's data needs further verification, however. Martin's study [1970] seems to substantiate it; the findings from Singer, et al. [1973–1974], and from Chester [1972] do not.

Finally, we cannot overlook the theory of reading by Frank Smith, which comments on the importance of context cues under the heading, "The Identification of Meaning." To Smith, ". . . *any* attempt . . . to identify words when the aim is comprehension, must inevitably result in delay and disruption of both identification processes." The child "may reduce his meaning uncertainty without making *any* prior decisions about words" [1971, p. 213, emphasis added]. For example, Smith believes that for a child to differentiate between

The horse fell down.
The house fell down.

does not mean that "differentiation of a word is required before differentiation [of the separate meanings] of the two sentences can be accomplished" [p. 214]. That is, "word identification is not necessary for the acquisition of meaning" [p. 216]; "identification of individual words merely gets in the way" [p. 217] of reading for meaning. It is almost impossible to read for meaning if words are identified, he insists.

For proof, Smith refers in part to the evidence of the timed exposure of words, which indicates that for mature readers "identification of a fragment of English text requires less than half the visual information needed to identify the same words individually" [p. 218]. Presumably the good reader will recognize "The house (or horse) fell down" in a single fixation, and in no longer a period of time than it takes to identify *house* or *horse*.

We doubt, however, that the extreme nature of Smith's remarks about this matter are supported by the evidence he provides. One fault of Smith's interpretation of the "evidence" seems to us to be his assumption that because good readers can recognize individual words faster when they are reading a book than when the words are flashed one by one on a screen by a timed-exposure device (tachistoscope), this proves they do not recognize individual words when reading a book. It appears to us, however, that the faster speed in reading the book can be explained by the format of the material, and purpose of the reader of the material, rather than in the "fact" that the fast reader gains meaning without recognizing any individual words. And, it is *not* true, Smith to the contrary notwithstanding, that persons "reading" a thousand words a minute will always be able to tell much more about the meaning of what they read than persons reading a hundred words a minute. This ignores the well-established evidence that speed of comprehension is much more complicated than this. Henry Smith and Emerald Dechant reviewed the research and show that both these assumptions are wrong: (1) fast reading is inaccurate, and (2) slow reading is poor reading [1961, p. 222]. As this research shows, "Flexibility of reading speed appears to point to a critical difference between good and poor readers. The good reader sets comprehension as his goal and adjusts his rate rather automatically" [p. 224].

It is also important to keep in mind that Smith is commenting about mature or fast readers. In this book we are concerned with how a child learning to read, an immature reader, uses context cues. Ultimately, of course, the meaning of the words *in syntax* does depend upon the age and character of its reader. A word in a sentence will still have different meanings to different people, although they generally can agree as to the part of speech it is, or the name of the slot, or the part, in the sentence it occupies. The meaning readers attach to a word also depends upon their attitude toward its author. Some beginning readers are very cautious and demand of themselves an absolutely certain knowledge of what an author of a word intended. Other of these readers, on the contrary, make easy-going personal decisions as to what words mean based on a bare minimum of other information from an author's sentence. It is not clear what causes such diverse attitudes.

We see some teachers demanding that children learn and parrot back a single meaning of a word. Such a practice usually reverts to a hollow exercise in which only the more anxious, clever, or crafty child succeeds, and then only by conforming to a definition of the word that is formalistic enough to satisfy such teachers. These teachers need to realize that the meanings of words in sentences that children know can be only those their past experiences will allow. Equally guilty are the authors of teacher education books who perpetuate such nonsense as: "Understanding [of written material] is the ability to decode the author's meaning without infusing it with individual experiences or applications" [Eash 1967, p. 3]. Such a cognitive act is impossible. On the contrary, vocabulary growth takes place in children only when they can relate their present stock of experiences and language to a new word that fits into these categories of experience and language. Consequently, teachers should always have children interpret a new word to be learned in terms of their language and experiences. If there are no bases in the child's language and experiences for making this connection, the child obviously is not ready at this point to learn the new word in question.

The Role of Context Cues

An explanation of the role of context cues in reading comes best through illustrations of how this works. After pupils have learned to recognize a few words, they would be able to read this sentence and put in the deleted word: *The dog wagged its* _____ *when he saw the boy.* Anyone would say that *tail* fits the underlined blank or slot. *Wag, tail, dog,* and *boy* obviously are words that facilitate each other's recognition in a reciprocal way.

It is apparent that this example of context cues suggests that in most, if not all, instances a child should apply a combination of phonics and context cues as help in recognizing unfamiliar words. The manner in which context cues can help a child correctly determine a *single* sound-spelling correspondence is easily shown. For example, let us assume that the child could read all but the deleted letter in this sentence: *Bill was a _all boy.* Bill could be a *b all boy,* but more likely the context would demand the child read *t all* boy. Another example: *Bill was a b__ boy.* Bill could be a *bat* boy, but the context more likely would say to the child *big* boy.

A less perfect utilization of context cues comes with this example: *Bill was a t__ boy.* Bill could be a *tanned* boy, a *tiny* boy, a *teasing* boy, a *thin* boy, a *thirsty* boy, and so on. Thus, the more options that can be employed, the less possible an accurate application of context cues that can be made.

A better utilization of context cues comes with this example: *Bill was a t_ll boy.* (We assume in this example that the child did not perceive the vowel letter.) In this instance Bill *must* be a *tall* boy. We have here a reliable way of exploiting context cues to their near maximum usefulness. We have described in Chapter 4 how the identification of phonograms is the basis for word-structure analysis. We noted there that a fluent identification of phonograms is the best preparation for polysyllabic word analysis. In *Bill was a t_ll boy,* the context could contribute the vowel sound of the phonogram.

A replacement of the deleted word in *Bill likes to* _____ *his bike* is a different example of how context cues can stimulate inferences to word recognition. Many verbs could possibly be used in the underlined blank. The child reader will probably reject all of these in favor of *ride,* however, since *to ride* is what anyone his or her age would *most* want to do with a bike. Thus, it can be seen that "guessing" at words in context must at least be called "intelligent guessing." In this illustration, to guess *ride* the child tries to infer correctly the intention of the writer of the sentence.

In the sentence *Jane found the __ll and put it away*, an identification of the deleted word ending *ll* would depend entirely on whether the previous sentence read: *Jane lost her doll (or ball)*. If a child had read this previous sentence, it would be relatively easy for the reader to identify __*ll* correctly. Without the previous sentence it would be likely that either *ball* or *doll* could be read. Perhaps a higher percent of guesses would go to *doll* (Jane-doll?).

This example illustrates the contribution that an ongoing discourse about a subject has on the fluency of the reader's ability to recognize words. It throws into question, however, measures of readability that suppose the *number* of repetitions of an unfamiliar word in a passage is one measure of the reading difficulty of the passage. We do not recommend the use of such readability formulas [Dale & Chall 1948]. For it seems to us that once an unfamiliar word becomes known in a passage, a continued repetition of this word in succeeding sentences would make the passage *less* difficult to read rather than more difficult to read. Another wrong assumption of many readability formulas has been their implication that the difficulty of a particular word is not related to the context in which it occurs. But good readers know the reverse; the ease in their identification of a word depends very much on the words around it.

Goodman shows that with context cues some readers can even make "sense" out of pseudowords. By using properly inflected pseudowords connected by function words and the word *be*, he presents material that almost seems to make sense, or, more precisely, to which the reader tries to bring some meaning:

> Gloopy is a borp.
> Bilt is a lof.
> Gloopy klums like Bilt.
> Gloopy and Bilt are floms. [Smith, Goodman, & Meredith 1970, p. 249].

This passage, Goodman contends, "presents, in extreme, the problem of the reader's meeting words he has never seen before" [p. 249].

The problem of immature readers meeting words they have never seen before is even more "extreme," however. They cannot respond to all the syntax cues that this passage offers the mature reader.

It is not true, moreover, that children who come to school with well-developed control over oral language production and internalized systems of response to oral language will *automatically transfer* these oral language abilities to written language. For example, Compton [1972] found that "verbal" first grade children did not learn to read any better than did pupils classified as "nonverbal." Principally this is so because written language is critically different from oral language in a number of respects.

Comprehension and Context Cues

The relationships between pupils' comprehension of written materials and their abilities to use context cues is also a significant matter. Evidence about this relationship has been discovered by John Bormuth. He analyzed children's abilities to guess correctly the words that had been deleted from sentences at regular intervals (every fifth word was deleted). He found children

> gained little or no information [from written material] when their reading ability was so low that they were unable to answer more than about 25 percent of the items on the cloze tests [that is, fill in correctly 25 percent of the deletions]. But when they had sufficient ability to answer as many as 35 percent of the cloze items, they were able to gain roughly as much information as students having a greater degree of reading ability [1970, p. 6].

This research suggests that while the young reader uses cue systems within sentences (nearby function words, inflections, the slots in sentences words normally are in, familiarity with sentence patterns, and the sound of a word read in a sentence) to identify unfamiliar words correctly, *this is a minor part of a pupil's comprehension* of written material. The majority of the factors that influence one's ability to comprehend a passage (be literate with it) are unknown "thought" processes. Literacy does not depend, in the main, on either phonics or context cue systems to word recognition within sentences. Most of the factors that make up what Bormuth calls literacy (comprehending the meaning an author intended for a passage) have yet to be experimentally verified. It is clear that ability with phonics does not insure literacy.

This should be sobering evidence for anyone intoxicated with the false notion that all poor readers need is more phonics, or more use of context cues. It is a forceful reminder of the limited role of phonics and context cues in reading for comprehension.

Nonetheless, literacy depends in part on the fluent recognition of words. Children who have yet to develop a fluent recognition of words (which depends to a degree on the ability to use phonics) read haltingly, dwelling on one word at a time, almost oblivious to the cues to word recognition that the sentence offers. To get a feel of the clumsy manner in which beginning readers necessarily operate with material that is prewritten for them,[1] read this list of words: *it, in, toys, the, on, up, check, to, box, the, into, looked, Bill.* Now reverse the order of these words; read the list

---

[1] Advocates of the language experience approach to reading [Hall 1970] say that if children's own language, written down by the teacher as they say it, is used for instruction in phonics that children will read their own sentences with *more* normal intonation and speed. This is opinion, however, and not a conclusion based on research. On the other hand, that these language experience children do as well on reading tests as basal reader children is an established fact.

backwards. Your first reading was the typical "shopping list," word-by-word, singsong manner of beginning readers who have yet to develop even fluent word recognition. These pupils must of necessity concentrate on word recognition so much that context cues help them very little. In your second reading of the group of words, however, you grasped almost immediately that this was not a list of words, but a sentence. Thereupon you began to utilize the context cues of the sentence. Had you tape recorded your two readings you would also be able to hear the different and proper intonations you gave to this second reading. There is little doubt that proper intonations when reading aloud depend on an understanding of the context cues offered by the sentence.

We can see, then, that to utilize the context cues of the sentence one must be able to recognize some words rather fluently. Up to a point, then, the greater the reader's ability to recognize words fluently, the greater the ability to use sentence cues to word recognition. Unfortunately, we have little—if any—research as to what this "point" is.

This is not a replay of the classic conundrum, "Which comes first, the chicken or the egg" (word recognition or comprehension)? We believe that recognition of some individual words in a sentence *must precede* the utilization of context cues. Context cues then can act to speed up other word recognition. At the point at which enough words in a sentence can be easily recognized, context cues to the recognition of the remainder of the words can be put into effect. How many words is "enough?" Who can tell? According to George Spache there is some recent evidence, however, "that the words that follow a strange word are more likely to aid in contextual analysis than those that precede it" [1964, p. 317]. This suggests, of course, that the beginning reader be encouraged to read past the unknown word for cues to its recognition. The question of how many words in a sentence a child needs to know to use context cues is beyond any precise answer, though, since virtually no research on the problem has been done.

Grammar and the Use of Context Cues

It is readily apparent that the meaning of a sentence involves more than an understanding of the meanings of the individual parts of speech in a sentence. One cannot total the different meanings of the individual words in a sentence and use that to represent the meaning of the sentence. For example, even a young child could use each of these four words in a separate sentence: (1) *bit,* (2) *dog,* (3) *man,* and (4) *the.* One never knows from this what the four words will "add up" to, however:

The dog bit the man.

The man bit the dog.

The dog man bit.

The man dog bit.

The dog bit the man dog.

The man dog bit the dog.

The dog man bit the dog.

Man, the dog bit.

The dog bit, man.

The dog bit, the man bit.

The man bit, the dog bit.

The dog bit the man?

The man bit the dog?

The dog man bit?

The man dog bit?

The dog bit the man dog?

The man dog bit the dog?

The dog man bit the dog?

The dog man bit the man dog?

In addition, each one of the words *dog, man,* and *bit* can at times be given the greatest prominence in a sentence, which somewhat changes the meaning of the sentence:

The *dog* bit the man.

The dog *bit* the man.

The dog bit the *man.*

Sometimes reading a sentence with a greater prominence given to a certain word is the only way to make its meaning clear:

Cooking apples can be enjoyable. (Cooking apples) or (Cooking)?

At other times, however, only the punctuation or capitalization settles the meaning:

I'd like to eat Mother. I'd like to eat, Mother.

Professor Rakes leaves at noon. Professor rakes leaves at noon.

The ambiguity of some sentences cannot be resolved. Unless the word order is changed or additional words or sentences are given, their meaning is unclear. For example:

The chicken was too hot to eat.

The shooting of the hunters was terrible.

The function of context cues is also affected by the number of alternative words that can be fitted into the slot an unfamiliar word occupies in a sentence. Obviously, the greater the number of unknown words in a sentence that can be guessed, the greater the function of context cues. For example, suppose one were asked to replace any word missing from this sentence: *The man placed the meat on a dish.* In line with the previous idea the easier words for one to replace would be *the* or *a:*

1. _____ man placed the meat on a dish.
2. The man placed the meat on _____ dish.
3. The man placed _____ meat on a dish.

The remaining sentences in order of the ease with which one could replace the missing word would likely be:

4. The man placed the meat _____ a dish.
5. The man placed the meat on a _____.
6. The man placed the _____ on a dish.
7. The man _____ the meat on a dish.
8. The _____ placed the meat on a dish.

Thus, we can see that the number of alternative words that can be placed in any of the slots is affected by whether the missing word is a function word (*the, a, on*) or a noun or verb.[2] Then, notice how one's ability to replace the missing word depends on how much semantic information one has and the grammatical relationships sentence 5 gives: how many things (a _____) can *meat* be placed on? How many things (sentence 6) can be placed on a *dish*? In sentence 7, how many synonyms are there for *put* or *place*? How many for *meat*? Or did the man *cover, change, slice, disguise, cook, heat, season, move, arrange, poison,* etc., the meat? Quite obviously the man could do something *with* or something *to* the meat (a grammatical fact), which greatly enlarges the possible number of alternatives for sentence 7. Even more numerous are the animals and humans of all kinds, including all the names of humans, that could fit the structure, The _____. Sentence 8 should have the most alternatives of all.

The utility of context cues is further conditioned by the fact that certain kinds of words in a sentence act to reduce its uncertainty more than others do. Function words carry very little meaning:

_____ man placed _____ meat _____ _____ dish.
(nouns, verb)
The _____ _____ the _____ on a _____. (function words)

Then, the more words we see in a sentence the more likely it is that we can use the sentence to guess intelligently about the remainder. Note how the missing words in these sentences are progressively easier to replace:

The _____ _____ _____ _____ _____ _____ _____.
The man _____ _____ _____ _____ _____ _____.
The man placed _____ _____ _____ _____ _____.
The man placed the _____ _____ _____ _____.
The man placed the meat _____ _____ _____.
The man placed the meat on _____ _____.
The man placed the meat on a _____.

---

[2] Phonics teachers are invited to test this assumption. Give to each of seven different groups of equal-ability children the eight sentences with the missing words, one sentence per group. Note the percent of children in each group that can replace the missing word in the sentence given them.

It is more difficult to use context cues, however, if the information is presented in the opposite direction:

_____ _____ _____ _____ _____ _____ _____ dish.
_____ _____ _____ _____ _____ _____ a dish.
_____ _____ _____ _____ _____ on a dish., etc.

We can see, too, that if the sentence is in the passive voice (rather than the active voice), or as said in transformational grammar, *a passive transformation* (rather than a kernel sentence), there is a reduction in the effectiveness of context cues:

1. The dog was chas— ing a cat.   (kernel sentence)
2. The dog was chas— ed by a cat.   (passive transformation)

In substance, context cues are easier to use in kernel sentences than in transformations.[3] It has been corroborated "that transformations take more time to understand than the underlying kernel sentences" even for mature readers [Schlesinger 1968, p. 45]. This suggests that the phonics teacher use kernel sentences rather than transformations, at least at the early levels of the phonics program. This is not necessary, however, if the teacher uses the language experience approach. This program uses the actual language children speak, which will be largely transformations. But since these children have produced this language, they have no difficulty in understanding its syntax when it is heard.

It appears that (with the exceptions given) the child should be able to determine from the first two words of a sentence whether the sentence is a question. Notice how the beginning words of these sentences signal that they will be questions:

> Is the girl taking her doll?
> Did the girl take her doll?
> Who took the doll?
> What did the girl take?
> Which girl took the doll?
> What is the girl taking?
> What did the girl take?
> When did the girl take the doll?

---

[3] A kernel sentence is a simple (not compound or complex), declarative, undescriptive (no adjectives), positive (no negatives) sentence in the active voice, with no words in the possessive case:

Kernel: The boy rode the bike.

Transformation:
(question)   (passive)   (adj.)   (relative)
Was   the bike ridden by the big boy who

(neg.)   (poss.)
would not share his bike?

On the other hand, it is not possible to use the first two words in this way for these kinds of sentences:

> She is taking the doll, isn't she?
> If she takes her doll, will you take yours?

Limitations of Context Cues

Context cues are not completely adequate for the recognition of unfamiliar words for several reasons. *One* is that the different words which conceivably could fit into slots in sentences often have very similar shapes (*doll-ball*). It is readily apparent that an author's intended meaning in a sentence would be lost to readers not attending to the letter differences in *doll* and *ball*. We have shown how a connected or continuous discourse, more than one sentence in succession, about *doll* or *ball* would condition this to some extent. So, beginning readers are well served by advice to check the letter forms of all the unfamiliar words they attempt to read. For *ball* and *doll* this could mean only a check of the beginning letter in the words. A knowledge of phonics is necessary, of course, for this kind of "checking." This "checking" means the pupil uses context cues and phonics (letter shapes and the sounds the letter stands for) together.

Two, we note that as a general rule one or two (or more) words can be used (be brought up in the reader's mind) to give some sense to a given context. But this may not be necessarily the sense intended by the author of the sentence. Intelligent guesses may be wrong ones. If so, a recourse to letter perception (phonics) is necessary.

Three, context cues are of little help for readers in efforts to recognize proper names, as for example in these sentences:

> Bill has a cat. He named him _____.

Too, proper names often are not repeated enough so that familiarity with them can be achieved by the reader.

Four, written language that is unnatural, that is not normally heard or spoken by the child, can also reduce the utilization of context cues. There is evidence, moreover, that many popular basal readers present written materials that contain sentence patterns unlike any the child has ever heard [Smith, Goodman, & Meredith 1970, p. 272]; for example, "See Tip run." Such abnormal sentence patterns work against the use of context cues since they sound strange and artificial to the child.

Five, the more complex the sentence the more unlikely it is that one can use context cues. It is obviously easier to utilize such cues in *Bill saw the dog*, than in *Just before Bill walked into the school yard, he saw a large, black dog, which was lying in the roadway gasping for air as if he were sick or had been run over by a car.* The tangled clausal structure of the latter sentence prevents children from easily applying the cues this sentence presents.

Six, function words, generally those parts of speech other than nouns, verbs, adjectives, and adverbs, also cause problems in the application of context cues. Compared to nouns, verbs, adjectives, and adverbs, function words are difficult for children to use as context cues. Words like *where, also, above, then,* and *but* do not refer to concrete objects or actions, or to modifications of these objects or actions. And yet, unless children recognize function words fluently, their utilization of context cues will be seriously hampered.

Seven, children are handicapped in their use of context cues when certain parts of speech take on functions they ordinarily do not fulfill. For example, a word ordinarily read by a child as a noun can function as an adjective:

He is a *bike* rider. He wore a *cowboy* hat.

(We know that *bike* and *cowboy* are not adjectives except in the previous function because they do not fit the test frame, "The _____ boy seemed very _____," in both blanks. They take only the inflection *s'* or *s,* another reason they are adjectives only by function.)

Eight, there are definite limits to intelligent guessing. If children read the sentence *Bill saw the dog* as *Bill was the dog,* it will do them little good to check the context to see if *was* would fit the sentence slot. Both *was* and *saw* will fit, because either sentence is grammatical. It becomes necessary for the reader at such a juncture to check the serial order of the letters in the little word *saw* to see if it is *w-as* or *s-aw.*

Nine, it is obvious that to make an intelligent guess about a single word in a sentence, one must be able to recognize practically all the other words that surround it. While the statement *Bill was the dog* is grammatically correct, it is logically improbable, since few dogs are named *Bill.* Therefore, this may in some way trigger the child's thinking from *was* to *saw.* It is reasonable to assume that the improbability of *was* would direct the child to make a check of the letters in *was* and *saw* and to make the necessary correction to *saw.*

Ten, teaching children to use context cues too soon may create in them a dependence on this mode of word recognition that can hinder their overall reading growth. The data from Andrew Biemiller's study of the effects of too early a dependence on context cues shows

> . . . that the child's first task in learning to read is mastery of the use of graphic information [roughly, phonics], and possibly, of the notion that one specific spoken word corresponds to one written word. The child's early use of contextual information does not appear to greatly facilitate progress in

acquiring reading skill. The longer he stays in the early, context-emphasizing phase without showing an increase in the use of graphic information the poorer a reader he is at the end of the year. Thus, the teacher should do a considerable proportion of early reading training in situations providing no context at all, in order to compel children to use graphic information as much as possible. As they show evidence of doing so (through accurate reading out of context) they would be given contextual material to read [1970, p. 95].

Francis [1972] also found that beginning readers are more able to recognize and utilize words than whole sentences. Chester's findings [1972] question their use of context cues.

Eleven, the value of context cues for beginning readers depends on the spelling-sound similarity of the words being taught. As Ruth Hartley [1971] has shown, if a list of words with minimal spelling-sound differences are taught (*hen-ten-pen-men*), the use of the words *plus* a context cue "seemed to have a depressing effect" on the learning of such words. However, "a graphic stimulus word plus a context cue was most successful when presented with a maximal contrast list" [p. 118] such as *rake-show-king-ten*.

This evidence suggests that when minimal contrast words (ones in which only one grapheme difference is apparent, e.g., *hen-ten*) are taught in phonics, the pupil may not attempt to employ context cues. Just as important, though, when words of greater contrast are taught, children should be increasingly encouraged to use context cues.

Twelve, the utility of context cues is conditioned as to whether an unknown word in context is a monosyllabic word or a polysyllabic word. It is true that the former, short words, often have several different or possible meanings. On the contrary, polysyllabic words usually have fewer, often only one, specific denotations. Thus, they should be easier to guess from the context than monosyllabic words.

Thirteen, it is axiomatic that the use of context cues can come into play only if a child can readily distinguish the boundaries of words. The phonics teacher cannot assume beginning readers know that spaces between words mark off their boundaries, however. Nancy Meltzer and Robert Herse [1969] discovered that the salience of space between words as a determinant of word boundaries is low for beginning readers. They found young children go through stages in developing this understanding. They first think letters are words, before they note a word is more than one letter. They move, then, to the use of spaces between words as signals for word boundaries, unless a word is short. Juxtaposed short words may be thought of as a single word. Long words, to the contrary, are often seen as two words. In this case, certain letters take precedence over spaces between words as the determinant of word boundaries. For example, beginning readers will say a word is two words if it has tall or ascending letters, like *t* or *l.* A word will be said to end at the tall letter.

With this in mind, it is clear the phonics teacher should take specific steps to condition a child to realize that the space between words mark off their boundaries. Using word cards, one word to a card, to make up and take down sentences from pocket charts one word at a time would be a way to show this. Leaving more space between words written for the child than is normally done would help (see Chapter 7). Taking care to remind children that words with tall letters are not two words is an appropriate precaution. Showing children that their rather continuous stream of spoken language when written is broken into discrete parts, by recording sentences as children speak them, would help point out the need to pay attention to spaces between words.

Teaching the Use of Context Cues

The descriptions of context cues given so far have suggested many different kinds of activities the teacher can use to enhance pupils' ability to utilize these cues. In general, we would agree that a good way to develop the use of context cues is through wide reading by pupils of subjects and books that hold a special interest for them. Thus motivated, they also have the incentive to work out, on their own, many recognitions of words through the context of the material they read. The wise teacher also will scan the reading materials that pupils are required to read in connection with the so-called content fields, mathematics, science, and the like, to find passages that contain potentially difficult words. These passages can be used to help pupils employ context cues for the recognition of such difficult words.

A third kind of practice is exemplified by the examples that follow. They are intended to be used occasionally to refresh children's understandings of the potential usefulness of context cues, to give initial practice in their use, to add variety and diversion to the phonics lesson, or to test whether children understand the function of context cues.

The teacher should note that any exercise in the development of abilities to use context cues generally can be put into one of three categories: (1) when the unknown word has a common meaning, (2) when the unrecognized word has a special or peculiar meaning, and (3) when the unidentified word is one that is not in the child's listening vocabulary. This list also represents the order in which these different kinds of words should be taught through the use of context cues.

We do not recommend one practice that has been advocated for developing context cues—that is the study of grammar for this purpose. Some think that teaching children sentence parts and the different forms of sentence structure will help them "learn how to cope with difficulties that stem from involved sentence structures" [Karlin 1971, p. 193]. There is no evidence, at least, that a study of traditional grammar has any such useful-

ness. Perhaps a knowledge of "new" grammar, the transformational-gener-
ative grammar, may prove worthy in this respect.

1. Even an apparently simple word like *show* can be put into different
    contexts, which require that different meanings be brought to it.

    Did he *show* the judge the photographs that were taken?
    (put into sight)
    Perhaps the judge will *show* him some mercy.   (grant)
    The evidence will *show* that Mr. Brown was guilty. (prove)
    The DA will *show* how the accident happened.   (explain)

2. Somewhat different contexts can be given from which pupils are asked
    to supply the missing word, concentrating on the context for this
    purpose. If these passages come from readings the pupils have selected
    themselves, so much the better.

    a. The unknown word is *defined* by the passage:
       Level lands between mountains are called _____.
       The name that is given for animals with warm blood is _____.

    b. A passage uses a word and its *synonym:*
       He is the meanest, most _____ man in town.
       The careless boy did the work in a _____ manner.

    c. A *familiar expression* is used:
       That pan leaks like a _____.

    d. A passage uses a word and its *antonym:*
       The boy awoke from a deep _____.

    e. An *immediate experience* helps.
       The baby lions were _____ with the ball just like kittens do.

    f. The missing word can *conclude* or *summarize* the passage:
       Each time he walked through the graveyard he became more
       _____.

    g. The passage has a *figure of speech:*
       The dam will be built to _____ the river.   (harness)
       The cat's eyes _____ like little lights.

    h. An *appositive* is a context cue:
       The minutes, a _____ of the meeting, were kept by Jane. (record)

    i. The appearance of a *series of items* can classify an unfamiliar word:
       He likes to write many different kinds of things—poems, _____,
       plays, and stories.

3. Use a paragraph in which the word to be determined by context cues is imbedded:

> The boys walked by the red circus tent. "Why are all the people going in there?" said Bob.
> "The menagerie is in there," explained his older brother. "Let's go in and find out what animals they have.

4. Use the "cloze" procedure. Delete every fifth, tenth, etc., word, replace it with an underline of uniform length, and have children fill in the blanks. This is good for testing children's ability to use context cues. Also delete only certain parts of speech. A variation of this procedure is to make a tape recording in which certain words, as above, are omitted. Give the pupils a copy of the script and have them fill in the omitted words as the tape is played.

5. Use pictures that can be matched with the omitted words in a prepared passage that is given to the children.

6. Give the children sentences in which only a part of the omitted word is spelled. Begin with the first and last letters. Then, spell only the phonograms.

> The boy's face was very c_____. _____d. c_____d.
> The boy's face was very _old.

7. Part of the use of context cues involves the knowledge that certain words (pronouns) can stand in the place of (fill the sentence slot) certain kinds of nouns. It is useful, therefore, to go through passages making sure that children are conscious of this, showing them how the pronoun referent works, and testing their ability to find the word the pronoun stands in the place of.

8. Have children restore the missing parts of common rhetorical devices.

> Both Bill _____ Joe were here.
> Not only Bill _____ Joe were here.
> _____ Bill was here, Joe left.
> _____ _____ Bill could come, Joe left.
> Joe came _____ Bill was here.
> Bill came, _____, after Joe left.
> If Bill will come, _____ will Joe.
> _____ Bill comes, Joe won't.
> _____ Bill came, Joe didn't.
> Bill came. _____, Joe didn't.

9. Have children replace words in slots. For example, have them think of words that would fit the slot occupied by *few* in *Few men were working.* (*Many, more, most of the, only a few of the,* etc.) This can be done with many adjectives and adverbs.

10. Say: "What word like the one in the slot is the word that makes the sentences a good one?" Write:

> The man was an *act.* (actor)
> She is very *music.* (musical)
> Did he use good *judge?* (judgment)
> Obey the *safe* rules. (safety)
> Always be *social* with strangers. (sociable)

11. Discuss with children the special meanings of idioms. For example:

> The man *had a run* of luck.
> The man *ran out* of luck.

12. To help children correctly assign the part-of-speech category that is needed before a word can be given its proper sounding, have children read sentences such as:

> Will you *permit* me to burn these papers?
> Do you have a *permit* to burn these papers?

Other words to be used: *conflict, contract, address, rebel, import, setup (set up), greenhouse (green house).*

13. Follow the general instructions for integrating exceptional words into the phonics program. See page 232.

REFERENCES

Biemiller, Andrew. "The Development of the Use of Graphic and Contextual Information as Children Learn to Read." *Reading Research Quarterly,* 6(1970):75–96.

Bormuth, John R. *Literacy in the Suburbs.* Chicago: University of Chicago, Department of Education, 1970, mimeographed.

Chester, Robert D. "Differences in Learnability of Content and Function Words Presented in Isolation and Oral Context When Taught to High and Low Socioeconomic Level Students." *Dissertation Abstracts International,* 32(1972):3833A.

Clay, Marie M., and Imlach, Robert H. "Juncture, Pitch and Stress as

Reading Behavior Variables." *Journal of Verbal Learning and Verbal Behavior,* 10(1971):133–139.

Compton, Mary E. "A Study of the Relationship Between Oral Language Facility and Reading Achievement of Selected First Grade Children." *Dissertation Abstracts International,* 32(1972):6448A–6449A.

Dale, Edgar, and Chall, Jeanne. "A Formula for Predicting Readability." *Educational Research Bulletin,* 27(1948):11–20.

Eash, Maurice J. *Reading and Thinking.* Garden City, N.Y.: Doubleday, 1967.

Francis, Hazel. "Sentence Structure and Learning to Read." *British Journal of Educational Psychology,* 42(1972):113–119.

Goodman, Kenneth S. "A Linguistic Study of Cues and Miscues in Reading." *Elementary English,* 42(1965):639–643.

Hall, Mary Anne. *Teaching Reading as a Language Experience.* Columbus: Charles E. Merrill, 1970.

Hartley, Ruth M. "A Method of Increasing the Ability of First Grade Pupils to Use Phonetic Generalizations." *California Journal of Educational Research,* 22(1971):9–16.

Hochberg, Julian. "Components of Literacy: Speculations and Exploratory Research," *Basic Studies on Reading,* eds. Harry Levin and Joanna P. Williams. New York: Basic Books, 1970.

Karlin, Robert. *Teaching Elementary Reading.* New York: Harcourt Brace Jovanovich, 1971.

Levin, Harry, and Kaplan, Eleanor L. "Grammatical Structure and Reading," *Basic Studies on Reading,* eds. Harry Levin and Joanna P. Williams. New York: Basic Books, 1970.

Martin, Ruth G. "An Analysis of Three Types of Visual Cues Used in Word Perception Under Four Types of Presentation." *Dissertation Abstracts International,* 30(1970):5169A–5170A.

Meltzer, Nancy, and Herse, Robert. "The Boundaries of Written Words as Seen by First Graders." *Journal of Reading Behavior,* 1(1969):3–13.

Schlesinger, I. M. *Sentence Structure and the Reading Process.* The Hague: Mouton, 1968.

Singer, Harry, et al. "The Effects of Pictures and Contextual Conditions on Learning Responses to Printed Words." *Reading Research Quarterly,* 9(1973–1974):555–567.

Smith, E. Brooks, Goodman, Kenneth S., and Meredith, Robert. *Language and Thinking in the Elementary School.* New York: Holt, Rinehart and Winston, 1970.

Smith, Frank. *Understanding Reading.* New York: Holt, Rinehart and Winston, 1971.

Smith, Henry P., and Dechant, Emerald V. *Psychology in Teaching Reading.* Englewood Cliffs, N.J.: Prentice-Hall, 1961.

Spache, George D. *Reading in the Elementary School.* Boston: Allyn & Bacon, 1964.

Weber, Rose-Marie. "First-Graders' Use of Grammatical Context in Reading," *Basic Studies on Reading,* eds. Harry Levin and Joanna P. Williams. New York: Basic Books, 1970.

GLOSSARY

Acoustics. Another term for sound and sound perception. Speech acoustics is *speech sounds* and speech sound perception.

Affixes. A collective term for prefixes and suffixes.

Allograph. One of the variety of graphic forms a letter may be given. For example, *A* and *a* are allographs of this letter.

Allophone. A sound that is part of a bundle of sounds that makes up a *phoneme*. The difference in sound among allophones is not enough to affect any meaning difference, e.g., *law—lit*. Since meaning is not affected, an allophone is not classified as a separate phoneme.

Alphabetic principle. Refers to the use of a set of letters, an alphabet, to represent the *phonemes* of a language. Chinese writing, as an example, is not based on the alphabetic principle.

Auditory blending. A procedure of *word recognition* in which the individual *phonemes* of a word supposedly are first isolated and then blended together one after the other to form the sound of the word.

Auditory perception. The ability to hear sounds, including individual *phonemes*.

Basal readers. A series of books written for each grade level in the elementary school that purport to provide the basic instruction in reading.

Blends. See **consonant-letter cluster** or **vowel-letter cluster**.

Checked vowels. *Vowel phonemes* heard in *closed syllables*, /i, a, o͝o, u, e/.

Closed syllable. A *syllable* that ends in a *consonant phoneme*. Also called *phonogram* in this book.

Code-emphasis method or **approach.** The method used in beginning reading instruction in which there is a direct, intensive, systematic, and early teaching of *phonics*.

Compound words. Words of two *syllables* in which each syllable is an autonomous word. For example, *outside, into*.

Comprehension. See **reading.**

Consonant. A *phoneme* made by an obstruction or blocking or some other restriction of the free passage of breath through the speech cavities as one speaks. We describe consonants as *plosives, fricatives, nasals, laterals,* and *semivowels*.

Consonant blend. See **consonant-letter cluster.**

Consonant letter. A letter used to represent a *consonant phoneme* in writing.

Consonant-letter cluster. Cluster of adjacent *consonant letters* in words, as *st* in *step*. Often called consonant blends.

Context cues. The cues to *word recognition* supplied by the remainder of the sentence, paragraph, or discourse in which the given word appears.

Cursive handwriting. The style in which the letters are connected, e.g., *cursive*.

Decode. To decode a word is to discover the *phonemes* its letters represent. Decoding is one part of *word recognition;* the use of *context cues* is another part.

Diacritical marking. A special mark added to conventional letters in dictionaries to indicate the *phoneme* the marked letter represents, e.g., ē (be), or ŧh (the). This system is used in this book to record phonemes in writing.

Dialect. One form of a given language, e.g., English, spoken in a certain locality or geographical area, or by a racial or social group. A dialect has different pronunciations from other dialects, and yet is not sufficiently distinct from other dialects in a language to be regarded as a different language. While dialects correspond roughly to speech regions, any speech region can have at least two dialects, represented by the *standard* and *nonstandard speech* of the region. "Black English" is thought of as a racial or social dialect.

Dictionary syllabication. The set of rules dictionaries have used to explain how they divide *polysyllabic words*, e.g., *chok-ing*. This can be contrasted by the way many dictionaries syllabicate words in their *phonemic spellings* of these words, e.g., *cho-king*.

Digraph. A pair of letters in a word that represents a single *phoneme*. For example *th* in *path* and *ee* in *meet*.

Diphthong. A blend or fusion of two adjacent *vowel phonemes* in a single *syllable*. Diphthongs begin with the first vowel phoneme and then glide or gradually change into the second vowel phoneme. Some phoneticians say all vowel sounds are diphthongized to some extent. It is easy, however, to hear diphthongs in the words *pay, hide, owl, cold,* and *boil.*

Distribution of phonemes. Refers to the permissible sequences of *speech sounds* that are found in English words. See **spelling patterns.** There are some sequences of sounds that English speakers do not make, e.g., /*shp*ild/.

Encode. To encode a word is to spell it. To encode is the opposite of to *decode.*

Exceptional words. In this book this term is used to refer to any word at a given level whose *spelling patterns* have not been taught to that point.

Eye-voice span. The extent of time in oral reading that the voice trails behind where the eye is fixated on the print. In oral reading the fixation of the reader's eye on the print of a text always is ahead of any word that has been read aloud in the text.

Free vowels. All vowel sounds other than *checked vowels.* Free vowels can occur in any place in syllables.

Fricatives. *Consonants* made with a continuously flowing but partially constricted breath stream. Notice this when you say words with the phonemes /s, z, sh, zh, f, v, th, th, h/.

Function words. Words other than verbs, adverbs, nouns, or adjectives. Also called *marker words* or *structure words.* In the following sentence the function words are in italics: *Who* were *the* man *and* woman *in the* big car?

Glide. A *phoneme* characterized by a rapid change in resonance that is produced by a gradually changing movement of the speech organs involved. Glides are often said to be /w, y, r, hw/.

Grapheme. The written representation of a *phoneme*. Graphemes can be single letters, e.g., *hit* equals three graphemes: *h-i-t*. This is not always so. For example, *though* has two graphemes: *th-ough*.

Graphemics. The scientific study of the manner in which graphemes are used to represent *phonemes*.

Graphonemes. Another word for *phonograms*.

High-frequency words. The most commonly spoken and written words in English. A small number of these words accounts for a relatively large percentage of all the running words one speaks or reads.

Homophone. A word that has the same *phonemes* as another word but has a different meaning, as in *bare—bear*.

Implicit speech. See **silent speech.**

Incidental or **indirect phonics.** A *phonics* program in which phonics is taught only when it is deemed the child needs it to recognize a word. This approach contrasts with *systematic phonics.*

Inflections. See **intonation.**

Informal reading inventory. A process of evaluation of oral reading that counts all omissions, mispronunciations, substitutions, additions, and repetitions of words, as well as the times the reader is inattentive to punctuation. From the scores thus obtained the reader is said to be reading at a frustration level, an instructional level, or an independent level.

Intonation. The pattern of changes in pitch that occur when one speaks or reads a word aloud.

Juncture. Points between two adjacent *syllables* or *phonemes* are called junctures. *Close juncture* is the normal transition between *phonemes* or between syllables, as in *fry* or *funny. Open juncture* is a more obvious pause or break heard between certain syllables. Two strongly stressed syllables do not exist next to each other without an obvious pause or break, an open juncture, between them. Sometimes this is the only means of establishing meanings for words, e.g., *nitrate* vs. *night-rate, I scream* vs. *ice cream.*

Lateral phoneme. *Phoneme* spoken when the voiced breath stream escapes laterally over the side of the tongue. Notice this in /l/.

Less-accented vowel. See **schwa.**

Linguistics. The scientific study of language. This includes *phonetics, phonemics,* grammar, *semantics,* and *morphology.*

Linguistic transcription symbol. A symbol especially designed by linguists to write spoken language. For example, the word *myth* could be written /mɪθ/.

Long vowels. The *phonemes* /ā, ē, ī, ō, ū/ are often called "long" vowels.

Manuscript handwriting. The style in which letters are not connected, e.g., manuscript.

Marker letter e. An *e* is called a marker letter when it occurs in words like *hate*. It is said to be part of the vowel *grapheme* for this word. It signals that the *a* in *hate* will be read with a given sound.

Marker words. See **function words.**

Meaning-emphasis method or **approach.** A method of teaching reading in which it is held if children are given "meaningful" material to read, this, in itself, will develop most of their *word recognition* skills. This method is the opposite of the *code-emphasis method.*

Miscues. The deviations from the actual printed text a child makes when reading a passage aloud.

Monosyllabic words. Words that have one syllable.

Morpheme. The smallest meaningful unit in our language. A morpheme can be a single letter, *s* in *cats.* The word *cats* is two morphemes since *cat* means one thing and *s* (pluralness) means another. Thus, it can be seen that the term *word* is not sufficient to explain what is meant by "smallest meaningful unit" in language. Some morphemes such as *dog, jump,* or *good* can occur without being attached to any other morpheme. They are *free* forms. Other morphemes such as *re, ex, ed, er* cannot occur alone. These are *bound* forms. Roughly, then, morphemes are the free form words plus bound forms represented by inflections (e.g., *s, ed, ing*) and derivations (words using prefixes and suffixes). The *syllable* is not the same as a morpheme. For example, *Mississippi* is one morpheme and four syllables; *goes* is two morphemes and one syllable. It is difficult at times to generalize about morphemes, however. "How do you do?" is one morpheme since it is a formalistic greeting and not a question. Dancer is two morphemes: *danc-er,* but *finger* and *father,* which have *er,* have one morpheme each. *Reread* is two morphemes; *remote* is one.

Morphology. Scientific study of morphemes.

Morphophonemic spelling. The relationship between the morphemes of a word and its sound-spelling correspondences. Often this involves the spelling in a derivation of a word in which a spelling-sound correspondence in a base word is different than in the derivation, for example, in *bomb* versus *bombard.*

Nasal phoneme. *Phonemes* spoken so that an opening is left for the speech breath to enter the nasal passages; heard when you say /m, n, ng/.

Nonstandard speech. A variety of *phonemes, intonation,* grammar, and vocabulary used by low-income, poorly educated people in a speech region. Each speech region has both standard and nonstandard speakers. "Nonstandard" should not be equated with "inferior."

Open syllable. A syllable that ends in a *vowel phoneme.*

Orthography. Another name for the spelling system. Sometimes referred to as the scientific study of spelling.

Phoneme. A discrete, identifiable speech sound. We say there are 41 phonemes in *"Western" dialect.* Other speech areas in the United States have more or different phonemes. *Speech sounds* and *phonemes* are synonymous terms.

Phonemics. The scientific study of the *phonemes* or speech sounds of a peculiar language.

Phonemic spelling. The spellling of a word according to some aspect of *predictable spelling.* For example, /rat/ is spelled phonemically. Its *phonemic transcription* /rat/ is the same as its letter spelling, *rat.* To the contrary, /uv/ is not spelled phonemically.

Phonemic or **phonetic transcription.** The manner in which one can record a phoneme of a language with a written symbol. Phonemic transcriptions are written between slant lines, / /. Phonetic transcriptions are put between brackets [ ].

Phonetic alphabet. See **phonemic** or **phonetic transcription.**

Phonetics. The scientific study of *phonemes* used in all languages.

Phonic analysis. The use of phonics information to *decode* words.

Phonics. The information taken from *phonetics, phonemics,* and *graphemics* that children learning to read and spell can use to help them understand the *spelling-sound correspondences* of English.

Phonics generalization or **rule.** A *spelling-sound correspondence* that occurs as a *predictable spelling.* For example, one rule is that the *vowel letter* in a VC spelling in *monosyllabic words* is read as a *short vowel,* as in h*a*t.

Phonogram. See **closed syllable.**

Phonology. Another term for *phonemics.*

Plosive. This is a *phoneme* spoken so that the speech breath is stopped and then subsequently released in a somewhat explosive puff of air; it is heard, for example, when you say /p, b, t, d, k, g/.

Polysyllabic words. Words that have more than one *syllable.*

Predictable spelling. A word or *syllable* spelled with letters that predict with a high degree of confidence for the reader which *phonemes* these letters represent. For example, the spelling of *rat* is predictable since *r-a-t* are letters commonly used to represent the three phonemes spoken in this pattern. Contrariwise, *of* is unpredictable since *o-f* are not commonly used to represent the phonemes /uv/. The term is also used in this book to mean any sound-spelling correspondence, at any given level, a child has not been so far taught to recognize.

Prominence. A collective term that includes all the aspects of pitch, *stress, juncture,* sonority, and loudness that distinguish the dominant sound of a syllable (usually a *vowel phoneme*).

Pseudoword. A series of letters seen in true words but never seen in the combination displayed in a pseudoword. For example, *tr* and *ut* are seen in *try* and *hut.* These letters can therefore be used to write the pseudoword *trut.* Pseudowords are useful in testing a child's ability to apply *phonics* information.

Psycholinguistics. The scientific study of the relationships of *linguistics* and human behavior.

R-colored vowel. Any *vowel phoneme* in a *syllable* that immediately precedes the /r/ *phoneme.*

Reading. In this book reading is defined as (1) the skills of *word recognition* and (2) the ability to understand (comprehend) the meanings intended by its author of a given passage of writing.

Reading readiness. The training children supposedly need before beginning to learn *phonics.*

Recurrent spelling patterns. See **closed syllable.**

Redundancy. See **sequential redundancy.**

Schwa. A *vowel phoneme* that is less accented, that has less *prominence,* than other vowels. Usually heard in *polysyllabic words:* c*a*nal, batt*e*r, penc*i*l, kingd*o*m, min*u*te.

Semantics. The scientific study of the connotations and denotations (meanings) of words.

Semivowel. A phoneme that can be either a *vowel* or a *consonant* depending on where it is heard. Linguists disagree as to what are semivowels. For the purposes of this book we call /w/ and /y/ semivowels.

Sequential redundancy. The likelihood that if a certain letter appears in a *syllable* or word, only certain other letters will follow. For example, *u* follows *q* almost always.

Short vowels. Said to be the *phonemes* /a, e, i, o, u/.

Sight words. Words said to be recognized by a beginning reader without any analysis by this reader of the letters of the word for cues to its recognition. This is a widespread but fallacious notion as to how beginning readers recognize words.

Silent speech. Subvocalization, or the inner, implicit speech one makes when reading. Mature readers use less silent speech in *reading* than do beginning or poor readers.

Sonority. This refers to the resonance of *phonemes*. The phonemes /m/, /n/, and /ng/ are sonorous consonants. Contrast these with /t/ or /p/. Vowels have more sonority than consonants.

Speech region. A geographical area of the United States where one hears a different *dialect* from that spoken in another speech region. The boundaries of some speech regions are blurred and difficult to define.

Speech sound. See **phoneme.**

Spelling patterns. Refers to the sequential ordering of letters in *syllables* allowed in writing English. For example, *rat* is a spelling pattern; *rta* is not. See **closed syllable** and **predictable spelling.**

Spelling reform. The attempts made to establish an English alphabet large enough to have the same number of different letters as we have *phonemes*. This reform proposes also that one letter and one letter only be used to represent each phoneme.

Spelling-sound correspondences. The relationships between the *phonemes* and the *graphemes* that represent them in writing. Some of these correspondences are said to be *predictable spellings;* others are not.

Standard speech. A variety of *phonemes, intonation,* grammar, and vocabulary used by higher-income, better-educated people in a *speech region.*

Stress. This is a combination of loudness, duration, and/or rising pitch in *phonemes*. Linguists also believe there are three or four relative levels of stress in words (not all words have all levels, of course).

Structure words. See **function words.**

Syllabic. The speech sound given *prominence* in a *syllable,* usually a *vowel.* Can be /m, n, l/.

Syllable. A syllable almost always consists of a *vowel phoneme* (its prominent sound) and usually one or more *consonant phonemes* that precede or follow the vowel phoneme. *Phonemes* must be spoken in syllables to be heard as such. Thus, the syllable is the irreducible unit of speech. How the boundaries of syllables are determined is a controversial matter in *linguistics.*

Systematic phonics. See **code-emphasis method.**

Unvoiced phoneme. See **voiceless phoneme.**

Visual perception or **discrimination.** The ability to see individual items in any larger visual display, or against a background. In *reading readiness* the term often refers to children's abilities to identify geometric forms, to match designs, to name parts of a picture, and to follow directions in displays where eye tracking or eye pursuit is called for.

Vocal cords. Two folds of ligament and elastic membrane located at the top of the windpipe (in the larnyx), directly behind the Adam's apple. Air pressure through the windpipe acts on the membranes, which are blocked, narrowed, or vibrated as various *phonemes* are made.

Voiced phoneme. A phoneme made when the vocal cords are in vibration. Heard when you say /b, d, g, v, th, z, zh, j, w/.

Voiceless phoneme. A phoneme made when the vocal cords are more at rest than when a *voiced phoneme* is said. Heard when you say /p, t, k, f, th, s, sh, ch, h/.

Vowel. A *phoneme* made with an unobstructed passage of breath through the speech cavities as one speaks. We have described in this book *checked, free,* and free, *less-accented* vowel *phonemes.* Vowel *phonemes* have greater *prominence* than *consonant phonemes.*

Vowel-letter cluster. Two or more adjacent letters in a *syllable* that represent a *vowel phoneme* or *diphthong.* If this is two letters, it is often called a vowel *digraph.*

Vowel letters. Letters used to represent vowel *phonemes* in writing.

"Western" speech or **dialect.** The set of *phonemes* used in this book based on general American speech.

Whole-word method. See **sight words.**

Word recognition. The ability to give the name of a word after seeing it in print. See **reading.** Words are recognized by a combination of *phonics* and *context cues.*

APPENDIX

Reading Games

Most of the following games are played with decks of letter, letter cluster, phonogram, or word cards. Have children make the cards for letters, word parts, or words.

1. **Fish. Old Maid. Rummy.** All these familiar games can be played.

2. **Password.** Second child guesses the card the first child has read silently. The first child gives letter clues.

3. **Vowel or Consonant Match.** Take turns in matching or reading cards whose letters, which represent a certain sound, are in color.

4. **Bingo.** One child reads cards while others place their cards on spaces.

5. **Picture-Card Match.** Children cut out and paste pictures on cards. Then, they match these with word cards.

6. **Dice.** Use 1" by 1" lumber. Cut off in 1" pieces to make cubes. Print letters, words, etc., on each block. Roll out and read.

7. **Scrambled Words.** Match cards in which letters are scrambled with those that use the same letters to make a word. A form of anagrams.

8. **Phonemic Words.** Match word cards spelled "phonemically" with those spelled conventionally, e.g., *cats-kats, laughed-laft.*

9. **Word Guess.** Child chooses word card from deck. Others try to guess what it is, letter by letter.

10. **Tachistoscope Game.** Cut out some familiar shape, e.g., a football. Print words, letters, etc., on continuing strips of paper. Slip the strips into slots in the football so one word shows for a brief time.

11. **Railway.** Each word card is in the form of a different railway car. Who can make up the longest train?

12. **Reader Words.** During each reader lesson have children write several cards from the lesson. Pair up and flash the cards to each other.

13. **Carpenter.** Read a card from a deck and add a shingle to the roof of a play house, or a board to its side.

14. **Checkers.** Paste word cards on checker squares. Play game as usual except child must call word for the space moved into.

15. **Picture Checkers.** Paste pictures on checkerboard square. The object is to cover pictures with word cards naming them.

16. **Categories.** Mix up many word cards that refer to several categories (home, play, etc., or parts of speech). First child to sort out the deck wins.

17. **Clothespins.** A part of a word is written on a clothespin. The other part is on a card. Pin the two together. Also use pins and pictures.

18. **Magnet.** Tape pictures on a cookie sheet. Glue small bar magnet to each card. Children attach cards to proper pictures.

19. **Fish.** Use same word cards as with no. 18. Here children "fish" in a bag or bowl for the cards with a fishing pole with a magnet for a "hook."

20. **Racing Game.** Make a race track divided into spaces. Use small toys or cars. Each card read from deck allows child to move down the track. (Do same to "climb" a mountain, stairway, or a beanstalk, to "slide" down a slide, to "land" a plane, to "score" a round of golf [have different par—words read—for different holes], or to "pull" feathers out of a turkey's tail.)

21. **Synonyms-Antonyms.** Make a chart with a list of words and adjoining spaces. Child puts synonym or antonym card into the spaces.

22. **Memory.** Players pick a card from the deck, look at it (or show it) momentarily, and place it face down. Players try to match it with one in their hands.

23. **Spin and Win.** Paste word cards on colored poker chips. Child uses a spinner, sees the color it indicates, and reads the matching poker chip.

24. **Ring Toss.** The number of the peg the ring lands on represents a deck of word cards. The higher the number, the more difficult the cards. Score equals number of cards read plus the number of the deck they came from.

25. **Basket Toss.** Same idea as no. 24. If children make a "basket" with a bean bag they get a card to read. Vary this by tossing the bean bag onto squares with different numbers that refer to decks of cards.

26. **Riddle.** Write simple riddles on cards. Have pictures or other cards to answer them.

27. **Shoestring Match.** Use shoestrings of different colors. Attach the end of each string to a spot on a chart of the same color, and to a word, letter, etc., of the same color. Print a row of words, letters, etc., in black on the opposite side of the chart. Children insert a colored string into a hole alongside the black words. Then they turn the chart over to see if the color of the string pushed through matches the color surrounding the hole on the back side of the chart. Use for matching and contrasting.

28. **Cloze.** Write a story on a chart. Leave every fifth, tenth, etc., word blank. Children fit in words from their decks to complete the story. If necessary, write the first letter of each omitted word.

29. **Synonym (Antonym) Search.** Underline words in sentences written on a chart. Children find words from their decks as synonyms or antonyms.

30. **Mix and Match.** One child spreads out cards face down. Second child turns over cards one at a time, returning them face down and tries to remember which cards are pairs.

31. **Pocketchart.** One child places cards face down in pocketchart then shows a duplicate card for one of those so placed. Other children try to remember where the matching card is on the chart.

32. **Writing.** One child begins to print a word, pausing after each letter. Other children guess from cards in their hands what the word is.

33. **Pairs.** One child places cards face down in a pocketchart. One of the cards so placed matches another. Child wins who can recall which are the pairs.

34. **Thinking.** One child with a word card concealed from other children says, "I'm thinking of a word." Others guess what it is from cards they hold. They can ask questions, e.g., "Does it begin with a *b?*"

35. **Parts.** Distribute word-part cards. One child holds up one part of a

word. The child who can match it wins. Also played so that two parts make a word.

36. **Whistle or Hum.** Children begin by slowly turning over word cards from their decks. Teacher whistles or hums a familiar tune. When the music stops, each child must read the card turned over at that moment.

37. **Dominoes.** Play dominoes with words or word parts. Tape words on dominoes.

38. **Pegboard.** Cut up pegboard into 12″ by 12″ sizes. Each child plays with pegs of a different color. For each card read, child may place a peg. At end of game count to see who has the most pegs. Also played so that first child to finish a design wins.

39. **Tick-Tack-Toe.** Make a T-T-T design on a chart. Cover each space with a word card, face down. Begin by turning over a card. If read, place a colored chip on it. First to read three in a row wins.

40. **Scrabble.** Play with Scrabble pieces, or make these out of small ceramic tiles marked with a felt-tip pen.

41. **Word Wheels.** Staple together, at the center, two circles cut from tag paper. One circle is larger than the other. On the inner circle write letters or letter clusters. On the outer circle write phonograms. To play turn the inner wheel so that words are made.

42. **Baseball.** Construct a baseball diagram on a chart. The players move their "men" around the bases as they successfully read cards. A miss is an "out."

43. **Envelope.** Have children place pictures in envelopes or shoe boxes labeled with cards that represent the name or some part of the name of the picture.

44. **Spinner.** Construct a circle cut into colors or numbers with a spinner in the middle. (Children can also bring these from home.) Designate decks of cards as 1, 2, 3, etc., or as colors. Child spins and reads from deck indicated.

45. **Phonogram.** Deal four or more word cards to each child. First child reads a card. All other children who have that phonogram in any of their cards give those cards to the reader. Game ends when one child runs out of cards.

46. **Syllables.** Three cards are dealt out. On each is printed a syllable. Players draw and discard from a deck until they can make a two-syllable word.

47. **Syllable Racehorse.** Have three decks of cards. Each deck is made up of 1-, 2-, and 3-syllable words respectively. If children can read a word from a deck, they can move their "horses" around the track 1, 2, or 3 spaces.

48. **Affixes.** Child draws a card from a deck of root words and then from a deck of affixes. The winner is the one who can make the most words before the time runs out.

49. **Compounds.** The same game as no. 48 except each deck contains possible parts of a compound word.

50. **Choose.** Children pick a word card from a deck and read it if they can. Score is the number of words read in 10 tries plus the number of letters in each word read.

51. **Blankety-Blanks.** Play the same as no. 50 except there are blank cards in the deck. If a blank is drawn child gets to draw a card from an opponent's discard pile (one the opponent has already read).

52. **Rhymes.** Child chooses from a deck of cards, in turn with another child, until one gets two words that rhyme. A phonogram game.

53. **Challenge.** One player reads word card, for example, with five letters. If an opponent has a five-letter word, he or she reads it. Otherwise the opponent must draw, and then challenge the first player.

54. **Blast-Off.** A child who reads the first ten word cards—10, 9, 8, 7 . . . 0—is the first to blast off a rocket.

55. **I Spy.** Display words. One child says, "I spy a *d* (for example)." Child wins who can guess what word this is.

56. **Lay an Egg.** Use egg cartons. First child to read 12 word cards fills up a carton and wins.

57. **Paper Clip.** Print words in a random order on a game board. Children throw two paper clips onto the board. They score a point for each word (letter, letter cluster, syllable) they can read (or spell).

58. **Change-Around.** Provide deck of cards with C-V-C spellings, e.g., *can*. By adding *e* to this word, pupils see if they can read a new word.

59. **Bowling.** Make up bowling score sheets.

Each player reads a word card in the shape of a bowling pin and marks the number on the card onto a score sheet. Player with high score after 10 "frames" wins. Play with words of 2, 3, 4 . . . 9, or 10 letters. Depending on word, child can score 10 points.

60. Maze. Create a maze with several dead ends. Each time a word is read a child moves a space (or indicated spaces) through the maze. If a dead end is reached, player must retrace steps to get back on the right path.

61. Function Words. Write sentences on game boards in which function words are left out. From their packs of function words, children fill in the missing spaces.

62. Who—What—When—Where. Have four boxes labeled with these words. Players read a word card and get a point if they can put it into one of the four boxes. No points for words that will not fit.

Spelling Games

Many of the previous reading games can be turned into spelling games by having the child spell the word, letter, etc., instead of reading a card. Others are as follows:

1. Endless Chain. One child spells a word. The second must spell a word that begins with the letter that ends the first word.

2. No Double Letters. Write the alphabet on the board. Say, "I'm thinking of a 4-letter word that has no double letters." As children guess the letters of the word, erase the *wrong* letters. The right letters will emerge, which allows the group to finally spell the word the teacher was thinking of.

3. Ring the Bell. Teacher pronounces word waiting for bell to ring. Child in group who spells a word right as the bell rings earns a privilege for that group.

4. All in a Row. One child writes one letter on the board. The second writes another, trying to avoid writing a letter that will make a word. Child who has to finish a word loses.

5. Crossword. Give players crossword puzzle blanks of various shapes. First player writes in any letter into a beginning blank. Second player writes in a second letter (if second player can). First player does same for third letter (if first player can), and so on. Winner is the player who completes a word. Draw is called if word cannot be finished by either player.

INDEX